THE POWER OF TOMORROW'S MANAGEMENT

THE POWER OF TOMORROW'S MANAGEMENT

Using the vision-culture balance in organizations

Marc van der Erve

Heinemann Professional Publishing

Heinemann Professional Publishing Ltd
Halley Court, Jordan Hill, Oxford OX2 8EJ

OXFORD LONDON MELBOURNE AUCKLAND SINGAPORE
IBADAN NAIROBI GABORONE KINGSTON

First published 1989

© Marc van der Erve 1989

British Library Cataloguing in Publication Data
Van der Erve, Marc
The power of tomorrow's management.
1. Management
I. Title
685

ISBN 0 434 92333 8

Printed and bound in Great Britain by
Biddles Ltd, Guildford and King's Lynn

*In support of governments,
corporations and individuals*

*To Mikhail Gorbachev and Margaret Thatcher, for their
natural example in using awareness concepts.*

*To the Digital Equipment Corporation, for its example in
using culture awareness.*

To my wife Karen and to Myrthe, Derk and Fleur.

Contents

Preface	xi

Part One Preparing for Tomorrow's Success

1 Dawning awareness — 3
 Change — 3
 Transformation challenges — 4
 A pragmatic transformation model — 6
 Awareness positioning — 7
 Reflections — 8

2 New dimensions — 11
 Activating the most valuable assets — 11
 Understanding the vision engine — 12
 The vision pattern trap — 14
 The heart concern — 15
 Breaking through trends — 17
 Putting on the new-old jacket — 18
 Reflections — 19

3 The corporate entity — 21
 'Corporare' — 21
 Exploiting cultural strengths — 23
 Synergy between corporate entities — 24
 Reflections — 25

4 The vision–culture balance — 27
 Logic in culture changes — 27
 Leaders in their environment — 30
 The vision–culture diagram — 31
 Critical continuity — 33
 Reflections — 34

Contents

5 **The new deal** — 36
   The great depression — 36
   Towards the new manager — 40
   Re-assessing management effort — 41
   Reflections — 44

Part Two Culture Engineering

6 **Culture performance** — 49
   Impact of culture — 49
   Culture — 52
   Culture performance — 53
   Culture trends — 55
   Reflections — 58

7 **Dynamic positioning plane** — 59
   The effort-result curve — 59
   The effort-result curve cycle — 63
   The continuity-discontinuity paradox — 64
   The dynamic positioning plane — 68
   Reflections — 72

8 **The positioning model** — 74
   The people model — 74
   Structure — 79
   Involvement — 85
   Responsibility — 89
   Identity — 94
   Goal-tuning — 98
   The culture positioning map — 102
   Reflections — 105

9 **Repositioning strategies** — 107
   The positioning process — 107
   Move strategies — 109
   Reflections — 112

10 **Managing transformations** — 113
   One step back — 113
   Managing future organizations — 116
   Reflections — 117

Part Three Vision Engineering

11 Vision, added value and change — 121
Vision in the clouds? — 121
Added value: vision's pivot — 123
The promise of change — 128
Reflections — 132

12 The vision model — 133
The body of vision — 133
The vision facilitation model — 137
Constructing the vision model — 139
Success only through follow-up — 149
Reflections — 150

13 The vision-operation connection — 152
The most common issue in planning — 152
The success-cube theory — 153
The completion of the total picture — 157
Reflections — 159

Part Four Improving the Vision-Culture Balance

14 Vision and culture engineering laws — 163
Towards a biological system — 163
The big difference — 168
Competitive culture engineering rules — 170
Reflections — 173

15 In nations — 175
Culture performance: more visible — 175
Positioning a nation for success — 177
Reflections — 178

16 In corporations — 180
Formidable change agents within — 180
The future mob — 181
In search of a suitable partner — 182
Reflections — 184

17 In careers — 185
What do you want to become? — 185
The employee career system — 186
Where do I fit? — 187
Reflections — 187

18   Preparing managers for tomorrow   **189**
  Some basic steps   189
  The workshop reference card   191
  Change, only through awareness   194

19   Framework for the future   **195**
  Culture expert framework   195
  Tomorrow .... the 'association'   197

Part Five   Appendices
  Appendix 1 Propositions   201
  Appendix 2 Glossary of terms   204
  Appendix 3 Bibliography   210

Index   217

Preface

When reading modern business management literature, I am often impressed by the incredible number of recommendations and examples. In general, the proposed strategies tend to be logical and sometimes decidedly interesting! However, most of them *seem* to apply in almost every case and from the looks of it, all corporate cultures are in need of roughly the same set of values. At least, that is the perception. The challenge for managers is enormous: 'What (if not all) should they select from this stock of, without doubt valuable, recommendations'?

In my view, too much effort has been put into the development of *treatments* and simply not enough into *diagnostics* and into the method of implementation. In that light, management by intuition, currently identified as 'avant-garde', is certainly not new nor state-of-the-art. As far as the *selection of treatments* is concerned, intuition has been used since managers became managers.

I felt a strong urge to develop a natural framework for diagnostic thinking and acting that could be used by people and managers in a social structure, such as a company. This framework should lead to the development of the *need* for *specific* change strategies, that match the particular operating culture. This urge has been based on my profound belief, which psychologists have demonstrated, that people (and thus managers) are driven by *their needs* when searching for solutions. Therefore, 'identification of the true needs' has been the starting point.

This framework for diagnostic thinking and acting should by no means 'equalize' national or corporate cultures. I believe that each culture should be cherished, as we cherish life. For example, with Europe growing towards a more committed unity in 1992, this in particular seems to be one of the understandable concerns of national leaders, such as Margaret Thatcher.

I claim that one should try to exploit the niches of naturally and historically evolved cultures. The focus should be on improving the *performance* of corporate and national cultures and not necessarily on changing them. The result could be very similar to that of the restoration activities in the Vatican's Sistine Chapel. There, age and time have covered the precious frescoes of Michelangelo. This book will help to restore and re-interpret the bright colours of corporate and national cultures by the improvement of *culture performance*.

The framework for diagnostic thinking and acting evolved into a *'vision and culture engineering framework'*.

On the recommendations of the publisher, I have (re-) structured the book in such a way that it becomes a practical guide for those who wish to apply the *'vision and culture engineering framework'* in their environments. Each main chapter includes a section with *'reflections'*. There, the key messages of that chapter have been summarized, as well as the references to the other subjects in the book. Several workshops have been identified to put the vision and culture engineering routines into practice. I have included *propositions* to remind the reader of the reasoning rationales. And in Part Four of the book, I have put the concept of *vision and culture engineering* into a *practical* perspective.

I have referred to many events in the world at large. These events relate to the dynamics of corporations and in some cases those of governments or nations. They are vital to the understanding and the development of the logic of the *vision and culture engineering framework*. They demonstrate the tendency of corporate entities to swing from one extreme to another. They should be interpreted as corporate and organizational struggles that clarify the basic dynamics of the framework. They are not necessarily examples of 'success', that one would want to follow.

The *vision and culture engineering framework* should really be the criterion for corporate entities when deciding upon the strategies they need.

Marc van der Erve

PART ONE

Preparing for Tomorrow's Success

1

Dawning awareness

Change

'The Power of Tomorrow's Management' is closely related to the awareness of change and to the impact of change on *corporate culture* and management *vision*. It is a *new way of thinking and acting* in tomorrow's nations and companies. For individuals it may have the power of religion, where faith has been replaced by 'constructive awareness.'

In the world of today and tomorrow one thing is certain: 'change is constant'. Statements like 'the natural state of the enterprise is to be unstable' appear more regularly in management literature. They confirm a growing awareness of the inevitable processes of change in our companies. The rate of change is increasing due to, for example, faster technological advancements and changes in society that are encouraged by intensified communication through television, telephone and the application of computer networks.

An additional complication is the fact that at the same time the business environment is becoming more competitive. As a result of the internationalization of trade, not only multinationals are confronted with foreign competitors. Medium and even small-sized businesses are increasingly subject to pressures from emerging challenges in the business world. Import, export and the related protectionist issues nowadays affect virtually every company.

As opposed to growth trends in the business world, you see a mirror image in governmental organizations. Significant change is experienced there as well, but nowadays caused by reduced budgets, a re-direction of capital and manpower towards the business world and competition between these organizations for whatever funds are left.

There is also another wave going through our corporations and we may not even fully realize it yet; we are moving from a post-industrial economy to an information economy. This transition is reflected in our societies as well as in our companies.

Information is increasingly considered to be a product. The way people provide added value to the *information product* differs from the past. In fact, it will produce entirely new working methods and a different relationship between the employer and the employed. Managers may already feel the impact when the usual hierarchical way of dealing with people does not always provide the results they needed or expected.

With all this going on, the burning question that this book addresses is: 'how should managers and individuals react and how should they position their companies and themselves for continued success in this world of change'?

Transformation challenges

A wide variety of suggestions for coping best with change float into the office through management literature and other media. Solutions cover quality circles, competitive strategy analysis, intrapreneurship, organizational networks and many more suggestions, all of which are valuable. Books talk about subjects that vary from 'passionate excellence' and 'chaos' to 'productivity'.

Although most of these recommendations make sense, management will most likely be confused when they have to make up their minds. Should they go for stricter controls or should they loosen them up? Is it management style, de-centralization and reduction in management levels or is it the education of staff and the workforce?

What makes some companies more successful than others? And why do certain strategies, such as joint ventures and diversification, work in one company while they do not in others? All these questions relate to how managers deal with corporate transformations successfully.

Management's role

The involvement of management in managing transformations follows a cyclical or sine pattern (see Figure 1). The first phase is absorbed by the development of a direction or vision for the corporation, division or organization for which the manager is responsible. The orientation of management in this phase is more or less outward-looking, because the market situation, competitors and suppliers are weighted against the corporate, divisional or organizational strengths. The result is a management vision or direction that needs follow-up in the entire organization in order to ensure its realization.

Fairly soon, therefore, the manager is increasingly drawn into actually selling and communicating the emerging vision to his own environment. That is, in fact, the beginning of the second phase, which is characterized by achieving 'alignment' in the organization. Obviously, it will take a number of steps, since the manager will have to deal first with those reporting directly to him (and perhaps the next layer of management) before he involves the rest of the organization.

This second phase is extremely critical, because it should result in a constructive response by the organization that helps to materialize the vision or direction. The manager now becomes more of a facilitator, as opposed to the developer of a vision. Therefore, somewhere between the first and second phase, management also needs to define ways or strategies that are focused on the stimulation of organizational response.

Challenges for leaders

The above demonstrates the qualitites required anywhere in the world, i.e. from Gorbachev to Thatcher and from Carlo De Benedetti (*Olivetti*) to Ken Olsen (*Digital*). It is the capacity to develop a mind-stretching vision. And in addition, it is the capability to generate and ensure a constructive and supportive response in their environments.

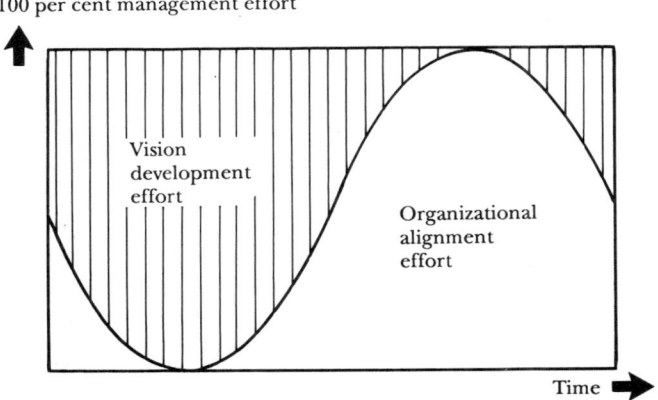

Figure 1 *Phases of management involvement in transformations*

Considering these qualities, one can spell out three major transformation challenges, that managers (and individuals) are confronted with 'in pursuit of excellence' in their environments,

1. How to design an outward-looking and competitive vision that ensures the success of the environment concerned;
2. How to develop and choose supporting strategies that result in optimal responsiveness of their environment; and
3. How to initiate and facilitate the actual process of transformation.

These challenges are inter-dependent, which means that overall failure is most likely to be the outcome if one of them is not realized. Management at every level in an organization has to cope with the phases of involvement, as in the sine curve model, as well as with the associated challenges.

A pragmatic transformation model

Due to the increasing rate of change in the business world, there is an outspoken awareness that the role of management is becoming increasingly complex. 'Adapting to change and marrying corporate goals to society as a whole' are seen as the major causes for this complexity. Management, in other words, is obliged to speed up the frequency with which it sets new directions. But given the change in society, strategies for realigning organizations will need to be adjusted continuously as well.

Alignment refers to having an organization or a group of people constructively accept and build on a given vision. (Proposition 1)

In fact, management has to drive many kinds of transformations at the same time, each being in phase one or two of the 'sine curve phenomenon'. As a result, the transformation challenges discussed earlier are becoming more complex and as such more difficult to handle for the 'traditional manager'.

Corporations (and countries) in Europe and the United States are indeed experiencing the need for transformation. World competition and continuous change caused by technological developments, have also forced the Japanese to look for alternative ways of managing their companies. Diversification, innovation, entrepreneurship and horizontal career paths are just a few components of the new management trend that is being observed in Japanese multinational companies.

But when and for how long are these management trends valid? They will have to be revised again over time in order to maintain organizational responsiveness under changed circumstances!

As such the requirement for a model that allows management to plot and understand the changing trends and values in an organization, seems almost like a natural consequence. However, a better insight into organizational 'value needs' only becomes effective when it is supported by a practical process for the definition and facilitation of management vision. At that moment, both the organizational 'foundation' (organizational values) and the 'incentive' for corporate activity (vision) have been addressed sufficiently.

Awareness positioning

Well-recognized models have been designed that are 'outward looking' and which focus on the development of a competitive direction or strategy. On the other hand, an increasing number of publications deal with corporate cultures and seem to focus on the improvement of organizational responsiveness.

The thinking advocated in this book is complementary to the views expressed in literature on corporate strategy and to the opinions about cultural levers that *currently* seem to be successful. However, *The Power of Tomorrow's Management* distinguishes itself by a break-through approach that applies to organizations of the future in spite of the changing environment. It will help to create a movement towards a time when we may be able to describe organizational and people phenomena in terms of statistical densities, as in quantum mechanics.

The key to the approach is an effective and ready-to-use *thinking and guidance framework (model)* that leads the reader through a gradual process of growing *awareness* of the corporate future in terms of the operating culture. This *corporate awareness* is an important incentive for change and organizational response. The framework addresses the selection of strategic ingredients for mobilizing the organization to support the corporate vision and goals and it formulates the actual facilitation process towards synergetic organizational activity.

Corporate awareness refers to a shared understanding of the corporate future, identity and culture by management and other people in the organization. (Proposition 2)

'Why *awareness* is important to successful change' will be discussed in the next chapter. The reference to *corporate* awareness relates to the 'corporate entity', as defined in Chapter 3. The corporate entity is one of the basic building blocks in the *The Power of Tomorrow's Management*.

In my previous book *Enterprise Dynamics*, published in 1986 in Dutch, I described the basics of the above mentioned framework by defining and demonstrating the two dimensional *dynamic plane*. It consists of a model to position and reposition people's awareness on where they stand as an organization. In this book the process has matured significantly and can indeed be characterized by *awareness positioning*.

The framework offered by the *The Power of Tomorrow's Management* constructively encapsulates views like 'Management By Objectives', 'Management By Motivation' and 'Incentives Management', but without forgetting the essence of corporations and organizations of any kind: '*performance*'. In fact, improving and expanding corporate (and individual) performance is the underlying and ultimate goal that justifies reading and using this book. In addition, I am tempted to predict that based on the conclusions derived in Part Four, 'performance' may get an extra dimension.

The *awareness positioning framework* in this book is backed up by a solid affinity to the real world. It is the result of a process of induction. In other words, it postulates logical and general rulings based on business events and changing management trends, as they have been reported in the different professional media. The pragmatic background also means that it emerged out of dialogue and working together with management. My responsibilities in the business world have made it possible for me to observe and work with true 'masters of change'.

In conclusion, it is my profound belief that the open-minded experience of organizational change itself has been an intellectual and emotional condition for the formulation of these positioning theories. This kind of experience will, I hope, also contribute to the dawning awareness of others on these matters.

Reflections

Key messages

Corporate evolution sometimes reminds me of a soccer game. Just imagine its basic elements, such as a goal, a soccer player who kicks the ball and the ball. Now, if one assumes the 'changing environment' to be the soccer star who kicks the ball hopefully in the right direction, one unfortunately has to come to the conclusion that the ball represents the corporation speeding through the air to (its?) goal.

The rhetorical question is of course: 'who controls the game ..., the ball or the soccer player?' The situation does not seem to be so glorious for the ball. However, if the ball could transform itself, say into a baseball, a basketball or a volleyball, it could actually select the game it wants to be in!

- Hence, in most cases, a 'corporation of any kind' (and an individual) can do only one thing to cope effectively with the challenges of a moving environment and that is to change itself first, rather than trying to change the environment.
- Change can only be achieved through people, because *they* make change happen. Systems don't. New innovative visions will indeed initiate change. But the capacity to change within corporations strongly depends on a constructive organizational acceptance and response. Because of this, the management task is increasingly developing into a dual task, i.e. one of designing vision and one of facilitating organizational acceptance and response.
- Most current literature focuses on success strategies. Evolution has only scratched the surface of awareness models that can be used by management to select and implement the appropriate strategy for optimum culture performance.
- Different environments may not only require different visions, but also different operating cultures. Therefore, vision development will need to be coupled to operating culture adjustments. This relationship needs constant tuning, because there is no one operating culture that guarantees success under all circumstances.
- The key to successful change is people's awareness of the corporate vision in connection with the operating culture, specifically *relative to* the dynamics in the environment. This awareness should be well structured in order to make it effective in the selection of the most suitable change strategies.
- The use of 'awareness positioning' will turn out to be the 'new way of thinking and acting' in tomorrow's world. The need for success tomorrow, especially given the increasing amount of change, will result in the emergence of the proposed reflex-like build-up of constructive awareness.

The attributes of tomorrow's manager will be discussed in detail in Part One of this book. For that purpose, the following chapters analyse what makes people tick, what is within their minds and guts and within groups (of any kind) by looking at the latest explanations on how people operate and how they currently or could perform. Through the definition of the two core concepts in this book (the 'corporate entity' and the 'vision-culture balance') the contours of the 'new manager' are sharpened in the last chapter of Part One ('The new deal').

As important for tomorrow's manager, as discussed above, is the ability to develop and facilitate vision together with the ability to adjust the corporate culture. In Parts Two and Three of the book, culture adjustment and vision development are dealt with separately. In Part Four, both vision development and culture adjustment are connected. The vision-culture balance is expanded into a new 'progress-spiral' for corporations of the future. Applications in various environments are highlighted and the book concludes with a description of the foundation to perfect its key concepts.

Steps to consider

A constructive response to corporate goals and to any other need for change may be obtained through a number of very simple and almost trivial actions.

Managers should improve *communication* with the people in their organizations about organizational challenges, goals and desired attitudes. Communication is a broad concept. It varies from traditional communication, through newsletters, posters, the media, video and cassettes to communication through formal interactive sessions with selected groups of people, and informal talks while walking around and most importantly, by giving the *right* (and of course visible) *example*. The latter, especially, is an extremely strong but under-utilized facility available to managers. Going back into history just a little, an impressive leader such as Gandhi managed to enforce peace between three hundred and fifty million Indian people, at that time, simply by force of personal example. What I am suggesting is that *Internal Communication* (of a new kind) needs to be looked at as a major management tool for successful change. To put *internal* into the right perspective, however, I would like to refer to an interesting finding in the Philips corporation. The public relations officer once said that Philips' employees view the public media, in particular, as a most important source for information about their own employer.

Managers should establish the *positioning of awareness* through workshops with their people. Ask teams to brainstorm and to think with an 'unlimited view' of what could be changed within the organization to cope effectively with the environment. The expectations on the outcome of such workshops should be clearly set, i.e. they should 'look for alternatives' and not for the final soloution. The outcome of these sessions is often a surprisingly logical answer that may come very close to a final solution. If not, the manager knows what needs to be worked on. In any case, the result is that people will get used to the idea and be prepared for change.

2

New dimensions

Activating the most valuable assets

There is a new focus on pictures and icons in our organizations. Just watch the fire exit signs at airports or the mouse driven personal computers that are being installed in the office. Strangely enough we seem to have forgotten that for ages people have communicated in pictures. The hieroglyphs in old Egypt are well known. Chinese and Japanese cultures are still the proud and convinced users of *kenji* pictures. Each of them can be associated with a concept, a certain meaning or action. The reason for their existence is relatively simple: when people think ... they only think in pictures and almost never in abstract signs. So, if you want to put a message across and you really want people to follow and understand you, then do relate to ... or even show it in a picture. That is what McKinsey tells its consultants. But that is also how Einstein explained his complicated theories ... 'Suppose you are standing in an elevator, that travels down with a certain speed...'. One of the first steps that managers therefore can take to improve their effectiveness is *to visualize what they want to achieve.* ...

The Dutch Ministry of Economical Affairs regularly issues interesting updates on the state of technology in the USA, Japan and Europe. They are written by Dutch governmental research staff, stationed in those countries. The difference in these reports is remarkable. The *European Technews* publication in most cases consists of an endless list of projects and procedures for requesting information and subsidies. The subjects are not necessarily related and seem to focus on basic research rather than imaginative and understandable end results. Apart perhaps from projects such as ESPRIT, a concerted vision or an overall goal seems to be missing.

The Japanese 'Technews' however, talks about the Japanese vision on for example, biotechnology and expresses this in a catch phase like 'the long sprint towards the twenty first century'. It incorporates a detailed description of what the results will look like and only reminds a careful reader that a 'few' problems need to be resolved in the meantime. The USA 'Technews' hovers somewhat between the styles of the European and Japanese updates.

These differences in styles seem associated with the challenging suspicion that there is a link between the impact of an inspiring vision on society . . . and success. Many cases of the use of vision to pursue success have been quoted. One of the outstanding examples on a national level is the announcement of John F. Kennedy in the early sixties: 'to put a man on the moon within the next decade . . .' There is no doubt of the achievement of that vision. Similar national visions have been stated today, such as the Strategic Defence Initiative vision in the USA, the fifth generation computer in Japan and *perestroika* in the Soviet Union. There is a high probability that these visions will come to fruition as well. What might influence the success of these visions, I will discuss further in this book.

Within the mini-societies of corporations, clearly stated visions are used very effectively as well. Peugeot's chairman, Jacques Calvet, with his strong and well communicated vision: 'to be Europe's number one low-cost car producer' proved to be very successful. After losing $1.3 billion in four years, Peugeot made substantial profits in 1986. Projections show the profit trend to be further improving. Within Peugeot, Calvet's vision led to the initiation of many supporting actions, from automation and Japanese quality control to workplace sociology.

In summary, what counts is: what a company wants 'to be', rather then what it has to do. *Vision* as such has the potential of activating people, organizations, countries and societies.

Understanding the vision engine

The understanding of the vision engine has been greatly helped by interpreters such as Maltz (Psycho Cybernetics) and Tice (Investment in Excellence). They have 'translated' complex psychological findings and conclusions into understandable day-to-day language. By doing just that, they also demonstrated the potential of people actually to influence and improve their *own* performance.

The basic model that they use to explain the thought process (see Figure 2), consists of three elements. The first element is human consciousness, which initiates a perception of the outside environment by observing or sensing it. At the same time it drives the actions of

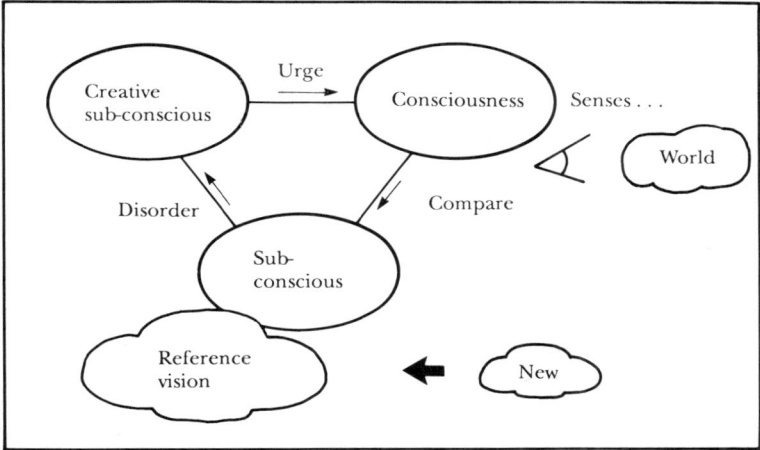

Figure 2 *Vision pulls the car*

human beings. When consciousness senses a certain situation, it passes on to the subconscious the observed picture. The subconscious compares the observation with a certain *reference picture* or *vision*, that has at one time been stored in the memory. A mismatch as a result of this comparison will create a disorder or a certain *awareness* that something is wrong, 'because what I see is not what I thought it to be'. This disorder is transferred to the so-called creative subconscious. The latter generates the urge and drive for the first element (consciousness) to take particular actions.

The reference 'vision' which has been stored in the memory is the item that draws most of the attention, because mismatching with it triggers action. For example, a person with a subconscious vision 'that he belongs in a higher wage group' will be triggered by his creative subconscious to take actions that eventually will match reality with the picture in his mind. In other words he will get the urge to undertake activities that may lead to a higher income. On the other hand, if he is earning more than his subconscious vision tells him he needs, the 'creative-subconscious' will trigger actions (through consciousness) to correct that as well. It means that this person may get the feeling that he does not want to take promotion after all! And the strange thing is that he will find very 'logical' reasons to justify this to the outside world ... and to himself. Although this is a very brief and simplified representation of what goes on in the mind, it explains where the opportunity area is.

It is the vision in a person's mind that determines his performance. Consequently, human performance may be improved by creating a new vision in the mind or a new *belief*. This train of thought raises a critical question: 'how does a vision get into the subconscious'? And also: 'how to change the vision'? In general, the vision is the product of the conditioning by, or influences from, the outside environment. This conditioning normally takes place without the person consciously realizing it, either by a consistently repeated pattern of similar impressions or by an experience with a certain state of emotion attached to it.

Similarly the vision in the mind can be changed. Based on this finding, one may take control of this change process consciously and as such improve the impact on one's own destiny. Because in general people only use ten per cent of their brainpower, vision may open the road to unknown and imaginative potential. Maltz and Tice have developed very challenging methods for individuals and groups to facilitate this process. *The Power of Tomorrow's Management* deals with the same subject matter: *vision*, but now related to corporate strategy. It can not therefore be presented without understanding this powerful underlying concept. Through *vision*, a tool for moulding and building a company to *'how one would like it to be'* is handed to management and the employees. In order to create effective change in an organization or corporation of any kind, as I have stated in Chapter 1, first of all one needs a certain awareness. With reference to the model for the thought process, awareness can be explained as creating a disorder between 'what the consciousness observes' and 'what the subconscious recognizes as a reference vision'.

Awareness concerns the mismatch between the 'observation' and the 'reference vision in people's minds'. This mismatch leads to corrective change actions (driven by the creative subconscious), that are geared to align 'what one observes' to the 'vision in one's mind'. (Proposition 3)

The above proposition identifies awareness as a prime driver for change. Two topics, related to the above, are extremely important. One is the development of an appropriate reference vision and one concerns the need for a process identifying a mismatch between this vision and the real world situation. The *awareness positioning frameworks* for culture and vision in the next parts of this book, deal with both.

The vision pattern trap

Creativity is the art of seeing and finding undiscovered patterns of thought that are hard to find or not easy to see. In many cases, we just don't see things because we don't expect to see them. We are too driven or harnessed by our own vision of what we ought to see. It is therefore a real challenge to find alternative thinking patterns, even if we suspect that they exist. So, a certain 'trick' is needed to escape a current flow of thoughts and find a new one. But why should we worry about this? Well, as we briefly discussed in Chapter 1, all facts strongly indicate that the change in the company of tomorrow will go beyond our comprehension. In addition, change will itself lead to more change and impact on every process in the operation. So, in order to stay competitive, it is of the utmost importance to develop the capability of finding new ways of doing business better and cope with this change effectively.

Edward de Bono, the well-known creator of the *lateral thinking* concept, developed the so-called *po*-device. It is simply a mental catalyst, or as he calls it, a 'provocation', that forces somebody through all sorts of techniques to approach a subject from an entirely different and even unusual angle. Statements like: 'suppose you have a car with square wheels ...', are encouraged and further developed into realistic and creative ideas. In summary, the *po*-device helps people to swing out of their current train of thinking by creating a willingness to look for alternatives. '*The Power of Tomorrow's Management*' aims to provide a '*po*-device' that helps management to develop new trains of thought on where they want to be as a company and what they want to have as a culture. By taking away the concern about the process of how to do the latter, thinking capacity for the achievement of originality and innovation will actually be freed.

The heart concern

Planning in companies is normally associated with an abstract chain of objectives, goals and targets, strategies, tactics, programmes, etc. (see Figure 3). I have never seen so much confusion about what these terms mean. Management teams really have to think about it to come up with a satisfactory answer. The result ...? Valuable management time is spent on semantics and on the clarification of these items. And even then it is not always realized that in essence these elements only differ in their level of abstractness. Corporate employees literally tend to be drawn into the formulation and checking of these terms without providing the necessary added value.

In addition, these terms create a hierarchy in strategy setting and therefore a hierarchy in strategic involvement of the employees. It is too much top-down orientated and may lead to unnecessary management levels and lack of feedback. In comparison to our discussion on the power of vision and breaking through thought patterns, this hierarchical

16   The Power of Tomorrow's Management

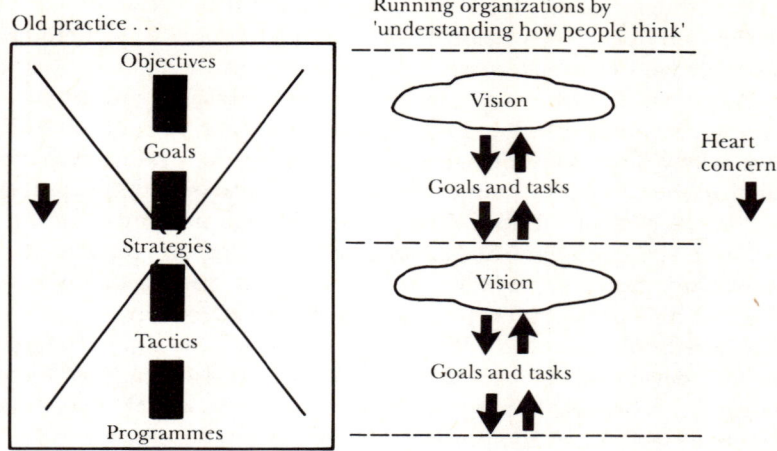

Figure 3   *The new chain of planning*

chain of 'planning terms' does not seem very inspiring. It is merely a way of formulating strategic conclusions, basically on paper. In order to recapture the innovative momentum in corporations and organizations, it is essential to create a planning chain that talks about elements such as vision, measureable goals, tasks and feedback (See Figure 3). The idea is to get back to the guts of planning and action, which are dormant in most management teams. These 'guts' can be found by understanding how people operate.

As we have seen, people think in pictures and are activated by vision. This is particularly so when the vision concerns what they would like to be as a team, as a corporation or as a country. The adjusted planning process therefore should exploit this. Although planning and vision are matters of the brain, it should be realized that the planning cycle is also a concern of the heart, since emotion and culture are heavily involved. 'Getting at the planning guts of a management team' can be stimulated by associative interacting. By having managers of different disciplines work together on the development of a vision that concerns them as a whole, interactive associations or new ideas may be found. In essence, this is because different backgrounds and disciplines encourage unconventional subject combinations. The drive to develop a vision of where they would like to be as a team, may lead to the selection and development of some unusual concept combinations. Interactive associations can be explained by a new and emerging approach in science called *ideonomy*, as developed by Patrick Gunkel. Ideonomy basically concerns the generation of possible ideas by connecting different subjects and concepts. Patrick Gunkel works out these connections through lists of subjects that he randomly connects to other lists using a microcomputer. The connections between these subjects do not always make sense. But some may stick out and lead to entirely new concepts related to artificial intelligence, medicine, clothing, sports, flowers, superconductivity, political systems and many more.

In conclusion, a strategic planning chain should be simple and related to how people intrinsically operate. At the same time, it should enforce the interactive association between the different entities in a team of people. Lastly, it should allow for an optimal response to the corporate direction. The success of the planning chain, therefore, is related to the corporate culture, since free interaction is its basic ingredient. The 'status free' planning chain and the related team concept are critical elements in the way the awareness positioning process works.

Breaking through trends

Some kids are not successful at school because they are bored. Or to put it differently, school is not challenging enough for them, it does not stretch their minds. Likewise, you may see in a manufacturing firm that when management sets a goal to reduce the production cost by ten per cent in one year, this goal is just not or is hardly achieved. Why? Because, in response to this goal, the manufacturing operation will start to tune its processes, work on its efficiency, initiate productivity teams, put in extra controls and do many other things. But really changing something...? That will most likely not happen, because 'it is not really needed', they argue!

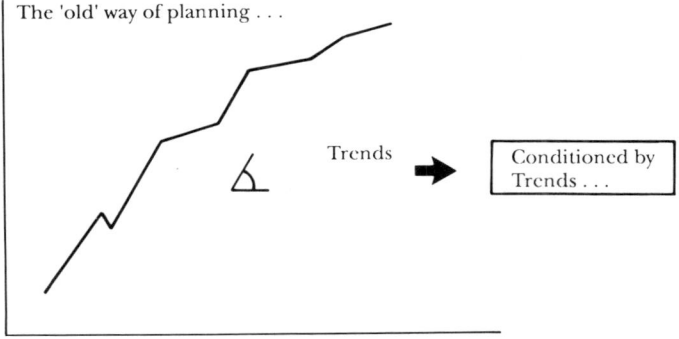

Figure 4   *The old way of planning*

Subsequently, ask that same operation to reduce its production cost by 40 per cent in one year! Now, perhaps after an initial panic, the operation will start to realize that this goal *truly* is impossible. No way can this cost reduction ever be achieved. At least not with the current product and not with the current processes and not with the current discipline. So, what to do? In order to be successful, they effectively have to start from scratch! The product is therefore re-designed to improve dramatically and simplify its manufacturing. New and entirely different processes are developed and tested. Working methods are re-thought. Other and better tools are sought and work disciplines are critically reviewed. Vendors are contacted to make special and well defined deals. And it's amazing what they find out! They not only reduce the product cost by 40 per cent, but it seems that further cost reductions are projected up to in total 50 per cent! They really have done a great job! At this point, we should not forget the manager who introduced the goal for a product cost reduction of 40 per cent. It seems that this 'impossible' goal provided the incentive for the operation to look at things totally differently. For management too, trends may have a 'conditioning' effect, that is when they make their long range plans. It is therefore worth considering whether management should always be led by trends and extrapolations. An inspiring example of this has been provided by Pierre A. Wack, who described a new approach of designing planning scenarios, based on his experience with the Shell oil company during the oil crisis. Wack explains how scenarios (in other words: alternative visions) can help companies in scouting the possibilities beyond the 'trends' in a certain time period. The success of Shell during and after the oil-crisis, compared with other oil companies, is based on its willingness not only to look at trends but to imagine the possible 'impossible'.

In summary, management certainly can facilitate trend-breakthroughs in their companies, by setting at least some 'trend-breakthrough goals' or 'daring visions'. This, in particular, is one of the success attitudes that play a role in the vision engineering section of this book.

Putting on the new-old jacket

The new dimensions discussed in this chapter are some of the basic building bricks for this book. They are new in the way that they have been explained, popularized and summarized. But in fact many of these concepts have been well known for quite some time and can even be interpreted as common sense. The renewed awareness of their existence and scope in the management world seems to relate to the appreciation and need for these concepts in today's corporations. In summary, new dimensions to be aware of are:

- People think in (and are triggered by) pictures;
- Shared visions activate people to find solutions to achieve them;
- People need something to help them escape from their existing thinking patterns;
- 'How we achieve' in our corporations should be based on our knowledge of how people think, since they are the most valuable assets in creating change momentum;
- New visions and ideas are achieved by the selection of interactive subject combinations;
- 'Trend-breakthroughs' may be achieved by setting daring goals and by developing mind-stretching visions.

Reflections

Key messages

1988 was the year of the Olympic games in Korea. The fight for gold, silver and bronze medals created impressive peak performers. Some made it and some did not. For some the challenge was so big that they ignored the rules and turned themselves into 'bio-chemical men'. Ben Johnson, after breaking the world record on the 100 metre dash, was disqualified, having used steroids. It triggered an intriguing article in the *Herald Tribune* of 30 September, 1988 by Grigori Raiport on how in fact the Russians have achieved such consistent results, that is, without the use of drugs. It turns out that dedication alone has not been the only reason for their success. In particular, the use of the mental capabilities of their athletes has caused major breakthroughs. Methods such as auto-conditioning, analysis of the opponents' psyche, etc. are considered as serious performance enhancing techniques. 'The Russians realized long ago that while the human body has its natural limits, the mind's potential is *unlimited*.' In fact, the findings in this chapter are in line with the above.

- Increasingly, the basis for effective change and breakthrough in every corporation is in 'how well we understand and adapt to the processes in the human mind'.
- Awareness is the prime driver of change. It requires the development of an ideal reference picture (a vision) and a process for matching it to the real world.
- Vision, and especially one expressed in a picture, has a strong impact on people's drive to achieve it successfully.

- The innovative and constructive payback of multi-disciplinary teams will be incredible when they have the freedom to interact.
- Breakthrough can be achieved by creating a true sense of urgency, for example, by setting stretch goals or by developing daring visions.

All of these messages are in support of the awareness positioning processes in this book. For example, those for creating team-awareness on culture performance through the culture performance positioning and re-positioning workshop in Chapter 9. Another example is the construction of the vision model in Chapter 12. The messages in this chapter form the pillars of the workshops on culture and vision.

The proposition on *awareness* in this chapter formulates the base assumption on how to create change momentum. The other subjects of trend-breakthrough, planning hierarchy and the catalyst for new views (de Bono) refer to ways of getting the best change results.

Steps to consider

This chapter prepares the reader for the discussion of the core models on culture performance and corporate vision in this book. However, a few practical steps for managers to consider have been abstracted from this chapter.

- Try to put your proposals in a picture. Also ask your people to summarize their suggestions and/or analyses in simple and easy to understand pictures.
- When designing strategy, do not see your people as a herd that needs direction. Their visions on how to do or achieve things may create a new spectrum of possibilities about which you may not have thought.
- In formulating goals for the organization, do define some goals that seem almost impossible to achieve. Support these consistently, as mind-set types of goals.

3

The corporate entity

'Corporare'

The dynamics of nations, companies and organizations have one thing in common: in every case they concern a group of people, that more or less act as one body. The aim of this book is to maximize an effective response from that 'body'. As such, it is important to improve our understanding of its basic building blocks. For the sake of identification, let us name these bodies: *corporate entities* simply because the Latin word 'corporare' means 'form into a body'.

A new appreciation of this 'corporate entity' is gradually being moulded by the efforts of management specialists all over the western business world. The contours of this 'new look' seem like the sum of the influences from currents like:

- Portfolio management, as designed for the manager to determine the investment priorities of the different business units in his company.
- Strategic planning, where planning experts have tried to formalize the assessment of the environment and the development of derivative strategies.
- Corporate and environmental culture analysis, which aims at understanding successful values and stategies in and around corporations.
- Human thinking performance, as captured by theories and terms, such as creative thinking, peak performance, lateral thinking and new age thinking.

Based on this perspective, a simple and straightforward model has been worked out in Figure 5. It shows the corporate entity as a square box with a particular outside environment, including the influencing forces

22 The Power of Tomorrow's Management

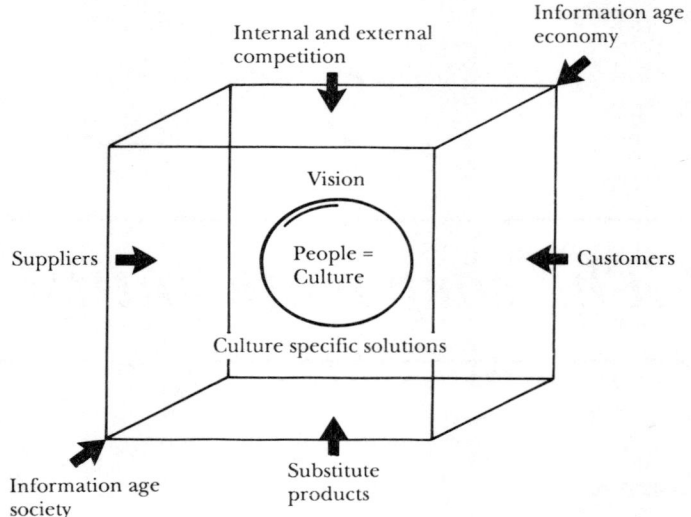

Figure 5 *Focus on the corporate entity first*

from customers, suppliers, competition and substitute products. The impact of the information age economy and the information age society has also been included as part of the environment, very much based upon the convincing assessments of John Naisbitt and Patricia Aburdene in their book *Re-inventing the Corporation*. Inside the box, which in essence represents a particular group of people, one finds the vision of how these people see the future and their operating culture. Together, these two elements cause a certain counter pressure in response to the influences or rather challenges from the environment.

This model leads to a definition for the corporate entity, which will be used to identify so called culture performance drivers. The corporate entity will also play an important role when establishing the scope of a particular vision.

The corporate entity comprises (any number of) people, who are tied together in a group by a certain commonality in their vision of the future and by a common operating culture. They face the challenges of a common outside environment. (Proposition 4)

The importance of the pressures on the corporate entity from the local and/or country environments should not be underestimated. This is demonstrated by a study of Kanter and Mirvis both from the Boston University on 'how employees view their work and private lives'.

Distinct differences between six European countries and the USA have been found in terms of attitudes in the workplace and the perception of management. Interestingly, the suggestion made by the researchers concerns the improvement of communication between management and the workforce by effectively creating two-way-communication.

Exploiting cultural strengths

A business, if you like, can be represented by a group of people and the internal culture that they have created to operate in. Again we must realize that this culture is influenced not only by the people that work there, but also by the culture of the environment. Within the boundaries of that particular corporate culture, the employees are driven by vision. This vision will lead to solutions and activities that are specific to the internal culture. In other words:

One and the same vision may create different solutions in companies with different corporate cultures. (Proposition 5)

Some companies are very much aware of this and have taken steps constructively to use the strengths of certain cultures. In spite of its late entry to the Japanese market, the Lotus company successfully established its name by realizing and exploiting the above characteristics of the business entity. With the same vision for the USA and Europe, that is to provide and sell an advanced spreadsheet program (Lotus 1–2–3), they decided to look for a culture-specific solution. Therefore, rather than convert its programs into Japanese as other software houses had done, Lotus totally rewrote 1–2–3 to reflect the differences between the US and Japanese ways of doing business. All of the development efforts were moved to Tokyo, where they hired a team of local computer programmers and entered into a licensing agreement with a local software firm. The result: a new product with more and typical Japanese features that eventually received the prestigious Nikkei Award for Creative Excellence. It reached the top of the best-selling software list at that time. This example not only demonstrates success in the (Japanese) market, but most importantly it shows the success of the Japanese subsidiary of Lotus, responsible for the product development. Being allowed to find *culture-specific solutions* to one and the same corporate vision, apparently created the super right spirit to excel. In a similar way, Hewlett Packard decided to create a research centre in Singapore, rather than only focusing on the traditional low cost manufacturing opportunity. By capitalizing on the strong points of the culture in Singapore. Hewlett Packard effectively tied product development to marketing, improved its return on R&D projects, reduced the cost of its products and shortened its product development time.

In summary, *The Power of Tomorrow's Management* should be based on the definition of the *corporate entity*. It concerns the total of the external environment with its specific influences and cultural aspects, as well as the business itself with its people, their operating culture, the vision they work with and their *drive* for culture-specific solutions, as natural ingredients. Corporate entities with the above definition can be found on every level in the organization. It means that not only the company, as a whole, should be considered as a corporate entity, but also a division, a subsidiary, a plant, a department and even the *employee himself*. All operate according to the model as provided in Figure 5.

Synergy between corporate entities

One of the main challenges for management, as I briefly indicated in the first chapter, is to obtain synergy between different corporate entities in support of an overall goal or vision. Management should get the best out of these entities individually and as a whole.

Synergy between different 'corporate entities' cannot be achieved just by commanding 'them' to do certain things in certain ways This will probably eventually invite resistance. Managers should in principle concentrate on creating synergy in vision and allow for culture specific solutions in order to utilize cultural strengths (see Figure 6).

Issues about culture differences and lack of vision synergy are often

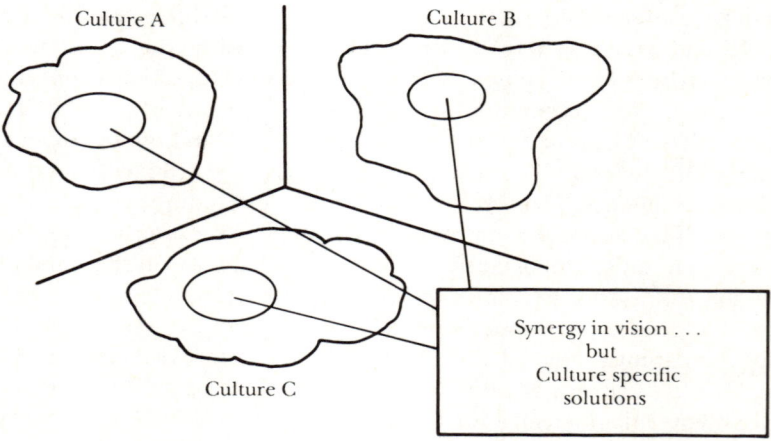

Figure 6 *Pulling corporate entities together*

confused. In 1982, a joint venture between Fokker, a Dutch manufacturer of medium-sized civil airplanes, and McDonnel Douglas for the development of a 100 seater airplane 'tragically crashed'. In an article about Fokker's plans to start up a production facility for a similar plane in the U.S.A. four years later, the president of Fokker recalled this event and quoted the then cultural differences between the two companies as the basic reason for the failure of this joint venture. However, based on the previous discussion, it may be apparent that not only differences in culture but the lack of true synergy in vision was the most likely cause of this failure.

It was presumably for the same reason that the initial joint venture discussions (1986) between McDonnel Douglas and Airbus Industries did not emerge. The background for this proposal was to maintain McDD's own long-term position in the U.S. market. Together with the drive for technological independence in Europe, true vision synergy turned out to be then imposible.

The open question is of course: 'how to get vision synergy and how to ensure that solutions are based on the strengths of certain cultures'? Having defined a model for the 'corporate entity', one has a base to determine these how's. . . .

Reflections

Key messages

From the time when evolution produced higher life forms, corporations or 'corporate entities' have existed. Even now, herds of animals are bound together by a natural urge to increase the probability of their survival. Similar patterns can be found all around us in the human world. However, in that world 'survival' has a different meaning, such as continuity, growth, profit margin and so forth. Survival of a corporate entity or corporation has everything to do with the short and long-term actions that it develops and undertakes. Quite different from animal herds, the survival of corporations is characterized by a pro-active rather than a re-active approach. Initiative and being the first is an essential success factor. Also, how corporations structure, manage and size themselves is of the utmost importance to their success. Whether 'small is beautiful' or whether you need 'scale' to be innovative (*Trading Places*, C.V. Prestowitz; Basic Books, N. Y., 1988) are subjects that seem to be addressed continuously in the business world.

- The understanding of the 'corporate entity' is basic to the development of awareness processes, that have as objectives its performance, its survival and its success.

- A corporate entity is not a legal entity, but a natural one, which consists of people, their vision, their operating culture *and* the environment in which they manoeuvre. As such, a corporate entity can be a nation, a corporation, any organization and even the employee him/herself.
- The challenge of management is to recognize the strengths of different operating cultures and to use them, not crush them.
- Synergy between corporate entities with different operating cultures can only be achieved by synergizing their visions *and* by allowing those corporate entities to provide culture-specific solutions.

These messages are the foundation of the different workshops that have been suggested and analysed in this book. For example, the workshop on 'culture positioning' in Chapter 9, or the one on 'vision engineering' in 12. Chapter 18 includes an overview of these workshops. More important is the role that the corporate entity plays in the definition of awareness positioning theories. It is used as a reference or thinking model, when defining so-called culture performance drivers, as in Chapter 8. In addition, it is useful when determining the scope of the vision, as in Chapter 12.

Steps to consider

The visibly improving awareness of culture specifics in this world really encourages management to change their initial reaction of rejection to one of openness, when they deal with alien approaches, views and behaviour. It that light, it may not be surprising that Mr Gorbachev, for example, views mass organizations and movements as a positive sign in the development of people's initiatives. One should try to improve the understanding of the culture-specific strengths in the different parts of the organization. Based on this understanding, one should decide the allocation of strategic resources. As result, strategic investments will be made where they have the best chance of leading to success. The eventual outcomes may later be cross-fertilized to other areas. When dealing with different operating cultures, that is within a company and within a management team or in collaboration with outside partners, managers should first define the synergy and acceptance of 'what will have to be achieved in the future', in other words, the *vision*. Only then should the culture-specific strengths be considered to divide the work.

4

The vision-culture balance

Logic in culture changes

Next to an appreciation for culture, as part of the corporate entity, the awareness that cultures are subject to change is growing increasingly and is being confirmed by several management specialists. Even successful cultures seem to need adjustment in order to maintain their competitive edge. Japanese corporate cultures, many times quoted for their productivity, are now being re-shaped in order to deal effectively with the new environmental challenges. The high yen in 1986/1987, the protectionist trade measures then in force, cheap manufacturing alternatives in countries such as Korea and Taiwan, and increasing technological change gradually led to the formulation of new management trends. These trends are marked by distinct shifts away from the traditional Japanese management orientation. Some of these, as noted by the Japanese Committee for Economic Development, are turning ...

- from operation-centred to strategy-centred strategic action;
- from sticking to the core lines of business to diversification;
- from being efficiency-centred to innovation-centred;
- from centralized to de-centralized power;
- from incremental to entrepreneurial behaviour modes.

And these are just a random selection of about twenty change characteristics.

In Europe too, many examples of successful shifts in management trends and corporate cultures are available. A frequently quoted example is the successful revival of British Airways. Specifically, their training programme 'Putting People First', is one of the recognized ways of changing the culture to a more creative and customer orientated one. SAS, Scandinavian Airlines (headed by Carlzon), has also been praised for similar successes. These shifts in fact represent the re-positioning efforts of companies towards more successful work environments.

The assumption is that a certain logic or rule exists underlying these shifts, with which repositioning efforts can be explained and anticipated. (Proposition 6)

At first sight, repositioning efforts in companies seem to indicate a certain dynamic balance between two different cultural extremes. In order to demonstrate this phenomenon, let us examine two examples of the evolving dynamic balance between entrepreneurship and control.

Kodak

Kodak, with a revenue of approximately $10 billion in 1984 and at that time known for its monolithic and bureaucratic structure, has since been changing considerably under the pressure of competition and fast technological developments. For example, the electronic products that were marketed by Kodak's competitors to replace chemically based film products (in addition to heavy competition on the chemical film market), gradually started to have a negative impact on the year-end results. The strongly centralized decision-making structure in Kodak prevented a fast and effective response to the changing market situation. As a result, Kodak's chairman, Chandler, decided to restructure the company into 17 entrepreneurial units, each having profit and loss responsibility. At the same time, Kodak also aimed to diversify its products by buying up small companies. The overall objective was to bring back entrepreneurship in the organization with enough incentives as well as flexibility to fight back competition. As we have seen in the meantime, this decision has been very successful. Both Kodak's growth rate and profits are climbing again, while its culture changed dramatically, to one where simply more risks are being taken. Kodak's position and repositioning effort can be graphed in a dynamics plane for structure related strategies, as a move up towards an improved balance between entrepreneurship and control (Figure 6). Similar structure related repositioning efforts are taking place in Nippon, Fuji Xerox, General Motors and many other companies.

Apple

We see the opposite in Apple, however, where the divisions for the Apple II and the Macintosh microcomputers were combined and rationalized. At the same time, more and effective controls were introduced by John Sculley, who eventually took over from Steven Jobs, the founder of Apple. In Apple's case, entrepreneurship and internal competition were not off-set by sufficient and effective controls that showed the impact and viability of new ideas. Its staff was more or less psyched-up by Apple's fantastic growth rate. Just too many ideas were generated. Sculley's structural strategies to improve control led Apple back to a better balance between entrepreneurship and control (Figure 7).

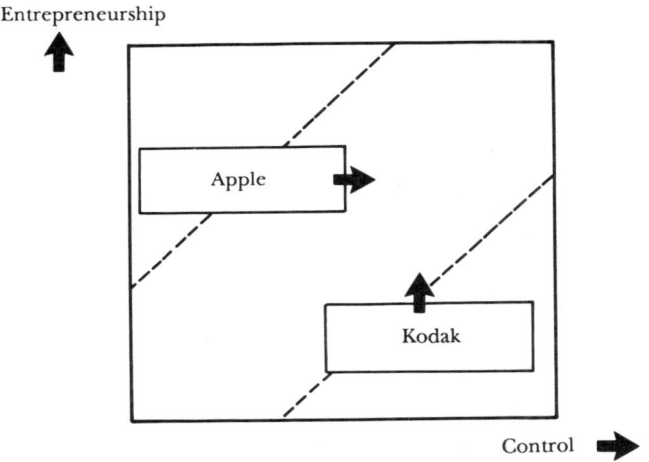

Figure 7   *Balancing logic in corporate culture shifts*

In summary, the positioning efforts, as reported in business literature, point in the direction of at least five basic dynamic balance situations:

1 a dynamic balance between entrepreneurship and control, driven by corporate structure adjustment strategies (as in Figure 6);
2 a dynamic balance between the vision development activity and 'alignment' in an organization, as driven by people involvement strategies:
3 a dynamic balance between the strategic and operational orientation of managers, driven by responsibility adjustment strategies;
4 a dynamic balance between employee and corporate objectives, driven by corporate identity adjustment strategies;
5 a dynamic balance between goal-tuning with external partners and internal goal-tuning, driven by goal-tuning adjustment strategies.

The above dynamic balance situations are just a prelude to a comprehensive 'culture-performance' engineering approach, which will be discussed and explained in detail in the next part of this book (Culture engineering). The point that I want to emphasize is that corporate culture adjustment efforts are continuous and that they are subject to a certain logic.

Leaders in their environment

A key finding relating to these observed culture adjustments is that they are often initiated and driven by (mostly new) corporate leaders. This applies to Apple (Sculley), Kodak (Chandler), General Electric (Welch), Philips (van der Klugt) and so forth. Not surprisingly, leaders play an important role in the development of a new corporate vision and in the adjustment of the corporate culture.

It is a well known fact, though, that not every leader is capable of managing a start-up company. Vice versa, leaders of start-up companies may not be able to effectively manage a matured or a maturing organization. Many examples are available today of company founders who are not willing (or able) to follow the transitions that their organizations have been going through. Very successful company founders, who eventually were confronted with this reality, can be found in the computer industry. Just look at the way John Sculley took over from Steven Jobs in Apple and why Rollwagen is in charge of Cray Computers, rather than Cray himself. One of the few exceptions, however, is Ken Olsen, the founder and president of Digital after more than 30 years. Apparently, Olsen has successfully managed himself through the same transition as his organization went through. In other words, the vision of Olsen on where the company has to move to in the future is in line with the state or sophistication of the current corporate environment. In addition, the cultural ingredients that he thinks are needed to be successful, have evolved and matured with the organization. But many people who helped to build Digital together with Ken have not made this transition and have left the company. This in particular explains the influx of new vice presidents and managers in the top layers of Digital's organization over recent years.

In summary, managers experience very specific challenges when managing their corporate entity over a longer period of time. These challenges relate to their ability to generate new and innovative visions when the old ones have been achieved, to their skill in getting a vision accepted in the organization and to their success in bringing about the necessary culture adjustments when they are needed most. The vision-culture diagram, as in the next section pictures and clarifies these challenges. The particular relationship between vision and culture is the principal concept in this book. The success-cube theory as in Chapter 13 and the vision and culture engineering rules will be based on it.

The vision-culture diagram

Management's tasks incorporate both vision development and culture adjustment. In essence, a certain balance should be maintained between vision and culture. For example, when management develops a new vision that applies to a certain organization, a potential vision-jump is generated. A vision-jump could be considered as a temporary dissociation from the existing environmental views or culture. Then, after the management vision has been developed and communicated, (assuming that the vision is not rejected), the environment goes through a period of transition, during which the management vision is absorbed by the adjusting culture. Culture should in this context be considered as a set of values, concepts and views, that are considered common sense in an organization. Hence, culture eventually includes or embraces new management visions.

There is a natural tendency towards the (re-)establishment of a balance between vision and culture, once a vision has been introduced. This balance is

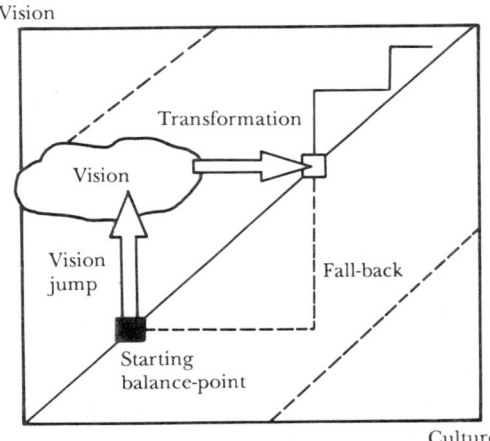

Figure 8 *Balance and imbalance between vision and culture*

achieved either by the absorption of the vision in the culture or by the rejection of the vision. (Proposition 7)

In Figure 8, the balance between culture and vision has been shown graphically. It describes the starting balance point with its characteristic equilibrium between culture and vision. Then, by developing a new vision (displayed by a cloud), management creates a vision-jump or a certain imbalance between culture and vision. Assuming that the environment accepts this vision as given, it will transform through its culture towards a new equilibrium, as on the equilibrium diagonal. Now that is 'how it should happen', when everything is all right! The first problem for leaders occurs when their vision is so far out that the cultural environment with which they are dealing refuses to accept it. Those situations are experienced by founders of companies in organizations that have matured over time. And new managers that come into an 'established' organization may also be confronted with this situation. Obviously, this model applies to corporate as well as political leaders.

Soviet analogy

The de-Stalinization programme in the Soviet Union that Nikita Khrushchev initiated in the sixties was not really there to discredit the name of Stalin. Above all, it was an attempt by Khrushchev to decentralize the centralized economical planning system of the Soviet Union that Stalin helped to develop.

As we know, Khrushchev did not achieve his goal. His vision was too far stretched for the Soviet environment at that time. Years later, after scene-setting attempts by Andropov, Mikhail Gorbachev should have a better chance. Although he has been helped by the economic problems in the Soviet Union and the inevitable influences from the rest of the world, Gorbachev has been careful in introducing the vision of *perestroika* or restructuring of the central economic bodies, such as Gosplan and the ministries. In order to get his vision accepted, he has initiated several strategies to prepare the cultural environment. One of the most quoted strategies is *glasnost*, which has been related to openness or publicity; in other words, as an approach to influence constructively Soviet society by bringing some of the truths and economic failures to the surface. Mikhail Gorbachev's vision will most likely lead to the successful transformation of the Soviet culture in line with this vision. This very visible process and struggle shows how hard it can be for top management to have their visions constructively adopted by the affected environment.

Critical continuity

After transformation of the environmental culture has taken place and a new vision-culture equilibrium has been reached, the next potential problem occurs: 'there needs to be a new vision'.

This is exactly when some leaders get into trouble. In many cases, leaders become burned out after surviving and achieving their major vision. It happened to great political leaders such as Charles de Gaulle in France and Winston Churchill in the United Kingdom after the Second World War. But in companies too, founders are being replaced and new top managers are moving in. When 'old leaders' stay on and when no new follow-up visions are launched, country and company cultures will slide back to the old situation along the dotted line in Figure 8. When that happens whatever progress has been made may be diminished and eventually lost. The challenge for every leader and management therefore is to come up continuously with new visions, i.e. after the culture has absorbed the previous ones. This will eventually result in an increasingly sophisticated environmental culture, where more advanced visions are acceptable and possible. In Figure 8, this is indicated through the subsequent steps along the vision-culture *equilibrium diagonal*.

Several challenging examples can be found in industry. In a previous chapter, I talked about Peugeot–Citroen and its chairman Jacques Calvet. In a subsequent article, Calvet confirms how important it is to set a *new* vision after successfully returning to the 'black' from the brink of disaster. After achieving the vision of becoming Europe's low-cost car producer, the new vision is to be the number one in the European car business. His determination is underlined by a heavy investment programme to modernize the company. Calvet clearly indicates that this new target vision is a way of motivating the company once again.

The right attitude ...

Do you need a special type of people who are capable of coming up with a new vision, after having gone through the same transition as their environment? The answer in essence is no! In general, the trouble is that there is too much focus on the achievement of a particular vision, which suppresses the awareness that 'there is life after death'. In other words, by creating the awareness that new visions need to be developed continuously, the attitude of management may be changed right from the start. Simply by maintaining the right attitude, management will continue to be focused on the future effectively.

34 *The Power of Tomorrow's Management*

The extremes meet

The vision-culture diagram in Figure 8 also incorporates some of the extreme cases where environments are characterized by an imbalance between vision and culture. Some of the Middle Eastern countries can be considered as examples of extreme societies, where a strong cultural impact and very basic visions rule the people; in the diagram these are shown down in the bottom right corner. On the other hand, dictatorships can be explained as extreme imbalance situations as well, where dictatorial vision overrules the culture; these are shown in the diagram in the upper left corner.

It is obvious that these extreme situations should be prevented for the sake of progress. One should always stay close to the vision-culture equilibrium diagonal. In accordance with proposition 8, the natural tendency towards a balance between vision and culture can be observed in history and in the many countries and companies of today, where internal revolutions manifest the re-balancing act.

Framework rather than intuition

With this chapter's findings in mind, it is evident that a process for maintaining an appropriate awareness of the vision-culture balance is essential. This process should ensure the continued development of vision and at the same time work the receptiveness of the cultural environment. There is just too much at stake to let things happen by intuition only. The vision-culture balance is a reality that needs to be taken seriously. It provides opportunities for continued and improved corporate success by showing the impact of vision on culture and vice versa. As such, it will be key to the conclusions of this book, as formulated in Part Four.

Reflections

Key messages

Just before the 1988 Conservative Party conference at Brighton, Margaret Thatcher mentioned that one of her challenges was to prevent the potential complacency of the top people in the party. Her aims were clear, that is to prepare for a fourth term in office. Whatever people's political preferences are, the sheer success of her long career is something that cannot be denied and can only be respected. She has out-managed a country with unions, a country at war and now she is planning to lead Britain into the 1990s by making its industries competitive enough to cope with the opening up of the European market.

The vision-culture balance 35

Thatcher is a leader who has been capable of developing vision after vision. At the same time, she managed the necessary adaptation of the cultural environment in the United Kingdom. The fact that she still is in office underlines the acceptance by the environment.

- Leaders greatly influence the cultural effectiveness of the environment for which they are responsible.
- They should ensure the acceptance and absorption of their vision by its careful development, in order to prevent its rejection, and by the introduction of supporting culture adjustments.
- A certain logic exists which explains culture adjustments in corporations. The understanding of this logic will help to improve the development of a more effective operating culture.
- The natural tendency for an equilibrium between vision and culture is a challenge as well as a blessing. It is a challenge for managers, when they create a temporary imbalance at the moment they launch their new vision. It is a blessing in extreme imbalance situations, when it causes a continuous force that only stops when a balance has been achieved that is acceptable to the environment. As a result one should be aware of organizations and countries where a continuous antagonistic force is observed.

The logic of culture trends, one of this chapter's key findings, will be explained in Chapter 7 by relating it to the basic characteristics of change. During the course of Part Two, it will finally be explained in a comprehensive model for the management and improvement of culture performance. The second major finding in this chapter, the vision-culture balance, will lead to conclusions on revolutionary and evolutionary progress in organizations or in any other corporate entities. In summary, effective management may have to be based on 'managing evolution, as a process of small revolutions'. This has in particular been addressed in Chapter 14, which is about vision and culture engineering laws.

Steps to consider

Managers should be encouraged to use their knowledge of the cultural characteristics in their environments. As such, managers should consider which strategies might be developed to facilitate or invite constructive support for their visions. The question that managers should ask themselves regularly is: 'what should the vision or goals be when the current ones have been achieved'?

5

The new deal

The great depression

After the Great Depression in the 1930s, it was President Roosevelt who initiated the New Deal in the United States of America. Along the lines of the British economist Keynes, he instituted a government spending programme to revitalize the American economy and to reduce unemployment. The New Deal in particular provided a new spirit to the American people, which in itself may have been one of its key success factors.

Like Roosevelt's programme, the New Deal in management aims at providing a new spirit to the management of corporate and national organizations. In a sense, it may be considered too as a spending programme on people in the organization, but now in terms of redirecting the focus and efforts of management. In an 'untraditional' way, the New Deal, as proposed in this book, homes in on bringing the strategic responsibility of management into the organization. From now on, whenever 'strategic planning people' are at work, they should mainly concentrate on process coordination and *not* on making strategy. *The Power of Tomorrow's Management* is a reinvestment in strategic activities with the objective to revitalize the corporate capacity to change.

The information age connection

One of the major corporate challenges today is the transition from a post-industrial era towards the information age via a period of change in terms of values, thinkings and strategies. Companies in the post-industrial age were mainly devoted to their physical operation. Now in a transition period, they are improving productivity by redefining those operations. Through simplification, innovation, automation and networking, companies will reach the information age, where resource management as well as information management are equally important. In this situation, people, functions and departments will be much more dependent on each other as planning partners. It will produce the need for improved or one plan synergy. In addition, the link with other outside environments will play a much greater role.

Significant, in relation to the above, is the intention of the Dutch electronics multinational Philips to invest two per cent of its revenues per year in the improvement of its internal communication networks. This amounts to an investment of billions of dollars, all dedicated to the goal of improving one plan synergy and planning flexibility across the world-wide product divisions of Philips. The network will allow Philips to obtain inputs and feedback from local market areas. Strategic directions will consequently be better tuned to these areas. A New Deal in management is of absolute importance when trying to maintain and increase organizational performance with the information age in sight.

Figure 9 *The new deal in management*

Old ways

Characteristic of the old way of management are top-down controls, the focus on analysis of trends and communication on paper. It is time we realized that reports and documents are two of the least effective strategic communication media, especially when they are not accompanied by an appropriate and interactive introduction. Just look at who reads and understands the strategy reports and check who actually touches policies and procedures manuals! Reports should be used as a reference guide or to prove that a certain event happened. And most of the value of internal strategy reports is in the feeling of identity that they may provide to originators and affected employees.

The old way does not sufficiently mobilize the brainpower and knowledge in the organization. It is a one-way instead of a two-way flow of strategic inputs.

Interaction

The New Deal or the new way in management very much concentrates on interaction between the people who have to make the continuous flow of new strategies happen, primarily, because they have to work the inevitable change, as caused by those strategies. In order to obtain synergy in action, it is important for people in an organization that they understand corporate vision and directions as a team. Only through interaction is this team understanding achieved. But interaction does more. Team members will also get a better understanding of the views, aims and strengths of others. It will lead to a better use of the available people potential.

The 'why' issue

The New Deal tries to provide a rationale or reason for looking ahead by understanding the *why* of planning, by understanding *change*. The basic characteristics of change in organizations will therefore be explained in Chapter 7. The 'why issue' in management teams (why change?) will also be resolved by creating an appropriate level of awareness of the possible change scenarios. In line with the findings of Pierre A. Wack (Chapter 2), management teams should develop alternative visions and work out particular strategic and operational responses.

Simple process

Only simple planning processes will have a chance of being used. The planning process for the New Deal in management therefore needs to be much simpler and more flexible than the usual planning approach, as developed by the so-called experts. The New Deal process should look like the example in Figure 10, where the next higher layer in the organization determines the vision of what it 'wants to be' first. Also the key measurable goals for that level should be quantified, as well as the required action and/or investment items. Complications such as objectives, strategies, tactics, etc. should just be left out. The managers of the

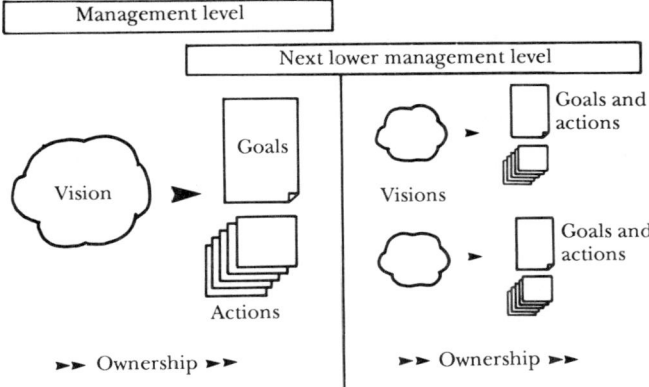

Figure 10 *Simple planning process*

next lower layer in the organization are assumed to participate in this interactive process.

Based on the outcome of the above, the management of the next lower layer should go through a similar process at their level. Of course, the vision they will develop will reflect the environmental influences and the particular strengths or ideas at *their* level. This approach stimulates a feeling of identity and ownership at each level in the organization. The available mental and creative capabilities will then have a reasonable chance of being mobilized. The proposed way of fulfilling the planning task does not necessarily do away with a certain planning hierarchy. It aims, however, to stimulate creativity by focusing on something simple that connects with the way the mind works.

Self sufficiency

The New Deal encourages self-sufficiency or self-management in terms of being responsible for the monitoring and feedback of one's own results. It requires an awareness that feedback is not there for the sake of control, but that it is needed for the achievement of the goal. Feedback should trigger corrective actions in case the goal is not achieved, and it should generate ideas when the goal is over-achieved. Therefore, why not have the organization monitor its own strategic progress? When monitoring and managing its own progress, it makes a lot of sense also to involve the organization in goal-setting and hence in having it create more responsive and supporting visions. This will allow a better use of the particular cultural strengths within the organization. Vision development and vision management should consequently be made part of the organizational responsibilities and toolkit. The question of 'What a vision really is' will be discussed in detail in Part 3 of this book.

Towards the new manager

In the previous chapters, a basic description has been given of the environment and approach in the New Deal organization, where both vision and culture play a critical role in successfully shaping the future. But what about the manager in that organization? What should he value in order to function effectively within this environment?

Ford, the American car manufacturer, has successfully reintroduced intuitive car design. But now the 'intuitive approach' in corporations is expanding more and more towards *intuitive management*. In the United Kingdom, another phenomenon has been discovered. A new elite of very results oriented people, such as Alan Sugar (founder of the Amstrad company) and Margaret Thatcher, seems to be emerging as the 'Disestablishment'. These managers exhibit a strong drive to break through old practices, class and habit restrictions and inhibitions imposed by governments and unions. Every organization should be run like a business. Social engineering and charity are seen as important for a happy and productive society. In short, these managers are characterized by their internationalism, their understanding of cultural differences and their rock-hard realism.

A new generation of Japanese executives is coming into the limelight. They are people with a cross-border type of mentality, capable of bridging cultures with entirely different backgrounds. This bridging capability is seen as critical to the success of increasingly international operating companies. The British Midland Bank has seriously invested in psychological training programmes with the objective of liberating the business creativity of their managers and people. Professor Ahmet Aykac, director of the MBA Programme at the International Management Institute in Geneva, has developed a model to capture the new modes of managerial thought and behaviour. He talks about holistic thinking, thinking in networks, subjective thinking and thinking in approximations, as complementary qualities for tomorrow's managers.

The spectrum of management education is constantly being broadened. Not only are different skills being taught, but also the forecasting ability of tomorrow's managers is being expanded significantly. The historically evolved prejudice about what *is* and *is not* possible, is constantly being broken down. The findings in Chapter 2 on the New Dimensions indicate that our potential and achievable visions lie far beyond the borders of our current assumptions. At one point people wondered 'will we ever reach the moon?' Now the questions are: 'will we ever find superconductive materials at room temperatures?', or 'will computers ever become intelligent?' and even 'will we ever travel faster than light?' However, an optimum state of mind will be required to materialize tomorrow's breakthroughs, whatever they may be. One should also realize that this state of mind is very much linked to the management of our emotional world and well-being.

The improvement of the vision-culture balance and the application of the associated culture and vision engineering processes, described in Parts Two and Three of this book, will help managers to grow towards a new set of values and success factors, such as:

- *the importance of* heart *(or guts) as well as brains;*
- *the appreciation of an* infinite *rather than a finite world;*
- *the need for a* subjective *as well as an objective world;*
- *the endorsement of* continuity;
- *the support of targets and their background*

(Proposition 8)

In Chapter 14, after discussing culture performance adjustments and vision development, a further assessment of this proposition will be made. These success factors will cause a re-assessment of the traditional management effort.

Re-assessing management effort

The values and success factors of the 'new manager', as in Proposition 8, will greatly impact on the essence of his efforts. Characteristically it will be a partial shift from goal-setting to facilitating vision development and vision specific organizational behaviour. The ultimate goal is to improve the performance of the corporate entity by making best use of its people's potential.

Numerous examples are known of people who have achieved successes that were beyond the expectations of their environment *and* the odds. That in itself should be an impressive argument in building the required management incentives for using the untapped and above all unknown people potential and energy by creating the right environment. Tough competition and the sheer amount of technological progress, however, emerged as two additional no nonsense reasons for increasing performance in an untraditional way.

In the introduction to this book, the two different phases of management effort over time were discussed, specifically in order to amplify the major challenges that each leader and manager faces, when dealing with his environment. The first phase concerns the development of a new

42   The Power of Tomorrow's Management

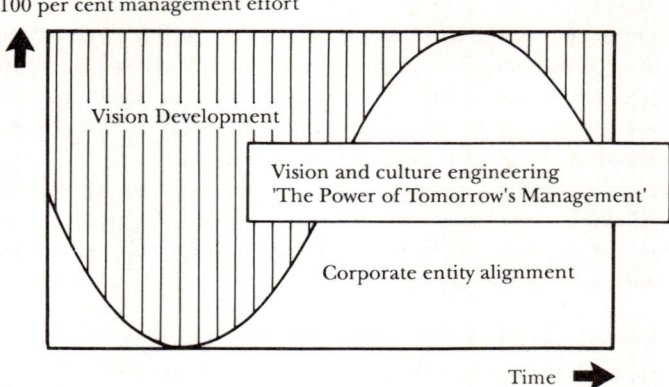

Figure 11   *The power of tomorrow's management*

vision for the organization. In the second phase the manager spends more and more time getting the vision accepted and ensuring a constructive response from the organization. Once the organization picks up the vision and starts to work on its realization, the manager can gradually spend more effort on the development of the next new vision. In Figure 11, the sine-curve in management effort is shown and in particular the area where the *Power of Tomorrow's Management* will be. The *vision and culture engineering processes*, described in this book, will indeed help in the development of a vision by describing and picturing it. But their major strengths are in the second phase, when interacting with the organization. The aim there is to understand and improve the performance of the organizational culture. How one should visualize culture performance will be discussed in Chapter 6.

A 'new' orientation

Many strategic planning methods deal with the development of a competitive strategy or vision that weighs the corporate strengths versus the outside forces of competition, technology, product development and marketing. These methods, one could say, have an outward orientation because they relate the corporation to the outside business world in pursuit of a competitive strategy or vision.

The Power of Tomorrow's Management may in fact take the results of these competitive strategy analyses and work on a constructive response in the organization for which the competitive vision or strategy is meant. Figure 12 visualizes this in a picture. The corporation is represented by

The new deal 43

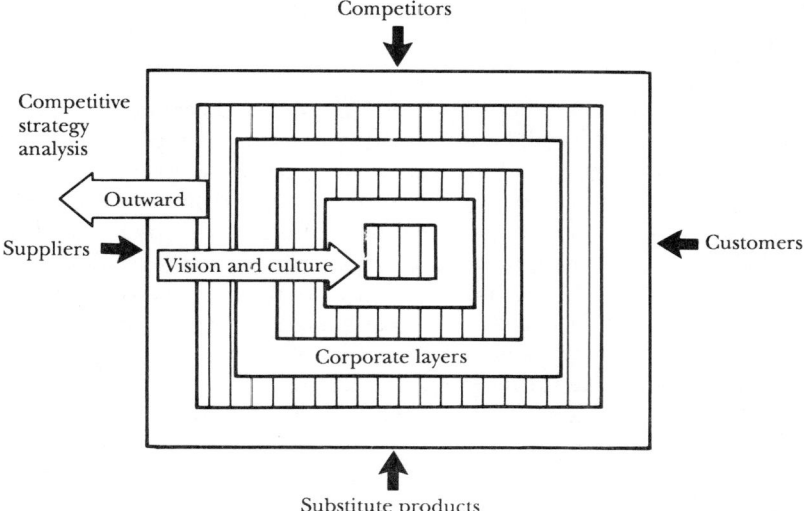

Figure 12   *Inward orientation*

a number of nested squares. Each square is a different layer in the corporate organization. Since this book, in particular, is focused on these layers, it could be considered as having an inward orientation. As such it is complementary to other outward-looking strategic planning methods.

Phasing-in tomorrow's success

In summary, this book incorporates two core management activities (see Figure 13).

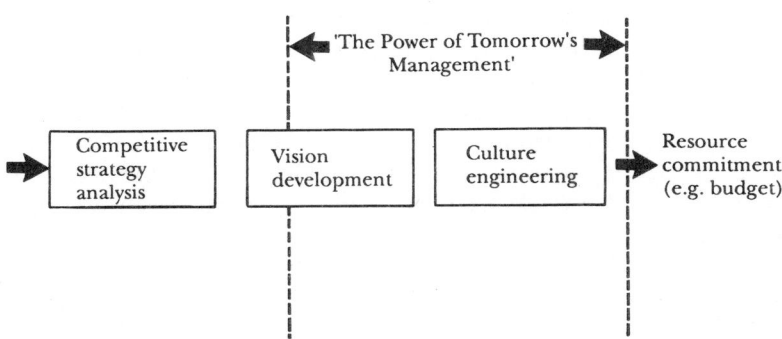

Figure 13   *Phasing-in tomorrow's success*

44   *The Power of Tomorrow's Management*

1   the facilitation of vision development and
2   the repositioning of culture.

During the development of a vision picture, management is guided towards a complete and understandable conceptual representation of how it sees the future and the role of the corporate entity. With this vision picture in mind, management may use the culture repositioning approach to determine the vital culture adjustment strategies that are needed to ensure an appropriate level of organizational receptiveness. *The Power of Tomorrow's Management* fills up the gap between competitive strategy analysis and the budgeting process. The budget process will hopefully become more a matter of number crunching, rather than the usual re-active fight for figures and funds.

Although vision comes first, I purposely decided to deal with culture engineering first, simply because in my view, culture engineering is going to have a great impact on the quality and originality of the vision engineering results.

Reflections
Key messages

Steve Jobs, the co-founder of Apple computers, may have done it this time! Within four months of being deposed as chairman of Apple, he had formed a new venture called NeXT. He gathered a cadre of new engineering talent and by 1988 he had launched a new, and on first sight innovative desk-top mainframe, as he called it. During those first three years, no press was allowed and almost nothing was communicated on what was happening inside NeXT. Applicants, after being screened by Jobs and other colleagues, would only be told about the operating style and the state of developments, when they seemed totally acceptable.

This secrecy obviously had to do with competition. However, it also characterizes the specific atmosphere that Steven Jobs used to create in Apple to make breakthroughs happen. When he developed the famous Apple Macintosh computer, he and a select group of extraordinary characters locked themselves up in a small building. On top of the building waved a pirate's flag! His management approach was dominated by guts and brains, by subjective as well as objective modes, by an infinite world and by a clear target, of which the 'why' was outstandingly clear and supported. The people in that environment did not represent the obvious choices, at least from a traditional point of view. For example, some of them hardly had any formal higher education. But Jobs created an environment or an operating culture, if you like, that led to a breakthrough product. This time, he may indeed have come close to a New Deal in management.

- A New Deal in management will emerge, as a new spirit in organizations that invests in vision and culture management, in creating the reasons for looking ahead, in stimulating self-sufficiency in monitoring and feedback and in the development of accepted work processes.
- Team interaction or active networking will be increasingly the dominating form for management to increase the performance of the organization concerned.
- The new spirit and interaction in tomorrow's management, will broaden the spectrum of success factors for managers significantly with items that deviate from the traditional western world views.

This chapter sketches the coloured window, through which managers of tomorrow will have to look, in order to be successful. It should set the scene for the development of the culture and vision engineering processes (as in Parts Two and Three).

Steps to consider

Based on the above, there are only two sensible steps that can be recommended, because transformation along the outlines of the New Deal will only then have a chance. One should set oneself the goal of reading the next two parts of this book in the next two weeks. One week on culture engineering, one week on vision engineering. In the third week, one should read Part Four about the *application* of these processes. Then make a decision either to follow the concept or to disregard it. If the former do not sleep before brainstorming where one could use the concept.

PART TWO

Culture Engineering

6

Culture performance

Impact of culture

About ten to fifteen years ago culture seemed to be the pet interest mainly of anthropologists. They were the people who made expeditions to far away and exotic countries to study rare tribes and primitive societies. Their observations were on the whole contemplative and as such seemed to dissociate these societies from events in our own environment. Successful elements in other cultures did not therefore consciously serve as examples that we would use to improve the performance of our own culture.

Awareness of culture impact

The impact of Japanese industry has become more and more apparent from the late seventies onwards. High quality and price-competitive Japanese products sneaked into our markets to build up a substantial market-share. After Japanese cameras came cars, watches, hi-fi equipment, calculators, shipbuilding, computers, chips, bio-chemical products and many others. The background to the success of Japanese industries became one of the frequently discussed subjects in the business world.

Interestingly, the Japanese seemed to apply theories that in essence were developed by a number of American experts, such as Drucker, Deming and Juran, on management and quality concepts. Since these methods were not drastically different from those known in the rest of the business world, there must have been another reason for their successful application. People started to become intrigued by Japanese culture and by the culture within the Japanese corporations. The findings indicated more and more that these corporate cultures played an important role as the driving force behind the success stories. *In Search of Excellence* by Peters and Waterman, confirmed to the world the importance of corporate culture by sketching dominating cultural elements that in their view led to 'success'. Therefore, in spite of its shortcomings (due to the later poor performance of many of the 'excellent' companies), it strongly contributed to the growth of culture awareness. But interestingly, the usefulness of this book may stretch further than the critics and the authors would like to believe. In fact, it proved that the characteristics of the companies referred to may have led to success in the past, but that these characteristics are not a guarantee for success under all circumstances.

Hence, as a result of change within corporate entities and the environment, the cultural characteristics of these corporate entities will have to be adjusted in order to maintain or improve corporate entity success. (Proposition 9).

This important finding provides a natural incentive for the development of the culture performance adjustment theory, as discussed in this part of the book.

More-impact

Based on the conclusion above, one could also say that in an unchanged (corporate) culture, *effort* will reach a maximum of usefulness. In other words, when the environmental challenges facing a corporation change over time and when something needs to be done, it may not be effective to put in *more* effort. Figure 14 shows the relation between effort and its usefulness, given a certain cultural environment.

Starting from zero gradually putting in more effort will lead to an increase in its usefulness, as shown in a climbing curve. Then, after putting in an optimum amount of effort, a maximum of usefulness is achieved, that is, given an unchanged corporate culture. When more than the optimum amount of effort is put in, we will see the usefulness of this effort diminish. The conclusion must be that 'just working harder', in an unchanged cultural environment, may eventually turn out to be counter-productive! In other words, a company or organization needs to adjust and improve its culture in order to increase the maximum usefulness of effort and achieve *more-impact*. This will move the entire curve upwards along the dotted curve in Figure 14.

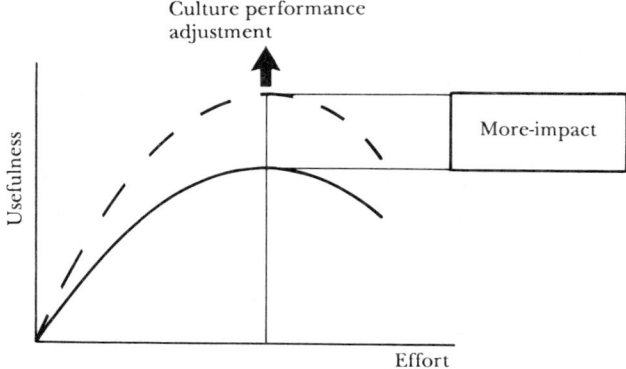

Figure 14 *'Just working harder' may not really be useful*

Some clarifying analogies

The relation between *effort* and *usefulness* is also known in marketing and tax-economics. Mathematically, it is the first derivative of the so called *S-curve*, which will be discussed in the following chapter.

The American economist Laffer for example, used a similar curve to explain the tax situation in the United States of America. Laffer referred to the amount of tax paid by American people and American companies. The assumption is that the useful spending of tax revenues increases to a certain maximum. When the tax yield grows further, its useful impact diminishes. Apparently, increasingly large governmental organizations that are funded with tax revenues run out of incentives and imagination effectively to allocate these funds. Hence, by reducing the amount of tax paid, one will not necessarily reduce and may even increase its useful application.

One of the more popular explanations for the effort-usefulness curve is the beer-drinking-analogy. Suppose you replace effort by the number of beers that one consumes. Similarly, one should replace usefulness by satisfaction. The curve now indicates that the more beers someone drinks the higher his satisfaction will be. However, after a certain member of beers, his satisfaction will reach a maximum after which it will tend to reduce. If the beer drinker keeps on drinking his satisfaction will reduce even further, until he is eventually sick! The satisfaction curve has then crossed the zero level again.

In summary, the effort-usefulness curve shows that there is a practical limit to the amount of effort that one should put into something. In addition, one will achieve more success with the same amount of effort by doing things entirely differently and/or by changing the corporate culture.

52   The Power of Tomorrow's Management

Culture

'We may achieve *more-impact* by improving or adjusting the corporate culture', was the conclusion in the previous chapter. But what is corporate culture? The usual discussion on culture relates to elements such as values, attitudes, behaviour, rituals and hymns. To me culture is more. Culture is a conglomerate of phenomena that determines the way a company works or operates, if you like. From the discussion on the corporate entity (Chapter 3), it is apparent that the environment influences the culture in a corporation. But vision also impacts culture, since vision tends to create new values. In other words, the true culture in a corporation is reflected in its corporate vision as well as in the related strategies and activities. Therefore, I just don't believe corporate officers who say 'so and so is our culture', when the corporate strategies and activities do not match the presented characteristics. Culture always 'puts its money where its mouth is'. And that in particular is what the 'vision-culture balance' (Chapter 4) proves for us.

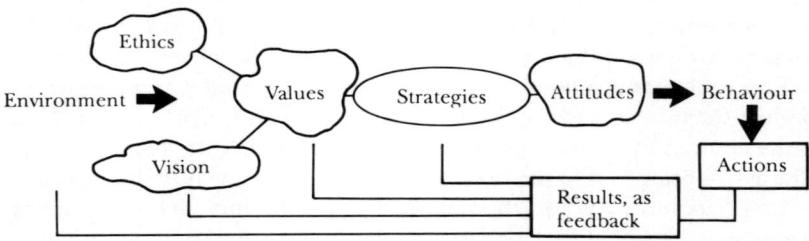

Figure 15   *Culture as a dynamic system*

In Figure 15, a model for corporate culture has been sketched based upon the above reasoning. Taking the definition for the corporate entity into consideration, one may choose to start from the environment, as the first element that helps to shape the corporate culture. As such, top management will develop a corporate vision, driven by the environment and their ethical values. These ethical values could be interpreted, as an inheritance from past environments. Subsequently, the corporate vision will generate additional or replacement values in the organization that has to respond to this vision. The values will allow certain strategies to emerge and strategies will influence the attitudes of people, which in turn determine their behaviour and actions. The outcome of the actions will have impact on the environment and eventually on the corporate vision as well. Of course, similar processes take place *within* the organization. Overall, the above is how culture 'lives' in a company. The sketch in Figure 15 is a simplified model identifying only the key elements of corporate culture. It shows that culture operates like a system or a process. Corporate culture can be interpreted as a dynamic system that operates to a certain extent with a closed and multiple feedback loop. In a sense, culture resembles a mathematical equation with only dependent variables, because culture as a whole influences its own characteristic elements.

In summary, culture not only includes values, attitudes and behaviour, but also the activity-orientated consequences such as vision, strategies and actions. Together these elements operate as a dynamic system.

Hence, by adjusting the vision, strategies and actions in a corporate entity, one will also influence its culture. (Proposition 10)

Culture performance

One place is not the same as the other. That applies to homes, restaurants and companies. In some companies, one finds cultures that are quite flexible and capable of quickly adjusting to new management visions. Other company cultures seem to be rigid. There, visions take ages to transform the culture (see Chapter 4 on the 'vision-culture balance').

Take, for example, a well-established company that decided to implement an electronic mail system. The decision was made based on a carefully computed cost-benefit analysis. It showed very attractive efficiency savings especially in the white collar area. In addition, the paper traffic would be reduced and the directness and speed of communication would be improved. Every manager received a computer terminal and the necessary printing equipment. After some time, however, it became clear that the projected savings had not materialized; that is, not according to the original plan. Too many managers were still communicating in the usual way, through their secretaries! It turned out that only a few were actually *using* the computer terminal. Apparently, managers, including senior management, were not prepared to sit behind a terminal. The 'social structure' did not easily accept it. It took this company quite some time and additional investment in training and encouragements to benefit from the investment it originally made. Another company that went through the same motions, had much less trouble. Fairly soon after the introduction of the electronic mail facilities, people started to use it. Eventually the électronic mail facility incorporated many interest groups who communicated frequently on

54   The Power of Tomorrow's Management

particular business subjects. The intensified communication resulted in a lot of new and creative ideas.

The cultures of the two companies must be different. Not only in the way the electronic mail was used, but also in the time it took to implement it. In other words, one could say that the *adjustment* or *change* performance of the culture in the one company was better than the 'culture-performance' of the other company. In Figure 16, the culture-performance lines of these companies have been plotted on a graph. Starting at a certain point in time, one and the same vision is introduced into both companies. The culture-performance lines show that this vision creates a vision-jump in both companies. That is from the culture-performance line, where a certain equilibrium exists between vision and culture, to the newly set vision. The vision-jump for one company is bigger than for the other. But also the time it takes for one company culture to go through a transition is longer. The transition time is the time needed by the corporate culture to encapsulate or be changed by a newly set vision.

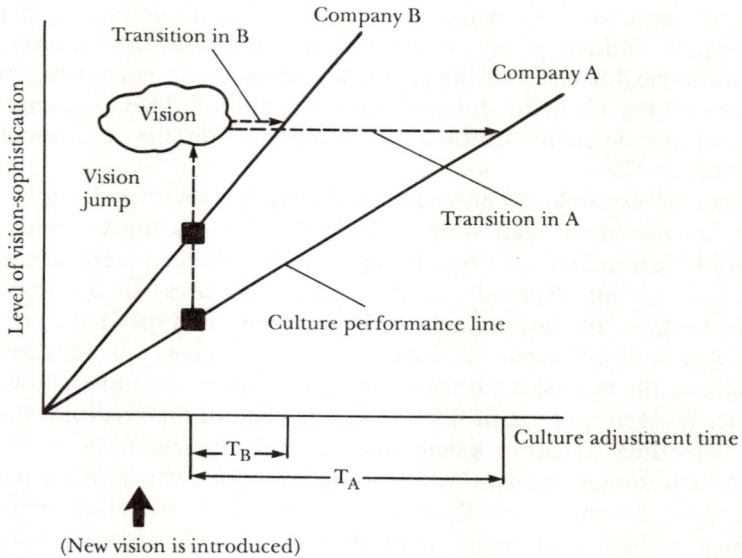

Figure 16   *Culture performance lines of companies*

In summary, corporate cultures may differ not only in their fabric, but also in their performance. It leads to a new definition for the performance of a culture or simply culture performance.

Culture performance can be explained on the one hand as the capacity to cope with sophisticated visions. On the other hand, culture performance refers to the time it takes to absorb a new vision (Proposition 11)

Learning from others

Just copying other cultures like those of successful Japanese corporations may not always work. In fact, it may work negatively on the feeling of cultural identity. It is much more important for management to discover *which visions* and strategies drive successful companies. Those should then be related to the vision and strategies in their own company. A careful assessment should lead to awareness and conclusions about what to adjust in the corporate culture to improve it. 'Culture positioning', as discussed in Chapters 7, 8 and 9, is such a process of assessment.

Culture trends

Most managers today have read about the industrial age, the post-industrial age and the coming information age. Many business publications and other media refer to these characteristic periods in industrial and social evolution. However, not only products and production technologies differ in these eras, but also the way companies are organized. In fact, their intrinsic way of operating, their culture, has been evolving in line with these particular ages.

Industrial age

Just after the war, we still lived in the remainder of the industrial age. Companies and cultures were based upon fixed hierarchical layers and relationships. Consequently, the organization of those companies was quite inflexible. As a matter of fact, there was no need to be flexible.

Management by coercion or by threat was still the undertone of the way employees were treated. Management worked through directives, i.e. by telling people what and how they should do things. People were used as machines or wherever mechanization could not be used either technically or economically. The demand-driven economy needed production capacity in terms of manpower or machinepower. This situation lasted until inflation grew out of hand and production capacity exceeded demand. Companies in the seventies therefore had to change in order to survive. Some companies that needed to change were not allowed to. Especially in Europe, companies were artificially kept alive through government subsidies. The aim was to prevent unemployment.

Post-industrial age

The new challenges of the changing economic environment forced companies to be more flexible. On top of the inflation problem came the oil crisis. At about the same time, industries from the Far East started to gain more momentum. It meant that companies were faced with a multitude of sometimes fairly rapidly changing challenges.

The necessary flexibility was achieved by changing organizations in support of goals. Organizations, however, remained hierarchical. The frustration of individuals in these changing hierarchical organizations was and still is considered a nasty but necessary side effect. Management By Objectives was a way to get the people moving, to a certain extent detached from organizational status and focused on goals. Corporate values in essence remained unchanged, black and white, not grey. It could be said that the stick had been replaced by the carrot, however, for the basic attitude and background of this approach did not change.

Towards the information age

In the late eighties and early nineties, we are in the middle of an industrial transition period. Technological advances seem to come more regularly. Products are rapidly developed and no time is wasted in bringing them to the market as soon as possible. The return on sometimes heavy investments in technology-driven production machinery are obtained by considering the world as the market. As such, internationalization is used by countries such as Korea and Taiwan, to position their industries strategically, as the suppliers of tomorrow's goods. Intensified communication facilities and the need for more and better information has caused the creation of a very competitive new product: *information*.

Information, as a product, creates new challenges for companies, since it is difficult to grasp and not easy to protect. It includes the knowledge of employees, as well as vital market and product statistics in corporate computers. Employees gain power by the information they possess. It provides them with the potential of starting their own business and they are stimulated by an increasing demand for information products! The investment in delivering value added information products doesn't have to be high, a personal computer is in most cases sufficient! So, corporations as such, may have to cope with internal as well as external competitors, in particular, the employees on whom they need to rely in order to be successful. In response, companies are allowing and even creating different work arrangements. Management of employees focuses on motivation. And even the goals of the corporation will eventually have to be balanced with those of the employee. What is more important, society as a whole seems to be becoming affected and involved.

Capacity to change

What is happening in the market, in technology and in society puts even greater pressure on the capacity of corporations to change. Change not only takes place more frequently, but also the usual way of changing seems not to be effective any more. The frustration of people in status layered organizations that are changed in support of goals, hampers the actual achievement of these goals.

Therefore, tomorrow's companies will most likely have simple but stable organizations with only a few layers. Networking within these organizations permits the necessary flexibility by linking individuals to certain goal-sets without changing their organizational status. In this way, flexibility is achieved through individuals rather than through the organization. New concepts like 'Change is nice' will therefore enter the corporate arena.

Corporations will also reconsider their core strengths or skills and limit the size of organizations to the people who have the chosen added-value capabilities. Non-core activities will tend to be subcontracted or realized through joint-venture type of arrangements.

Value flexibility

The need for change in corporations emphasizes the need for a review of existing corporate values that may block the road towards new approaches and breakthroughs. Values cannot all be maintained unaltered without endangering the survival of the company concerned.

It is like the change in values that one observes when people or countries get into a state of war. Certain things that would seem impossible in peace time are all of a sudden common sense. People who were considered dull and remote, seem to become enthused and show a tremendous inventiveness and drive. In the same way companies need to prepare themselves for change by reassessing the need for different values and consquently the need for culture performance adjustments – all with the objective of igniting the right spirit and character for tackling the job ahead. It obviously means that a company needs to understand change first, before it can actually take any such action. The appreciation of the oncoming change will put management in the best position to determine the necessary cultural set-up. Now, if one wants effectively to assist management in the above assignment, one needs to relate in a more structured way *effort to culture*. In particular, the development of the right culture performance strategies should be facilitated.

The challenges of tomorrow will fuel the need for new management tools, one of which is a framework for the repositioning of corporate culture and the development of change strategies. (Proposition 12)

Reflections
Key messages

In Chapter 3 about the 'corporate entity', we concluded that one and the same vision may lead to different solutions in corporations with different cultures. It means that the type of solution may be fairly culture-specific. However, it did *not* say anything about how fast a solution or a response was obtained after a vision was introduced! And rightly so ... Cultural strengths may not have much to do with the performance of the culture, that is in terms of its capability to cope with sophisticated visions and the time to realize a vision. Especially in the light of the amount of change in the business environment, culture performance (rather than culture) seems extremely important. Culture performance, however, may be part of the culture, but in its own right.

A difference is emerging between culture in general and culture performance. Culture seems based on the past by its hymns and rituals and by the inertia of its historically evolved traditions. Culture performance is aimed at the future, because it relates to anything that makes change successfully happen. Change in itself may eventually lead to culture performance adjustments. These adjustments, however, are effectively driven by plain strategies and actions. The culture performance adjustment–framework that is part of *The Power of Tomorrow's Management*, is a natural answer to culture trends and the associated change. The findings in this chapter are important for the development of the culture engineering concept. Based on an understanding of culture performance, culture performance drivers may be sought that can be applied to increase the probability of quickly realizing sophisticated visions in an organization. What then are we looking for in Japanese companies? Is it the centuries old culture with its samurai and martial arts or is it something else? Considering their well proven capability of quickly developing new products, it must be the latter.

7

Dynamic positioning plane

The effort-result curve

In order to design a framework that can be used to position the performance of corporate culture, one has to be able to connect effectively culture change and the required effort. Effort refers to the actions that management has to initiate, to adjust organizational values in support of the organizational capacity to change.

Pattern of change

In the previous chapter, the effort-usefulness curve was discussed. It is the first derivative of another interesting relation that exists between effort and results. The shape of the curve for the relation between effort and results is that of a stretched S. The top-end seems to have been pulled to the right, the bottom-end to the left. The result is a smooth curve, that rises first slowly, then fast and then slowly again until it ends (Figure 17).

It has been used in economics and performance studies. In economics it functions by relating marketing effort to sales. In other words, the more marketing effort a company puts in, the more its sales may grow. In performance studies, it shows the relation between effort, as provided by an organization, and the resulting increase in performance of products, processes, technologies and last but not least corporate culture. Effort is normally expressed in funds.

At any point in time, a company deals simultaneously with many of these characteristic effort-result curves. A sales department deals with the question of where to invest in advertising and the expected response

60   The Power of Tomorrow's Management

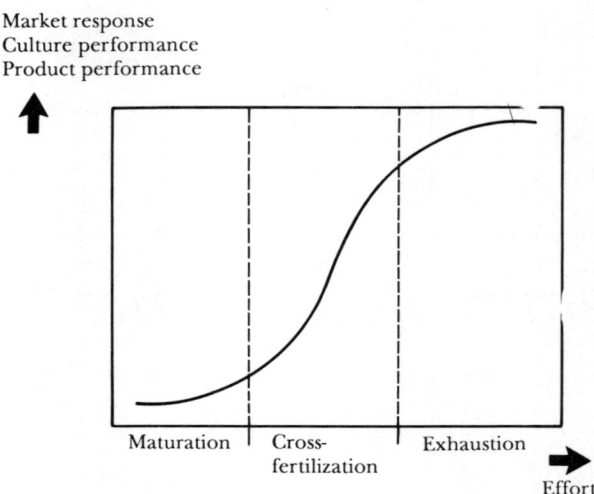

Figure 17   *The effort–result curve*

in the number of units sold. Management with input from the development division tries to anticipate the performance potential of its products and processes. Based on this assessment, decisions will be made on where to put in corporate funds.

Similarly, corporate management will have to watch continously the performance of particular operating cultures *and* the overall culture in order to decide whether to put in more effort, that is based on an anticipated culture performance potential.

The effort-result curve, in essence, shows the basic pattern of change of so many corporate action elements. All these action elements together impact on the overall performance of the company. Understanding the effort-result curve appropriately is therefore a key condition for management success. The effort-result curve or S-curve can be divided into three distinct sections: the maturation phase, the cross-fertilization phase and the exhaustion phase.

Maturation phase

During the first phase on the S-curve, the basic features and characteristics of, for example, a product, a process, a technology or culture are defined. In other words, corporate funds are spent on perfecting and out-developing so called future performance drivers, such as new products, new processes, new technologies and new corporate culture performance drivers. The resulting increase in performance initially is not that great yet. What emerges from this phase in particular is the performance potential. During the maturation phase, therefore, management will have to judge whether or where to put in corporate funding.

The maturation phase to which companies may be relating, in many cases concerns developments in the environment outside rather than within the company. In fact, any company may be triggered to invest in certain perceived performance drivers.

Cross-fertilization phase

Once the basic characteristics of a product, process, technology or culture have been defined in the maturation phase, the emphasis is on further improving their performance. That is assuming sufficient competitive impulses from outside the company are there to do this. Hence, when funding is continued and increased, the performance may go up increasingly faster than in the maturation phase.

Corporate disciplines, customers, suppliers and even competitors may play a role in this process. Results and ideas from anywhere may serve as the base for performance improvements. Similar to brainstorming, findings and refinements through cross-fertilization lead to new added value ideas and strategies. All these cause a steeply increasing performance result. The cross-fertilization phase is characterized by rapid change. Strategies to realize the potential of a performance driver seem to apply only for a short period of time. Since progress in performance is going so fast, *new* strategies are continuously required to stay ahead of this growth. Consequently, the life span of investments is becoming shorter, because they are based on strategies that are subject to change as well. Therefore, in order to achieve a satisfactory return on investment, high volume sales aiming at a quick pay-back are becoming key management priorities. Management's alertness during the cross-fertilization phase, in particular, is and should be stretched. Because of the speed of change, management is driven into quick decision taking on new strategies and their associated investments. The danger always is, that at some point in time the end of a cross-fertilization phase is reached. At that moment, the performance growth gradually flattens out. Investments from then on may not fully yield the anticipated returns, because the performance potential has been exhausted. Worse, however, is the chance that a replacement performance driver (through a new S-curve) introduced by the competition. That may make the old way of doing business obsolete, sometimes overnight!

The following are some examples of typical performance driver replacements:

The Swiss (mechanical) watch industry was almost wiped out when the Japanese industry introduced electronic rather than mechanical watches. And so was NCR, when its mechanical cash-registers had to compete with electronic calculators.

The steel industry is still largely hanging on to a flattening steel performance S-curve. With the breakthrough materials age ahead of us, new and more competitive materials that seem to replace steel as a construction material, are being introduced almost yearly.

In summary, the cross-fertilization phase in the effort-result curve results in two major management challenges. The first challenge deals with managing rapid change in order to stay ahead of the competition. The second challenge relates to developing an overall awareness of new performance drivers, that may make the current effort-result curve obsolete. It is important to understand that these challenges apply not only to technology but also to new and emerging culture performance drivers.

The exhaustion phase

When the intrinsic potential of a performance driver has been exhausted the effective result of continued corporate effort starts to diminish. It means that the S-curve flattens. In other words, the performance improvements are not as great any more in spite of continued investment. At that moment, the performance potential of a certain process, technology or culture performance driver has been exhausted.

Steel, for example, has its physical performance limits in terms of strength, weight and cost. New production methodologies aimed at stretching that performance are costly and offer only marginal results. Industry therefore is focusing on ceramics and composites that have a very much greater potential as compared to steel. Steel, one could say, is in the exhaustion phase, which is causing a reduced demand on the world market. Rolls-Royce, the UK aero-engine manufacturer, is seriously planning the design of a 100 per cent steelless (or ceramic) engine, sure of achieving a considerably reduced weight, higher operating temperatures and, as such, higher performance. Steel as the traditional construction material, is rapidly being replaced by ceramic and metal composites.

The effort-result curve cycle

As we have seen in the discussions on the cross-fertilization phase, another performance driver may, and most likely will, take over when the effort-result curve flattens out. It means 'jumping' from one S-curve to the next, as shown in Figure 18.

A transition along one S-curve is like managing a certain stage of continuity that consists of three evolutionary phases, the maturation phase, the cross-fertilization phase and the exhaustion phase. All relate, in essence, to one performance driver, for example, 'steel', as in the case of Rolls-Royce. Jumping from one performance driver to another means managing a discontinuity. It can be like a shock wave. In other words, it is like going through a total 'soil-switch', for example from mechanics to electronics as in the watch-industry.

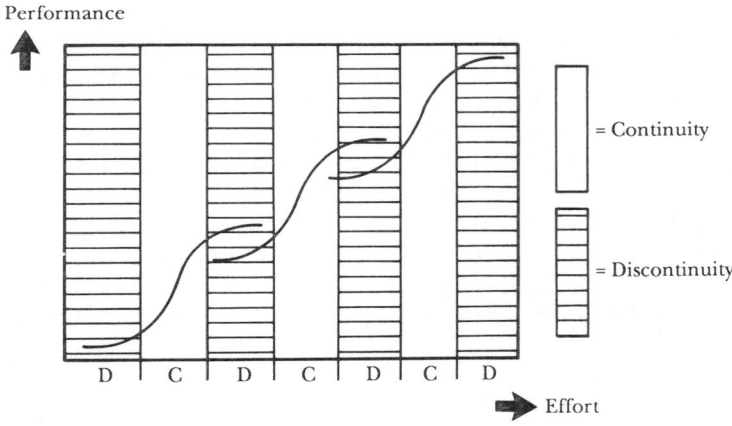

Figure 18   *Managing the continuity–discontinuity cycle*

During this discontinuity, a strong connection between originality and innovation is required, in order to become successful. Both of these elements are key to a successful S-curve jump. These S-curve jumps are critical for companies in their efforts to maintain their long-term market lead. They prevent companies from being out-manoeuvred by the performance drivers of known and unknown competitors. One of the many available jumping S-curve examples is found in the computer industry. There, an S-curve jump is being made in relation to the design of computer architectures by moving away from sequential processing to parallel processing. At a relatively low cost, tremendous computer processing performance improvements can (potentially) be realized. However, parallel processing is still in its maturation phase. New software strategies need to be developed in order to exploit fully its performance potential.

Large companies, in general, seem to have trouble in implementing these S-curve jumps. The required flexibility, as part of the organizational culture, often seems to have faded away. Small and start-up companies have the advantage both in terms of originality and culture performance. Much can therefore be learned from how the small ones operate.

The 'effort-result curve cycle' indicates that companies over time will have to cope with continuously succeeding S-curves. As such, they are moving through an alternating cycle of continuities and discontinuities. (Proposition 13)

Therefore, the first complexity that any corporate entity has to deal with is the management of the continuity and discontinuity stages. This is an inevitable condition for long-term success. The second complexity refers to the number of different S-curve cycles that impact on a corporate entity simultaneously. Just think of the technology S-curve cycles and those related to processes, materials, products, culture, etc. The third complexity is the challenge of choosing the right moment for jumping from one S-curve to the other. It means one has to have an integrated awareness of where one stands on the S-curve. In addition, it requires appropriate awareness of the state of the art outside the company.

Culture positioning

Management cannot effectively handle all these S-curve cycles alone, nor the other management complexities. Their major interest *must* therefore be to create the right cultural environment for the organization to perform these tasks to a certain extent. Culture positioning aims to achieve the awareness of the required culture performance changes in a corporate entity that are needed to cope with the above challenges.

The continuity-discontinuity paradox

We are now close to our major target in this chapter, that is the actual culture positioning tool or the dynamic positioning plane.

A balancing act

Management complexities seem to revolve around the right balance between continuity and discontinuity stages. Continuity in this case means sticking to the performance S-curve, while discontinuity relates to jumping performance S-curves.

From the previous discussion, it is clear that sticking to the S-curve is only wise for a certain period of time. Then a switch or jump to a succeeding S-curve needs to be made. On the other hand, jumping S-curves all the time is not recommended. The consequence would be an

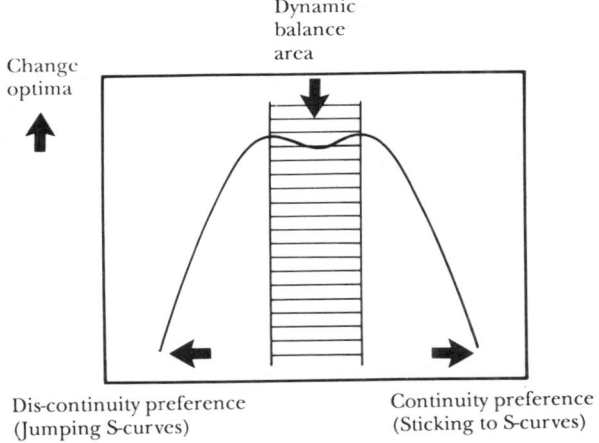

Figure 19 *The dynamic balance area*

unproductive repetition of cultural shock waves that do not get a real chance to settle in the corporation, with the result that future success is endangered. In other words, somewhere between 'jumping S-curves' and 'sticking to the S-curves' must be a practical optimum. In fact, not one but two practical optima must exist. Simply because one optimum would mean stagnation, that is *not* jumping S-curves *nor* sticking to them!

When one pictures the above as in Figure 19, it shows like a dip in a 'mountain', that lies between jumping S-curves and sticking to the S-curve. Right within this dip is a dynamic balance area. The corporate entity should stay within this area either on the left practical optimum or on the right practical optimum, depending on the environmental situation. It means cautiously moving from the 'sticking to the S-curve' optimum to the 'jumping S-curves' optimum and vice versa.

Management's game

It is all a game, they say and they are right! By adding a third dimension (time) to the graph in Figure 19, one will see the practical optima change over time as result of the environmental influences. One needs to visualize this again in order to understand it. In Figure 20, therefore, a number of these practical optima curves have been drawn, each representing the situation in a different time frame.

One may observe that these curves, together, move like a mountain ridge through time, influenced by the environment, they meet en route. The shift of this 'mountain ridge' to the right or to the left is indeed the result of environmental pressures. It represents the need for culture performance adjustments in order to ensure that the corporate entity stays close to the practical performance optima. The mountain ridge dip, or the dynamic balance area, represents both a tension and an equilibrium. It is a tension between 'jumping S-curves' and 'sticking to the S-curve', because neither of the two should be too dominant. It is an equilibrium, because of the natural inclination to stay within the 'dip'. The game that one has to play is simple ... one needs to keep the ball rolling in the tension-equilibrium area or in simple terms 'in the dip'!

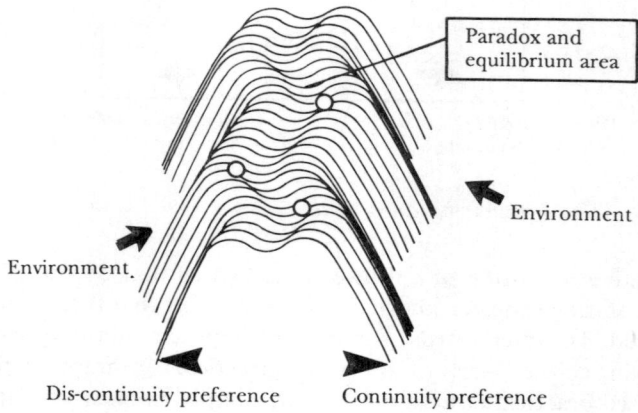

Figure 20 *Keeping the ball rolling in the mountain ridge*

Preferably, the ball should be rolling within the dip from one top edge to the other, on and on. It is like a swinging pendulum that shows the evolutionary movement in corporate entities between the emphasis on 'jumping S-curves' and the emphasis on 'sticking to S-curves'.

The management of the corporate entity encounters a number of obvious risks in this 'game'. The first is the problem of staying too close to the middle or low part of the dip, generally when management manoeuvres too cautiously. It causes stagnation as result of indecisiveness in respect of culture performance adjustments. The second is somewhat easier to imagine. When management is too strong in its measures or after a heavy environmental push, the ball may roll over one of the top edges of the dip, ending up on either side of the mountain. When that happens the corporate culture is really out of balance. Restoring the dynamic balance will require drastic management action, as I will explain later. From the above, it is clear that the dynamic balance refers to the delicate movement from one practical optimum (jumping S-curves) to the other (sticking to the S-curve) and vice versa.

Culture performance drivers

Within a corporate entity, a number of these 'mountain ridges' may be found. Together they determine the 'corporate entity's landscape'. The forces that keep the ball rolling within the dip of these mountain ridges are part of so-called culture performance drivers, that are similar to product performance drivers.

Culture performance drivers determine the inclination of people within corporate entities to stick to S-curves or to jump S-curves through two culture elements or culture forces. (Proposition 14)

One culture force encourages 'jumping S-curves' and the other one causes people to 'hang on to S-curves'. In Chapter 8, five possible culture performance drivers will be selected in support of the proposed culture positioning process. Examples of culture performance drivers (that incorporate the above mentioned culture elements) are structure, employee involvement, management responsibility, identity and goal-tuning with internal and external business partners. The motives for their selection are discussed in the following chapter. It is obvious, however, that over time, new culture performance drivers may be found or developed, depending on the needs of corporate entities. Since culture performance drivers can be represented by 'mountain ridges', it would be helpful to draw a map of the corporate entity in which those mountain ridges are shown. As such, one obtains a culture performance map or culture map in short. It will play an important role in this book by visualizing the actual culture positioning effort.

In conclusion, it should be clearly emphasized that culture performance drivers do not necessarily change the overall culture of a corporate entity. No, they only impact on the performance of a culture in terms of its capability effectively to cope with new challenges and

68 The Power of Tomorrow's Management

change. One could say that culture performance drivers help in constructively exploiting the uniqueness and strengths of a particular culture!

The dynamic positioning plane

A dynamic positioning plane is a key element on the culture map. It shows an abstract representation of a mountain ridge that can very well be used in the culture (re)positioning process.

Photographs from a high altitude

Let us return to the area or corporate entity landscape, where a number of mountain ridges can be found, each representing a certain culture performance driver. Suppose that one could find a pilot who is prepared to fly over this landscape in an orderly way in order to scan every bit of it. A positioning plane is obtained by making photographs of these mountain ridges, while flying at a high altitude.

Figure 21 shows such a photograph of a mountain ridge. The photograph, in fact, *is* the two-dimensional positioning plane. The dynamic balance area that is represented by the dip on top of a mountain, is the band that runs diagonally from the corner down the left of the 'photograph' and upwards. Along this diagonal, the results of any (re)positioning efforts can be visualized, the zig-zagging line in the dynamic balance area band, for example, is the optimal repositioning path. It represents the ball rolling in the mountain-ridge-dip. Preferably, positioning efforts should result in a move within the dynamic balance area band width. Ending up in one of the shaded areas in the top

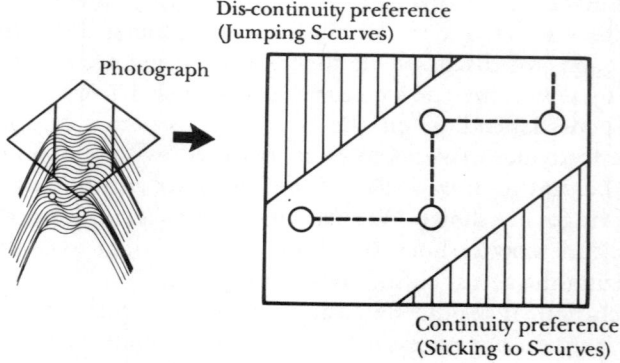

Figure 21 *The dynamic positioning plane photograph.*

left or bottom right corners of the positioning plane is like falling from the (corporate optima-) mountain ridge. The culture map will consist of several of these (dynamic) positioning planes, in which the entire repositioning effort takes place.

Hate-love relationship

Let us investigate the working of the positioning plane by first identifying two example culture elements. One should stimulate 'jumping S-curves', while the other should ensure 'sticking to the S-curve'. The examples of Apple and Kodak discussed earlier will come in handy when demonstrating the positioning plane in action.

A creative entrepreneurial environment may be defined as encouraging 'jumping S-curves'. It is an environment, or corporate structure, where new business ideas are generated, tried out and effectively realized. The reward and, what is more important, the 'image' of the performers in such an area is related to the development of new and successful strategies and objectives. However, entrepreneurial developments may cause a certain organizational ecstasy when an adequate verification structure is lacking, especially when the initial results point in the right direction. This ecstasy is characterized by a lowering level of discipline, by management 'shooting from the hip' and by an increasing number of wild cat people with even less inclination for control. Eventually, the impact of this state of creative entrepreneurial 'hypnosis' is reflected in declining financial results. When that problem occurs, the organization is unable to correct itself effectively. New management and mostly drastic actions are required to normalize the situation towards more productive levels of entrepreneurship.

An efficient *control structure* will generally be associated with 'sticking to the S-curve'. Such a corporate structure ensures that new business proposals are related to sound financial and business justification criteria. It facilitates appropriate approval and implementation processes. A control structure should in principle provide the necessary feedback to management, feedback that should result in appropriate corrective actions to keep close to the previously designated target. The implication of control structures that are too dramatic in their design is over-control. In those situations, the control structure is gradually turned into the goal of the organization, while it should only be regarded as its instrument. New business proposals may turn out to be smothered by its 'system'. Because of a number of accepted and unchanged review criteria, imaginative and quite lucrative business ventures may be turned down unjustly. At that time the organization has been trapped by its own enthusiasm for control.

70 The Power of Tomorrow's Management

In the longer term, over-control impacts negatively the financial results, in many cases indirectly for example, by the success of more flexible competitors, who swiftly invested in new promising ventures and developments. Reshaping the organization away from its over-control focus again requires drastic actions. Senior management replacements, lay-offs and restructuring are a few of the reported measures to restore the balance between entrepreneurship and control. Both entrepreneurship and control are important culture elements or culture forces for a company. They are projected on the sides of the positioning plane. A certain imbalance between these two culture elements is essential to keep the organization alive and non-stagnant, that is as long as the imbalance is well within the dynamic balance area. Too much of one or the other will have a negative impact on the organizational culture and its self-correcting capability.

Positioning efforts

In order to reposition the corporate culture, management has to assess first how far culture elements have been incorporated in the organization. For the purpose, scores should be indicated on the axes of the positioning plane, for example high, medium and modest. As such, they will indicate the presence of culture elements in the subject organization. Management should try to get a broad input before setting the score. The scores will then point to the position of today's corporate entity in the dynamic positioning plane (Figure 22).

The organization needs to reposition its culture towards the balance diagonal, if the resulting position is too far away from it, especially when

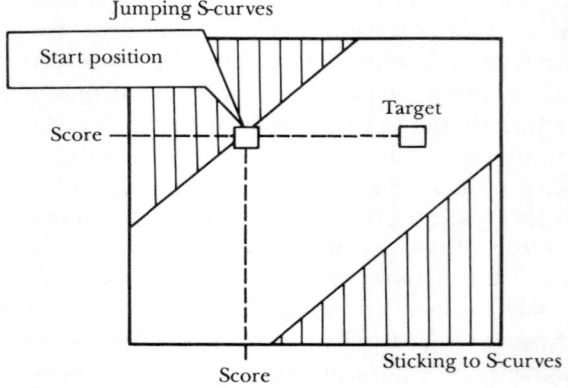

Figure 22 *Scores and position in the positioning plane*

one ends up in the shaded areas. The final objective should be a repositioning pattern that is relatively close to the diagonal, as mentioned earlier, like a zig-zagging line, representing the rolling ball in the mountain ridge dip. After having defined the current and the desired position in the dynamic positioning plane, how does one actually create movement towards the target position? It turns out that each culture element requires specific strategies in order to increase its presence in the corporate culture. One could choose to identify existing strategies that are known for being successful in other corporate entities. But one may also develop and brainstorm completely new ones that fit the requirements of the particular culture. The selection and successful implementation of these move strategies will drive the actual repositioning effort. Move-strategies are associated with culture performance drivers. It means, that move-strategies for the positioning plane, that is related to *structure*, concern the redefinition of the corporate entity's structure. In Chapter 9, these so called re-positioning strategies are further discussed. Many reported 'real-world' strategies will be categorized there and linked to several positioning planes.

Summary

The following summarizes some of the essentials on dynamic positioning planes. Understanding these will help management in defining positioning planes other than the ones discussed in this book. The functioning of the dynamic positioning plane will become even more apparent when the culture positioning model is worked out further in the next two chapters. The culture performance of a corporate entity is characterized by a number of key culture performance drivers, such as structure, people involvement, etc. Each culture performance driver can be represented by a positioning plane that is stretched between two culture elements or culture forces, one on each axis. One culture element in the positioning plane on the vertical axis encourages 'jumping S-curves'. The other one on the horizontal axis leads to 'sticking to the S-curves'.

The presence of two culture elements in a corporate entity determines its position in the dynamic positioning plane. For that purpose, scores are indicated on both culture-element-axes, for example: high, medium and modest. The preferred position is close to the balance line, that is in the dynamic balance area. Over time, the position of a corporate entity should zig-zag its way up, along the dynamic balance diagonal. The movement from a certain position in the dynamic positioning plane to another more preferable position can be achieved by the selection of re-positioning or move strategies. These strategies impact on the presence of a culture element in the corporate entity. They relate to a particular culture performance driver. For example, the performance driver 'structure' covers strategies that change the business entity's structural set-up. The application and characteristics of the dynamic positioning plane will become more familiar after discussing the total culture positioning model in the next chapter.

Reflections

Key messages

A high performing European project manager, who travelled frequently through Europe to facilitate the implementation of a complex information system, once explained to me that he had to 'change face' and strategies in every country he dealt with. And by the way, he sometimes visited two countries on the same day! It became clear to him that in order to achieve similar successes with French and German management teams, he needed to propose different strategies. And even 'French strategies' would not be successful in Belgium!

In the same way, Tonka toys, the US multinational, still believes in national differences. The performance of the national markets in terms of sales is strongly dependent on how well they tune their strategies to the traditional preferences for toys. The above examples more or less quantify the importance of culture-specific approaches and strategies that are the result of some form of culture positioning.

Change is based on a relation between effort and results with three phases. The first phase of slow change, one could call the maturation phase, where a particular driver of technological, product or culture performance is being shaped. The second phase of very rapid change, one could characterize as the cross-fertilisation phase. Results are steeply improving because of the cross-fertilization of ideas and findings. The third phase of considerably slowing change is the exhaustion phase. There the intrinsic possibilities of the technological, product or culture performance driver have been exhausted. At that moment, one should have 'jumped' to a new performance driver again with three phases. This three phased relation between effort and results is called the S-curve.

One should jump to the next S-curve when it does not give sufficient performance improvements, in spite of continued efforts. However, one should not jump too quickly, nor should one stick too long to one and the same S-curve. In other words, one should maintain a *dynamic balance* between jumping and sticking.

- Culture performance drivers determine the inclination of people within an organization to stick to S-curves or to jump from one to another.
- A culture performance driver consists of two *culture elements* or *culture forces*, one that makes people jump S-curves and one that makes people stick to them.
- In order to manage a dynamic balance between two culture forces, organizations need to determine what their inclination is in order to make corrections when necessary. This can be done through a *culture positioning plane*.
- One may define several culture performance drivers and each can be represented by a culture positioning plane.
- One needs to identify or develop *move strategies* to move from one position in the positioning plane to another, when the dynamic balance needs to be restored.
- Each culture may need different move strategies in order to restore the dynamic balance between two culture elements or culture forces.

In this chapter, the fundamental concepts of culture performance engineering have been defined. It may therefore seem rather theoretical, in spite of the frequent reference to real world examples. The dynamic positioning plane, as it has been defined, will be used in the next chapter to work out the model for the repositioning of cultures. Many examples of organizational and corporate dynamics will then be referred to in order to demonstrate the logic and the use of the model.

The conclusion in this chapter about the two culture forces that give shape to the positioning plane of a particular culture performance driver, is intriguing. One leads to 'jumping S-curves' and seems to invite fundamental change, while the other tends to encourage 'sticking to S-curves', and inhibits fundamental change. Since we are talking about the behaviour of humans, it is probable that these culture forces in essence can be related to the physiology of our brain.

8

The positioning model

The people model

One may learn from one of Mao's generals, who said that in order to be successful, he would not only need a conventional army but what he, above all, was looking for was a *culture army* to change the mind-set of the Chinese people and to make the revolution successful. He understood that certain awareness 'weapons' or 'tools' were required to guide people through change effectively. The culture positioning model is such an awareness guidance tool.

The definition of the corporate entity, introduced in Chapter 3, forms the basis of the culture positioning model. It consists of a box, which represents a subject group of people with their operating culture, their vision and their culture specific solutions. On the outside, one finds the different environmental influences. The challenge now is to define a number of culture performance drivers, that together sufficiently represent the corporate entity's capacity to change.

Responding to environmental influences

In the search for key culture performance drivers, it seems logical to be led by the internal and external environmental influences on the corporate entity. Both types of influence have a shaping impact on the culture of nations, corporations and individuals.

Structure

The structure of a corporate entity is one of the key tools to position people in reaction to the challenges and opportunities of the environment. Structure contributes to, for example, corporate success by ensuring effective interfacing with customers, competitors, suppliers and competitive products or technologies. In a sense, one could say that structure is the orientation within a company, say by customer segment, by supplier segment or by product segment. It may even be by major manufacturing process steps. In particular, the steel industry has historically been organized like that, until it (wisely) decided to reorganise into product groups.

The structure of a corporation is not only reflected in its organizational linkages but also in its control systems, for example, through management layers and systemized review and approval levels. In addition, the degree of centralization and de-centralization is included in the structure concept.

As such, structure is one of the key culture performance drivers *because it impacts on how people operate together in any organization.* (Proposition 15)

Structure can be seen as the heart of the corporate entity, because it interacts with all outside and internal influences.

Involvement

People's involvement is the second key culture performance driver. (Proposition 16)

Involvement relates to the awareness of customer needs and competitor threats. It drives people's actions and activities in response to the influences from outside their environment. Involvement is reflected in the degree of vision and idea contributions, as well as in the wholehearted support of related corporate goals. In Figure 23, the people model with the key culture performance drivers has been worked out. It shows involvement in the top right corner, facing customers and competitors as external influences. Involvement is not only dependent on external influences. Its location within the corporate entity links it with other key culture performance drivers, one of which is structure.

I once attended a strategy meeting of a management team that had just been made part of a large organization. As the planning manager of the organization that they had been integrated with, I was invited to explain how we tackled planning. The key to our approach in planning was to get people more involved in ensuring their own success. That aspect and 'how to involve people' was obviously part of my presentation. It turned out to be a traumatic experience. These people did not know yet how

76   The Power of Tomorrow's Management

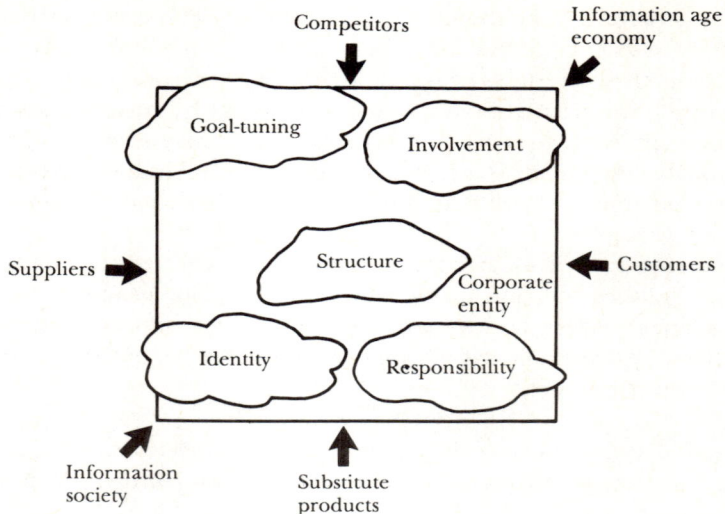

Figure 23   *Key culture performance drivers in a corporate entity*

they exactly fitted in the organization. And I was there to suggest to them how to get involved. Structure was what they needed first! With hindsight, it was obvious that the invitation came too early. Structure is definitely required before one can effectively address people involvement in a business entity. Involvement requires *two way communication*, that is, from the top down and from the bottom up. It requires a working harmony between management and employees.

Responsibility

The third culture performance driver ensures an effective future response towards customers and products that may replace the current success products of a company. It means a different mind-set on the concept of operational responsibility. The traditional operational focus of employees and managers needs to be broadened.

Strategic responsibility or responsibility for tomorrow's results should be as important as the responsibility for today's results. Employees and management need to be able and should be allowed to make investments for tomorrow in terms of time and resources. International competition and increasingly fast technological developments drive the need for mobilizing the brains as well as the arms and legs of corporate employees. The focus, as opposed to *involvement*, is more on 'tomorrow' and less on 'today'. 'Thinking of process rather than task' and 'preparing today for tomorrow's success' are phrases that characterize the essence of the *new* responsibility. In a world of new product announcements and continuously developing customer needs:

Responsibility (strategic versus operational), as a key culture performance driver, is increasingly important for maintaining responsive and 'state of the art' corporate entities. (Proposition 17)

Identity

Lamborghini, the Italian company that designs and produces sports cars, was bought by Chrysler in order to provide this 'people's-car-giant' with a position at the top end of the market. The acquisition was quoted as 'marrying the approach of an artist to that of an aristocrat'. Important to the management of Lamborghini was 'the maintenance of a family spirit, in which each man wanted to contribute all his intelligence to the task'.

Corporate identity is related to the uniqueness of the marketed products and to the added-value that a company provides in comparison to its suppliers. Consequently, corporate identity is very much linked to employee identity, when creative performance is the key to the success of a product, as in Lamborghini's case. The Japanese seem to struggle with a similar problem. that of creating a work environment that will encourage true creativity rather than adapting. One of the ways to achieve this has been to designate noted scientists as team leaders of research projects. In order to breakthrough the Japanese collectivism and stimulate independent individual peak performance, they named the projects after their team leaders. This identity-focused approach has eventually proved to be very effective.

When we look to the corporation of the future, we see something else coming up as well, that emphasizes the need for identity. Many of tomorrow's products will consist of information. Information products will require a manufacturing process that is based on expertise, originality, creativity, logic and philosophy. Corporate employees are and will be the major suppliers of information products for internal and external use. Hence, future corporations will be increasingly dependent on their own employees. Corporate identity, therefore, *must* be related to employee identity, because that will drive employee motivation and the quality of their contributions. A 'family feeling' or a 'cosa nostra' attitude seems to provide that balance between corporate and individual goals.

Corporate identity, linked to employee identity, is and will become even more a key culture performance driver. (Proposition 18)

Goal-tuning
After optimizing all previous key culture performance drivers, the company is in a good position to work effectively together with outside partners. Customers, suppliers and competitors may turn out to be the partners with whom to expand the corporate potential. Linking up with business partners makes it possible to access and develop new and different markets. Alien technologies, processes and products may well complement the current corporate capabilities. A mature corporate culture, however, is essential for successful and straightforward tuning of strategic goals.

Goal-tuning with external or internal partners is the fifth and (for the moment last identified) *major culture performance driver.* (Proposition 19)

It expands the success of the organization beyond its own borders and it implies linking to other corporate cultures. The location of this culture performance driver in the corporate entity (Figure 23) confirms the above reasoning.

Preparing for tomorrow's success

In summary, we have found five major culture performance drivers, using the earlier developed model for the corporate entity. They are,

- structure,
- involvement,
- responsibility,
- identity and
- goal-tuning.

Other culture performance drivers may be developed. However, the five key ones have been identified by taking into account the major and generally recognized influences on the business environment. The sequence in which these culture performance drivers have been explained matters! One should not pursue involvement before making sure that the right *structure* of the organization is in place.

Responsibility, which in many cases means increased strategic contributions, should not be dealt with before the corporate structure and people involvement are appropriately determined. Encouraging strategic responsibilities in a sub-optimal structure with uncontrolled people involvement may not be productive.

Goal tuning with other business partners may not yield the anticipated benefits when the underlying culture performance drivers have not been considered sufficiently. For example, a well balanced corporate identity is almost conditional. In addition, however, the other culture performance drivers should have been positioned properly to ensure a sufficiently mature corporate culture.

The cycle of positioning continues after all culture performance drivers have been reviewed. Change, as caused by the environment and by the process of working culture performance drivers, leads to a newly required balance of culture elements. If, for example, a company decides to work together with outside business partners, it will usually require an adjusted structure, another sort of involvement, a revisited responsibility balance and refined identity.

Evolutionary as well as *revolutionary* developments in companies, countries and individuals heavily drive the need for certain culture elements. The review of the above mentioned culture performance drivers is therefore important in preparing a corporate entity for tomorrow's success.

Five positioning planes

In the previous chapter, the working of the positioning plane was discussed. It allows the repositioning of an organization per culture performance driver through repositioning or so called move strategies. By understanding the positioning planes of all five key culture performance drivers, the people model can be turned into a practical management tool.

Structure

Each culture performance driver (in this case structure) has its own positioning plane. In fact, repositioning a company in the positioning plane for *structure* means changing the structure of the subject organization. The positioning plane (Figure 24) is stretched between two culture elements or culture forces. For structure the characteristic culture elements are.

1 the degree of creative entrepreneurial activity and
2 the degree of a control.

It means that the structure of a certain organization determines the creative entrepreneurial activity and the degree of control.

80 The Power of Tomorrow's Management

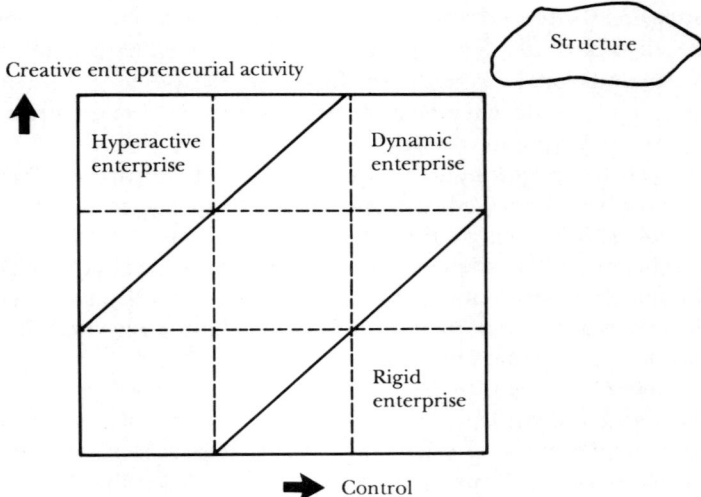

Figure 24 *The dynamic positioning plane for 'structure'*

Culture element attributes

What seem to be the characteristic attributes of the two culture elements for corporate structure?

The degree of creative entrepreneurial activity very much depends on the degree of decentralization in a corporation. That is decentralization of authority, for example, by creating relatively independent or autonomous groups under one corporate umbrella. These autonomous groups may consist of country organizations, product divisions and even sub-companies each with their own typical product set. Mostly these autonomous groups have (to a certain extent) the responsibility for their own profit and loss performance. Obviously, the management in these autonomous groups is forced to be more entrepreneurial. Growth and profit projections on the short and long term are dependent on it. The degree of control in terms of structure is related to the degree of centralization in a corporation. It means a corporate structure that forces central decision taking on operational and strategic investments. Consequently, it also tends to centralize the profit and loss responsibility. It is applied in companies to drastically cut costs, to streamline diverse operations and to reduce overlaps and organizational redundancies. Companies that are dependent on the success rate of high investments tend to centralize and improve the degree of control. The management in a more control oriented organization tends to be less entrepreneurial and more control focused.

Characteristic environments

The positioning plane for 'structure' shows three typical company types, the hyperactive enterprise, the optimal dynamic enterprise and the rigid enterprise. They represent the extreme cases for companies where one (or both) of the above culture elements is dominant. It is important to understand these extreme situations. They may or may not be found in the real world. They are important because they project the warning signals that management has to be aware of when repositioning their organization.

The hyperactive enterprise

In the hyperactive enterprise, the organization seems to be in a state of ecstasy. In many cases, this is caused by excessive growth of the company or group. It results in an organization that acts as if under the influence of drugs and feeling high and management tends to shoot from the hip. Ideas of the people and the management count. The feasibility of the ideas that have been put forward doesn't get appropriate attention, while the verification of success or failure is not done or just not possible. In general, the necessary controls of the operation have not been implemented. It is circumvented by management 'by gut feeling'.

The culture of the hyperactive company is inflexible, it has lost its capability to correct itself. The company is obviously not part of the dynamic balance area, it has slipped off the mountain ridge on the side where S-curve jumps take place too frequently. Corrective actions need to come from outside, mostly through painful measures, such as senior management replacement, corporate restructuring and employee lay-off's.

The optimal dynamic enterprise

In the optimal dynamic enterprise, both culture elements are dominant. Since they are in balance, this is the preferred situation for a company to be in. It means, a dynamic harmony between entrepreneurship and control that results in cultural flexibility. The culture is capable of changing its focus from control to entrepreneurship and vice versa, whenever needed. Adjustment and change are perceived as normal. The culture performance driver (structure) is in the dynamic balance area or in the mountain ridge dip.

The rigid enterprise
In the rigid enterprise, the organization is driven and almost obsessed by controls. Controls and control systems are considered as goals rather than as tools in support of the operation to generate profit and revenue. Good ideas are smothered by a control structure that consists of just too many approval levels and/or levels of management. The justification criteria of the control system are rigid and number oriented rather than vision oriented. Entrepreneurial ideas will therefore fail to float to the right level of top management. As with the hyperactive enterprise, the culture in the rigid enterprise is highly inflexible and incapable of correcting itself. Only now the culture flexibility is reduced by too much sticking to the S-curves. Actions to get out of this mode of operation are very painful as well. Replacement of senior management, drastic restructuring and pushing the decisions down the organization are just a few of the characteristic solutions.

Real world positioning examples

Many corporations, organizations and nations today are in a state of flux and changing their structure. They are repositioning themselves in order to cope better with competitive pressures, either by improving entrepreneurship or by increasing their controls.

Companies moving towards an entrepreneurial structure

Many respectable companies have decided to provide incentives for entrepreneurship by adjusting their organizations. They have all moved *up* in the positioning plane for *structure*, which indeed proves to be one of the prime culture performance drivers. Kodak was once recognized as a bureaucratic mammoth that was unable to move fast enough to cope with competition. In 1984, it successfully split-up into 17 product divisions each with profit and loss responsibilities. Sales and net earnings, since then, have shown this change to have been very effective. The Digital Equipment Corporation in Europe opted for a decentralized approach by increasing the independence of the different country subsidiaries since 1982. Growth and profit margin improvements show the unquestionable results of this move up in the positioning plane for structure. Many Japanese companies seem to create more entrepreneurial environments by moving up in the positioning plane for structure. Companies like Fuji Xerox, Nissan Diesel, Tateishi Electronics and Nippon Telegraph & Telephone show similar structural changes by splitting up into product groups, inside ventures, in-house firms and semi-autonomous divisions.

The positioning model 83

The Dutch steel industry 'Hoogovens', like presumably other national steel industries, has decided to step away from an organizational structure that was based on the steel making process. In 1987, it changed its structure into decentralized product divisions. This will certainly prove to be effective in stimulating 'jumping S-curves', that is towards the development of the next generation materials. In the car industry, one observes structural changes to reduce the lead time of car development and to improve flexibility in support of market requirements. For example, Volvo and Renault are implementing project structures that ensure overall focus on the entire life cycle of a particular product series. It means a decentralization into different product groups through a matrix structure (functions vertically, projects horizontally).

Companies moving towards a control oriented structure

Although the general restructuring trend seems to be moving to more entrepreneurial environments, there are a few well recognized companies that have chosen for more control.

Philips

In the year 1991, the Philips corporation will celebrate its hundredth anniversary. By that time, Philips will have changed significantly from what it was from the second world war until the early 1980s. Historically, the Philips corporation has been organized with strong national organizations in approximately 60 countries, as major elements in its corporate structure. Each national organization has a high degree of autonomy in terms of profit and loss and even country manufacturing. This structure was developed right after the war in order to cope with 'empty' and relatively closed national markets.

Today, the national markets have been developed. They contain, however, more and more international competitors. The trade barriers between European countries are disappearing and even those between world markets. Factories need to produce not only for one particular country but for the entire world in order to exploit economies of scale benefits. Technological changes and the associated investments are so dramatic, that these cannot be left up to the management of the national organizations alone, according to top managers of Philips. Altogether, the organizational overlaps and redundancies in the different countries also impacted the corporate results. Therefore in 1987, Philips initiated a companywide restructuring programme. The main theme is a new form of centralization. The entire company is being split up into four core activities or product divisions. The profit and loss responsibility has been taken away from the national organizations and brought back to each of the four major product divisions. The corporate activities will be managed by the centralized management of those divisions. What one observes in Philips is a move to the right in the positioning plane, that is to a more control-oriented organization. It is clear that it has been preceded by a move up in the positioning plane, right after the war. At that time the structure of the company required country market entrepreneurship. The shift to more control, in the case of Philips, not necessarily implies reduced entrepreneurship. In fact, improving control may be a necessary step before revitalizing entrepreneurship of a different kind. By focusing the divisions on the economic and technical performance of products in the world market, entrepreneurship is maintained, specifically, by the improved management awareness on the product-customer relationship. The move in the positioning plane therefore follows a horizontal path (maintaining entrepreneurship) to the *right* (improved controls).

Next to Philips, Apple sticks out as a corporation that has successfully consolidated its fragmented structure for product development. The size of the company required a different, more control oriented structure. John Sculley, chairman and chief executive of Apple, has been the key driver of this restructuring. Atari and People's Express seem to have moved effectively towards more control. The emphasis on more control in these cases has not led to a reduced entrepreneurial drive. It merely guided entrepreneurship to a more quantified and predictable environment. This, in fact, results in a horizontal move to the right in the positioning plane for structure.

Conclusion

Companies change their structure, either to improve entrepreneurship or their degree of control. It is a continuous alternating process that moves corporate structures from control to entrepreneurship and vice versa, depending on the evolutionary state that these corporations are in. Apple, after having gone through the above mentioned centralization effort, a few years later (1988) decided to decentralize into four autonomous divisions. The decentralization in 1988 was of a different kind. It shows a breakdown both in terms of functional and geographical responsibilities, i.e. Apple Products, Apple USA, Apple Education and Pacific and Apple Europe.

It is not clear, however, whether the timing of company re-structuring has been opportune in each case. Companies seem sometimes very much in a reactive mode when changing their structure, as a result of, for example, unacceptable financial performance or outlooks. A study,

McKinsey, published in 1988, rightly or wrongly criticizes the British Electronics industry for operating in a structure that seems too decentralized and which may have prevented it from making the mammoth investments needed for the development of a long term competitive product base. It seems therefore useful and recommendable to management to regularly position their awareness of the structure of their organization through the dynamic positioning plane. Efficiency losses and negative performance signals may be prevented by the pro-active application of the culture (performance) engineering approach.

Involvement

After reconsidering the structure of a company, the involvement of people in the new structure should be worked out. When management decides to reposition the corporate entity in the positioning plane for *involvement*, it means they intend to change the active involvement of people. The positioning plane for involvement (Figure 25) can be drawn between its two characteristic culture elements, these are,

1 the degree of idea development in the organization and
2 the degree of effective alignment in the organization.

The above implies that the *involvement* in an organization determines the degree of idea development and the organizational alignment.

Culture element attributes

Let us embrace the above mentioned culture elements by explaining their particular attributes. The degree of 'idea development' relates to the attitude of management towards bottom-up ideas. In other words, an open ear and a serious and positive management response to any ideas emerging from the lower levels in the organization greatly stimulates the idea development activity. In addition, the availability and effective allocation of funds for ideas generated on the floor propels the idea development activity to a higher level in terms of quantity and quality. The idea development activity may be handled in a more structured way by formalizing the approach for the involvement of corporate employees. Education seems to be essential in letting people exploit their given freedom to initiate and improve. In general, the idea development activity is required to achieve a more flexible and pro-active organization that easily and independently copes with competitive pressures and customer requirements.

Effective alignment in an organization is needed for managing top-

86 The Power of Tomorrow's Management

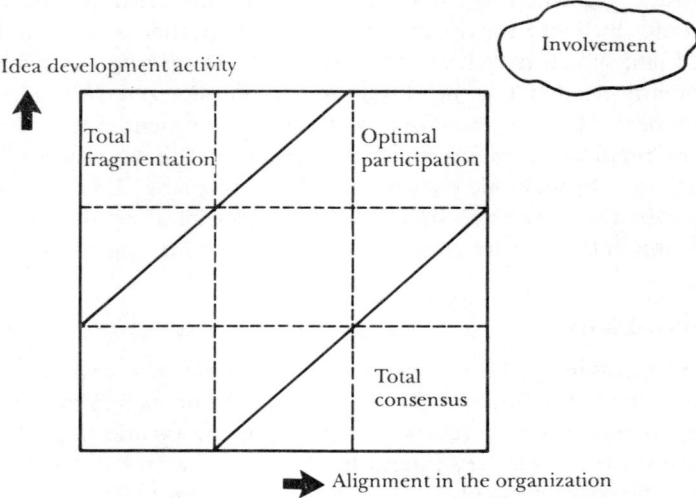

Figure 25   *The dynamic positioning plane for 'involvement'*

down innovation and investments. It requires the understanding and support of the rest of the organization in order to be successful. It is driven by the attitude of the organization towards directions from the top. Most of management effort is spent on working towards sufficient follow-up and support of top-down directions and goals. However, when alignment has been achieved, little management effort is required to keep the organization on track, as planned. In particular, the Japanese culture seems to incorporate alignment as a natural ingredient. It is the result of a certain collectivism that has the advantage of providing a formidable disciplined work force and mobilization power. On the other hand, it may lead to a relative inflexibility, because management tends to deal with the total organization rather than with a group of 'individuals'.

Characteristic environments

The positioning plane for involvement, like that for structure, shows three typical company types, i.e. one characterized by total fragmentation, one by optimal participation and one driven by total consensus. These are indeed extreme examples that may not be found in real life. But they are important, because they project the warning signals that are relevant to management, when deciding where their organizations are located in the positioning plane.

Total fragmentation

In a corporate entity that is characterized by total fragmentation, people are highly independent and overactively involved in their day-to-day operations and tasks. Employees are motivated to perform well, but in line with their own interpretation. Personally perceived goals for the organization rather than the overall corporate directives do really count. Corporate directives may not even exist. In environments where the independent idea development activity prevails, the profit and loss concept seems almost to be linked to individuals. All in all, it leads to employee opportunism, which does not turn out to be productive to the total company. Consequently, a certain cultural inflexibility emerges, that makes it difficult or even impossible for the organization to correct itself. Corrective actions therefore need to come from outside the organization. These are considered as painful, because they need to break through this dominant cultural element. 'Jumping S-curve' situations seem to occur too frequently. It resembles the ball rolling over the edge of the mountain ridge dip.

Optimal participation

Optimal participation is achieved, when a balance exists between the idea development activity and the alignment in an organization. This actually is the preferred state for a company to be in. The dynamic harmony between idea development and organizational alignment results in cultural flexibility. In other words, the culture is capable of changing its focus from alignment to idea development and vice versa, whenever required. When optimal participation has been achieved, adjustment and change are perceived as normal. With reference to the mountain ridge example, one could say that the ball is rolling within the dip.

Total consensus

In an organization where alignment is the dominant culture element, matters tend to be worked through total consensus. It means that a disproportionate amount of management time is spent on the facilitation and acceptance of corporate directions. It seems obvious that this will lead to a slow down of the organization, because consensus is pursued first and everywhere. In addition, such organizations are characterized by too much interaction, while only a few decisions are being made. Here again, the one dominant cultural element traps the culture by stifling its flexibility to change. Only dramatic management actions seem to have the power to swing the organization back to a state of optimal participation.

Real world positioning examples

A large diversity of companies are consciously working on getting improved people involvement, which in a sense seems logical. Management just cannot cope with the increasingly complex challenges in their organizations without the brainpower of the people who work for them. Companies range from high tech to low tech and from retail businesses to airlines.

Companies improving the idea development activity

Boots, Britain's leading chemist, has taken firm measures to improve the involvement of their local shop employees. By installing a new system in a number of their stores, they decentralized to a certain extent the stocking, pricing and display decisions. It opened the way to optimizing the merchandise mix in particular shops based on local competition, tastes, spending power and climate. Local shop managers now have the greatest influence. Club Méditerranée, the company that arranges classy vacations, has a culture in which employees have a natural attitude towards generating new and useful ideas. Perstorp, the Swedish speciality chemicals maker, encourages employee involvement by creating a climate for innovation and through a special budget to fund creative ideas. Nordberg, the general manager for corporate development, calls himself a sly corporate deal-maker. He helps subordinates go behind the backs of their bosses if they want to make a feasibility study on a good idea that has been turned down. This practice has successfully been used since the early 1970s, that is long before concepts surfaced such as internal 'venture funds' and 'intrapreneurship'.

Companies improving organisational alignment

Alignment of employees very much depends on the capability of top management to communicate vision down through the organization, specifically, by knowing how to motivate people to generate activities that will shape and implement the corporate vision. Cornelis van der Klugt, president of Philips, talks about creating one face to the world, one strategic command and one central policy. Philips is serious in its efforts to improve organizational alignment. It intends to invest yearly 2 per cent of its turnover on the improvement of internal communication systems and private networks. The objective is to centralize the planning and coordination of the product divisions. Matsushita in Japan is the largest electronics manufacturer in the world. In 1986, for the first time in eleven years, it experienced a decreasing financial performance, mainly caused by a reduced growth of the Japanese market and by *Endaka*, the climbing value of the yen. Matsushita was able (and still hopes) to inhibit the reduced financial performance through a huge alignment programme, called 'ACTION 86'. It stands for Action, Cost reduction, Topical product, Initiate markets, Organizational reactivation and New managerial strength.

Conclusion

Appreciation of the importance of employee involvement is certainly increasing. Top-down orders seem to be gradually combined with a bottom-up flow of ideas. At the same time, top-down orders are translated into top-down visions, which shows a definite change in the attitude of senior management. John Sculley, in his book Odyssey, seems to confirm this observation, based on the way Apple communiccates and sets its goals. The awareness of what is needed in terms of organizational alignment or idea development will help management in paving the way towards a smooth mobilization of the workforce. Understanding the position of the organization today and tomorrow in the positioning plane for 'involvement' is the first step. The selection of the appropriate strategies will come second.

Responsibility

Responsibility, in particular, refers to the responsibility of managers in the organization. So, when top management decides to reposition the corporate entity in the positioning plane for responsibility, it means they intend to change the way managers and people view their roles. The positioning plane for responsibility (Figure 26) is in principle based on two typical culture elements,

1   the degree of strategic orientation of people and managers and
2   the degree of operational orientation of people and managers.

The position of a corporate entity in the positioning plane for responsibility determines the degree of strategic orientation and the degree of operational orientation of managers in that entity.

90 The Power of Tomorrow's Management

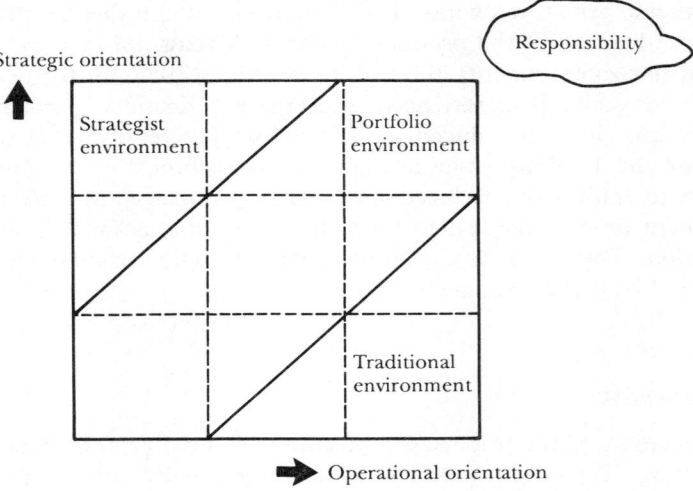

Figure 26 *The dynamic positioning plane for 'responsibility'*

Culture element attributes

The above mentioned culture elements again are best understood after discussing their particular attributes. The degree of strategic orientation of managers refers to the essential capacity of managers to *pre-view*. In other words, the basic quality of looking into the future and understanding what this future needs in terms of customers, products and processes. It is essential for ensuring continuity of the corporate entity concerned. The real challenge is to define what *success* in the future looks like. In fact, it is the most difficult part: picturing success and determining how to *measure* it.

Visualizing future success relates to the manager's forward looking time-span and to his capacity to disassociate from day-to-day issues. It requires courage, conceptual thinking, intuition, gut-feeling, realism, daring, spirit, and planning skills. A special difficulty exists in the eventual connection with the operation. That is how to translate the future into action today. Being locked into trends or having blind spots are just a few of the other problems one may encounter. In short, the strategic orientation of management 'occupied with the future', is an essential condition for maintaining or improving corporate success. '*Gouverner, c'est prevoir*' or 'the future is behind us' are just two of the many expressions used to confirm that. Strategic thinking ought to result in investments in terms of time and money that have a pay-off in the future and are not necessarily linked to today's operations.

One of the natural responsibilities of a manager is the performance of the operation that he looks after. In general, performance has been spelled out in an operational budget. The current trend, however, points in the direction of measuring managers not only on how well they do against their budget, but also on what they could have achieved. It requires managers to look at the total throughput, in terms of sales or production volume, relative to the total cost of their operation. This measurement approach requires an improved grasp of what the potential throughput could be. In addition it needs a good understanding of how the total cost is built up. In order to be successful in this both managers and employees need to think increasingly in terms of the *total process*, rather than in fragmented tasks. Significant results can best be achieved by linking up with suppliers and by being led by customers.

Characteristic environments

The positioning plane for responsibility shows three typical environments. One characterized as the *strategist environment*, one as the *portfolio environment* and one as the *traditional environment*. They are defined below. They are meant to project the warning signals that are relevant to management when deciding where their corporate entity is located on the positioning plane.

Strategist environment

In a strategist environment, the strategic orientation is dominant. A high degree of strategic orientation tends to make managers remote from and out-of-touch with the actual operation. In other words, in a strategist environment, the strategies are developed far from the operation by management with only strategic responsibilities. An unnecessary and impractical amount of theorizing rules the way of working. It increases management's dependency on the operational environment in terms of getting operational data for strategy models. It is obvious that the operations do not always cooperate effectively with these 'foreign spies'. Therefore, when strategies are made, they often do not sufficiently represent operational truths and possibilities. In the strategist environment, the success or failure of the developed strategy is not related to the salary or reward of the managers. The incentive to perform therefore tends to be lacking. Relative to the basics of the positioning plane, one can say that too many S-curve jumps tend to take place in this environment.

Portfolio environment

Both strategic as well as operational orientations are equally dominant in this environment. Managers there have the ability to initiate and achieve successfully. They know how to handle a portfolio of operational and strategic responsibilities, that is by moving consistently and when opportune from strategic to operational issues and vice versa. Adjustment to change is normal, without surprise and effective. It is the preferred state to be in, one of cultural flexibility or one of rolling the ball within the mountain ridge dip. The awareness of S-curve stages is optimal. For example, products and technologies are replaced at the right time by new and innovative ones after their major performance potential has been exhausted. To return to our principal metaphor, it means management is appropriately 'sticking to' *and* 'jumping S-curves'.

Traditional environment

Industry of the past encapsulates the *traditional* manager, one who focuses on his major performance targets, for example, the planned output of his department or organization. It is an environment that is strongly directed and ruled by short term operational goals. The initiative is smothered by the pressure to meet the budget as planned and as directed from the top.

Operational directions are clear cut and spelled out in detail. Over time, they have conditioned operational management even to ask for directions, as well as taken away their incentive to look into the future and initiate development. The authority of the traditional manager has been well described and limited to his accountability in terms of providing the calculated operational output.

This environment is characterized by a sticking to the S-curve attitude and behaviour.

Real world positioning examples

International competition today tends to provide the natural force for moving to a portfolio environment. As Roger Smith chairman of General Motors, mentioned in one of his speeches: 'managers should outwit and outstrategize competition'.

Companies emphasizing strategic responsibility

General Motors, through Smith, talks about 'shaking-up the environment to restore responsibility to lower management'. It seemed that decisions were handed down from the executive suite by managers, who seemed afraid to take risks. This behaviour was related to the 'sluggish and bureaucratic nature of the vast corporation'. Smith reduced the centralized corporate planning group. Instead, he sent the corporate planners to the operational plant managers in the field to teach them how to do their own strategic planning. Under its new head, Raymond Levy, Renault is progressing on the road to recovery. In order to be successful, Levy is aiming to reduce the number of intermediate layers and structures of management. The objective is to make the remaining management strategically active and more responsible for the overall corporate goals. Integration with the other functions is required, which is only possible through the right strategic mind-set.

Companies emphasizing operational responsibility

Companies that are critically dependent on operational management responsibility are relatively rare but at the same time easy to find. Such companies include those that supply general services and whose performance has a tremendous potential impact on the public, for example, electricity generating companies, nuclear reactor plants and water supply plants. The impact of unauthorized experiments by managers in those companies may cause disasters, like the one we have seen in Chernobyl. Space flight crews and NASA operations at the time of active space flights are tremendously dependent on the performance of operational managers. The vulnerability of the astronauts, the complex equipment and not least the tremendous public exposure made these types of operations move to professional operational management. But airlines are also as much in need of operational focus and responsibility.

Conclusion

More and more companies are requesting their managers to fulfil or take on strategic or longer-term responsibilities, relative to customer, product and organizational development. This is not just to provide management with the incentives to contribute. It is primarily in the interest of companies to mobilize the strategic capabilities of their managers. The increasing complexities in the world make it impossible for an oligarchy of top managers to develop all strategies for change and efficiently to facilitate frequent change throughout the entire organization.

The variety of companies today, however, also results in the need for managers with a specific operational focus. In general, a *portfolio manager*, who can switch from an operational to a strategic focus when required, is presumably what companies need most. Something that can definitely be obtained by appropriate management education.

Identity

The identity of a corporation is shaped through its products and its people. When management decides to reposition the corporate entity in the positioning plane for identity, it means they intend to reassess the corporate goals versus those of their employees. The positioning plane for identity (Figure 27) has been based on two characteristic culture elements, that is

1 the appreciation of employee ideals or goals and
2 the appreciation of corporate goals in the organization.

The position of a corporate entity in the positioning plane for identity determines the appreciation of employee ideals and the appreciation of corporate goals.

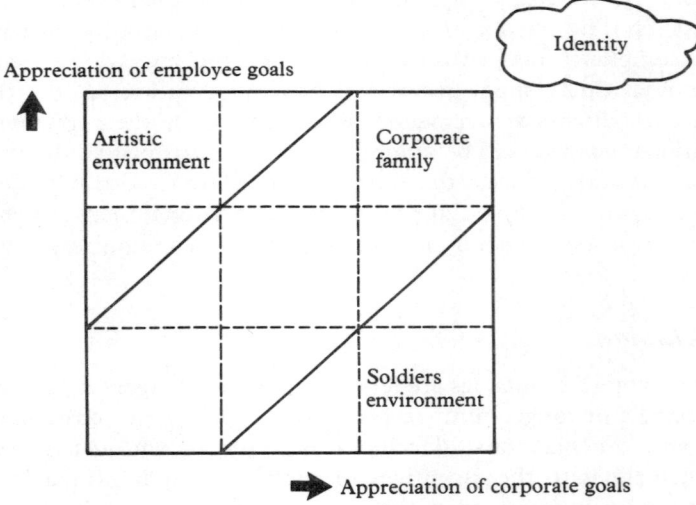

Figure 27 *The dynamic positioning plane for 'identity'*

Culture element attributes

The attributes of the culture elements mentioned above will provide a more complete background on the concept of identity, as it is meant here. The appreciation of employee ideals or goals in corporations determines the employee's willingness to relate to corporate goals. That means in terms of his effective support in realizing them and his loyalty. To put it in more straightforward terms: in all cases, people will consciously or unconsciously ask the question 'what's in it for me?', when deciding to join, stay with or support a company. In the past an employee's ideals were satisfied, when *he* earned sufficient money to buy food, clothing and keep a roof over his head. It related to his principal necessities of life. But over time, the standard of living has been increasing and so has his goals. Higher salaries and all sorts of company benefits are now the norm. With the information age in sight, employees now have other goals, such as the work environment, nice people to work with, interesting work and challenges, personal development, change of work or a specific job, just to mention a few. Achievement or fulfilment of these goals, as mentioned before, determines the well being, good feeling and eventually the performance of the employee in the corporation.

Today's shortage of qualified personnel (in spite of unemployment) leads to a further evolution of employee ideals and goals. Corporations will have to look for other untapped sources of qualified people. Especially in Europe, the female resource potential will certainly become a target for corporations and organizations to satisfy their need for brainpower and social skills. Even more so when national populations are greying and when the supplies of the young gradually dry up. It implies that the ideals and goals of females will need more attention and that cultural prejudice needs to be overcome. Tomorrow's employees will tend to become the key suppliers of information products. This, in itself, causes other personal goals to emerge. For example, the need for independence, the liberty to seek particular goals and the need for self-expression. 'Avant garde' examples of the latter, are found in very creative software development companies (e.g. for computer games), where programmers work in unusual ways. On first sight, their work habits seem totally irrational, undisciplined with outbursts of high productivity after days or weeks of 'thinking' when they are apparently doing nothing. The appreciation of employee goals also associates with the concept of the *family*. Family members tend to be allowed to pursue their own goals, but in harmony with family interests. The appreciation of organizational or corporate goals, like the appreciation of the family interests, is key to the success of a company. The successful corporate identity very much depends on a realistic interpretation and understanding of the corporate goals by the employees. In a sense, it can be interpreted as the binding ingredient (glue) for an effective corporate entity. The appreciation of corporate goals relates to their simplicity, their attractiveness, their appeal and their imaginativeness to the corporate employees. Employees, enthused by what their company stands for, should almost spark a certain envy with business partners and customers. It should drive their urge and need to be connected with this band, one way or another. Top management's focus is or should be on the development, facilitation and consistent communication of corporate goals. Their aim should always be the appreciation of these goals by their work force and management.

Characteristic environments

The positioning plane for identity again shows three typical environments, that is the artistic environment, the corporate family and the soldiers environment. Although they represent situations that may not be found in real world organizations, they demonstrate the signals that management has to look for when positioning their corporate entity.

Artistic environment

In the artistic environment the appreciation of employee goals and ideals dominates the situation, while the appreciation of corporate goals is hardly noticeable. The environment can almost be characterized as anarchy, where egos predominate. Ideas are not related to true company needs. Consequently, the family feeling in such a corporate entity is practically non-existent. The loyalty of employees in that environment is obviously limited. Eventually this attitude is reflected in deteriorating cooperation with suppliers, and what is worse, *with customers* In addition, the product range may show signs of the artistic environment, as result of numerous pet projects. Again, this is a state where S-curve jumps take place too frequently, because corporate needs and goals are insufficiently appreciated.

The corporate family

Those who think that the family concept will disappear eventually, may be very surprised when the opposite happens. In the organizations of tomorrow, where the structure is simplified by having fewer management layers and less hierarchy in order to facilitate change a different binding ingredient from coercion through hierarchy is required. The corporate family environment substitutes the usual norm through its dynamic balance between corporate and employee goal appreciation. It creates the conditions for change and the 'change is nice' concept, because it allows and enables the individual, rather than the structure, to change by providing a base of trust and identification. Its cultural flexibility and self-correction is possible through a manageable process of emphasizing 'the appreciaton of corporate goals' or 'the appreciation of employee goals', whenever needed.

Soldier environment

In a soldier environment, corporate goal appreciation is dominant. The employee is ordered to die, figuratively speaking, for the sake of the corporation. On the other hand, though the employee has the 'right to kill' for the sake of the corporation, since the appreciation of the employee's goals is very basic, their vision tends to be limited by the corporate direction and commands. Permission to break-through or propose is not granted, orders count. Eventually this will lead to a feeling of dissatisfaction by being 'harnessed' all the time. Employees then will either leave or look for other outlets for their ideals. Another opportunity to use the potential of employees will have passed.

Real world positioning examples

Both corporations and nations are subject to identity positioning plane situations. Companies today show an overall trend of moving up in the positioning plane, i.e. towards a broader appreciation of employee goals and ideals. The personnel market situation and the rate of change in technology and in society indirectly drive this trend. Royal Dutch Airlines (KLM) is recognized for its family spirit. This applies not only to the people who work at its base in the Netherlands, but also to the people at its many overseas subsidiaries, where all sorts of nationalities work. When asking a KLM employee 'what he does for a living', his answer will be: 'I work for the KLM'. His actual function there seems to take second place.

Britain's universities, faced with mounting financial and administrative pressures, have been planning a shake-up of their computing systems to improve their management services. They plan to organize themselves into 'families' to spread costs and share expertise – a novel approach to high tech developments for these independent institutions.

Quality circles in general are an attempt to create a type of family environment, where both the individual and group focus together lead to improved quality and productivity.

Conclusion

The awareness of the goals of employees versus those of the corporation is conditional to the success of the necessary and continuing change processes in our organizations.

The family concept (*cosa nostra*) is 'in' rather than 'out'. It is increasingly recognized as the optimal state in the dynamic balance between overall and individual goals. However, it goes hand in hand with a redefinition of the core activities of corporations. When companies are going to invest in the goals of employees, they will make certain they focus on employees who will contribute to core activities which directly support the charter of the company. Improvements through positioning in the plane for identity are still needed in many cases. Just take, for example, the male dominance in our organizations and societies, which will presumeably continue until the moment we realize it is not in our best interests.

Goal-tuning

Awareness of all previously discussed culture performance drivers is essential before considering focused actions to increase corporate growth. When management decide to reposition the corporate entity in the positioning plane for *goal-tuning*, they, in fact, determine the approach to achieve corporate growth. The positioning plane for goal-tuning (Figure 28) has been founded on two characteristic culture elements or culture forces,

1. the degree of goal-tuning with *external* business partners and
2. the degree of goal-tuning with *internal* business partners.

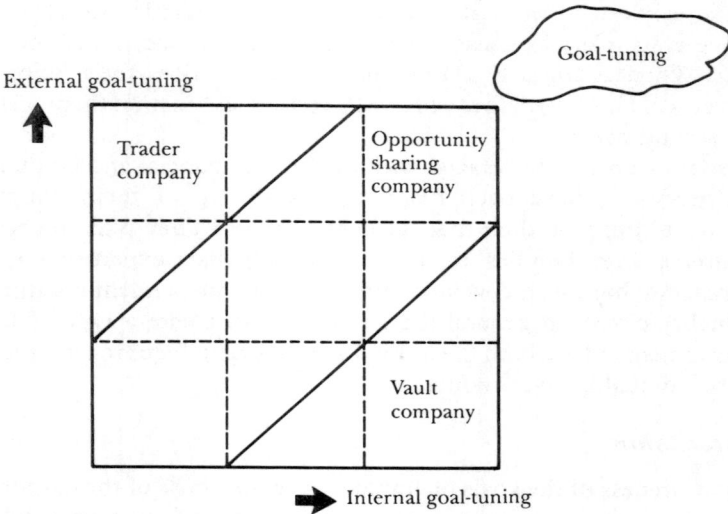

Figure 28 *The dynamic positioning plane for 'goal-tuning'*

The position of a corporate entity in the positioning plane for goal-tuning indicates how far it effectively uses external or internal business partners.

Culture element attributes

Internal and external goal-tuning and their relation to corporate growth are explained through their attributes below. Linkages with external business partners determine the degree of external goal-tuning. Outside business partners are acquired through major sub-contracting, joint ventures, acquisitions and mergers. One can distinguish two ways of working with other companies i.e. through *vertical goal-tuning* and through *horizontal goal-tuning*.

Vertical goal-tuning refers to relations with suppliers and customers. In fact, by the exchange and actual *tuning* of particular strategic goals, one may create mutual opportunities. An example of vertical goal-tuning is the approach of Heineken breweries, when they needed to replace their huge stock of glass bottles. By linking with the glass and plastics industry, they designed a superb new bottle and crate. The bottle through its size and shape significantly improved storage density and reduced manufacturing costs. As a result, transportation and warehouse cost savings were achieved for both Heineken and its suppliers.

Horizontal goal-tuning relates to linking with competitors. Through a combined approach of particular strategic goals, companies connect complementary findings, skills, capabilities and resources. Those may lead to an imaginative performance and growth improvement but also, by linking complementary markets, a vast increase in sales volume may be achieved, that can be used to finance further product development. Examples of horizontal goal-tuning are Siemens and Philips with their memory chip project, AT&T and Philips in telephone network systems and AT&T and Olivetti in computers.

Through *external goal-tuning* companies are able to achieve growth in revenue and to a lesser extent *organically*, that is, growth from within the intrinsic corporate structure. In addition, external goal-tuning provides companies with a method of coping with change fast. 'Jumping S-curves' is facilitated by external goal-tuning. In general, external goal-tuning also impacts on the individual cultures of the corporations concerned. Typical challenges for management in those situations are the definition and facilitation of one vision and/or vision synergy between the participating companies.

The degree of internal goal-tuning is determined by the number of business partnerships within a company. Those can be partnerships between different product groups or between different functions. Some companies favour growth by internal goal-tuning, which, if successful, leads to strong organic growth. Companies with a high degree of internal goal-tuning rely heavily on their internal cultures, when coping with change. Change-management therefore is one of the major challenges for the management in those companies. Digital Equipment, in particular, has until now been a company that did it on its own. The impressive growth over the last couple of years has been achieved without major take-overs or joint ventures.

Characteristic environments

The positioning plane for goal-tuning distinguishes three characteristic environments, i.e. the *trader company*, the *opportunity sharing company* and the *vault company*. These environments may not actually be easy to find in real life, but they do show management the key characteristics to watch for when evaluating the position of their own company.

Trader company

When companies are totally dependent in their success strategies on external business partners, they function as 'trader companies'. Trader companies show an opportunistic tendency in their attempt to achieve revenue growth by changing partners, whenever it suits them most. Their way or operation resembles that of brokers. By becoming highly dependent on their business partners, they end up being quite vulnerable, particularly when they are either very successful or out of luck, they may become victims of being sandwiched by their business partners. In general, the core activities of trader companies are not unique in comparison to those of their business partners. In other words, the value they add to the final product is hardly quantifiable. It requires very drastic management action to spin out of this cultural environment, particularly because the true corporate core is limited and does not provide many alternatives.

Opportunity sharing company

In these types of companies the right balance between internal and external goal-tuning exists. It is the preferred state for a company to be in. The opportunity sharing company has defined its core activities and value added well. It has sufficient uniqueness relative to its suppliers and competitors. Internal goal-tuning ensures the continuation of this uniqueness through new product introductions and market developments.

The corporate culture is flexible enough to go for external or internal partnerships, whenever it makes most business sense. Adjustments are normal and timely managed.

The vault company

The vault company tries very much to do things on its own. It seems to be closed to the outside world. It is not regarded as a potential business partner mainly because of its management's attitude which is a reflection of existing corporate culture. Whenever there are problems, vault companies manifest an inward looking search for solutions. Major business opportunities from outside may therefore be overlooked. People are typically asked to be their own consultants. Vault companies are sometimes like sleeping beauties who need to be discovered by a promising and fortunate prince. But sometimes vault companies are very aware of their attitude and consider themselves 'too good for the companies of this world.' In general, vault companies have the tendency to stick to S-curves too long. Drastic management actions are required to escape the dominance of internal goal tuning.

Real world positioning examples

The internationalization of trade and increasing investment in fast changing products drive companies into more external goal-tuning. The need for integration of technologies and skills continues to increase the trend for joint-ventures.

Positioning for external goal-tuning

Amstrad, the consumer electronics group in the United Kingdom, invests heavily in relationships with external business partners. Its Far-East operation aims for a stable set of sub-contractors, so that they can learn to take Amstrad into their confidence about their future plans. Amstrad has been dealing with one of its main suppliers for more than 14 years. The trust is mutual, sub-contractors do indeed keep Amstrad informed of their plans for expansion and development. General Motors has acquired EDS (Electronic Data Systems) and Hughes Aircraft Industries. But it also set up a joint venture with Toyota, much to the disgust of Lee Iacocca (of Chrysler). General Motors, if it is not careful, may have a tendency to become a trader company. Its cultural clashes with EDS, in particular with its previous boss H. Ross Perot, may make it a possible victim of its own policies. Daimler-Benz, like GM, has been acquiring high tech companies, such as AEG and Dornier, in order to get the know-how for its future car products (electronics and possibly gas turbine techology). The maturity and success of these partnerships seem to characterize it as an opportunity sharing company. Unilever has decided to sub-contract the operation of some of its manufacturing plants. This has been based on the assessment of what Unilever's true core activities and added values are.

The economist Professor Lester Thurow of the Massachusetts Institute of Technology has suggested a certain form of external goal-tuning between nations. In order to control and manage the world currency situation, he suggests a move to a new trading and financial system, preferably in an organized fashion.

Positioning for internal goal-tuning

ITT, during the power regime of Harold Geneen, diversified for years. Over that time, this multinational may have shown some of the characteristics of a trader company. Since Geneen left, ITT has been redefining its core activities and value added. It resulted in the selling of the European telecommunications group to the French company CGE.

Conclusion

The trend today seems to point in the direction of external goal-tuning. More and more corporations are appointing managers and vice presidents who are responsible for strategic investments and joint ventures. The repositioning of companies in the positioning plane for goal-tuning, however, is not possible without the reassessment of the core activities and the value added of the company concerned. What is more important, the decision to link up with other business partners will also result in the need to revisit the company's positioning in the other positioning planes for structure, involvement, responsibility and identity. The same applies to companies that decide to limit the number of external business partners. Although the promise of having external business partners is great at first sight, many companies have not been successful, because they have overlooked the impact of matching different visions and cultures. Part Four in this book pays focused attention to this subject.

The culture positioning map

Now, after the discussion of the dynamic positioning planes of all five culture performance drivers, one can draw up the overall culture positioning map, as in Figure 29. It can be used as an overview of the organizational repositioning efforts and progress. In addition, the con-

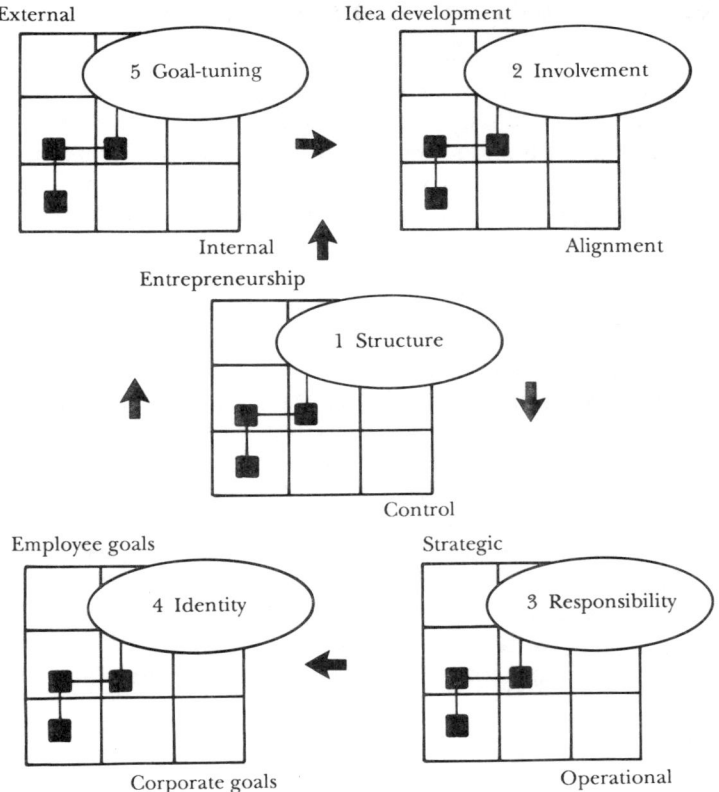

Figure 29 *The overall culture positioning model and map*

sistency between the repositioning efforts and progress in these planes can be monitored more professionally. Again, the impact of culture postioning on management will be much greater by visualizing what is happening. Each dynamic positioning plane quantifies its culture forces or culture elements in terms of basic, medium or high. A standard of measure that is easy to understand and use. On the culture map, a particular organization can be drawn, as well as the company to which it belongs. This leads to the idea of plotting successful competitors on the same map. By bringing in competitive pressures on the culture map, an extra incentive for culture performance adjustments may be obtained. It incentive for culture performance adjustments may be obtained. It implies that the 'competitive analysis of the future' may also include an assessment of the competitor's culture in relation to its product strategies.

Understanding the state of the industry

Another way of using the overall culture positioning map would be to show the general culture positioning trends in a particular industry, for example, the car industry, the steel industry or the electronics industry. The same could be done for certain countries, for example, the third world countries, the Eastern block countries, etc. In fact, many other valid groupings could well be plotted on the overall culture positioning map.

In order to visualize the state of the industry, one has to plot the positioning *and* the repositioning efforts of the major companies in that particular industry segment, like the car industry. The zig-zagging path that organizations follow in the dynamic balance area (the mountain-ridge-dip) indicates fairly well the evolutionary stage that companies may be in. We have seen how Philips decided after the second world war to decentralize its structure in order to cope better with different national markets. This is shown in the positioning plane for structure as a move up. They are however, now, centralizing on product groups to cope with the new world trade situation. Other companies for example Amstrad, may still be in the decentralization phase for different reasons. The insight into the overall industrial culture performance will also lead to projections of what may happen in the future. It will encourage more anticipative but also trend-break-through management attitudes.

Wrap-up

The positioning model has been developed as a practical tool for the improvement of the performance of corporate entity cultures, whatever they are. At least five culture performance drivers are believed to be key to the success of a corporate entity culture. By plotting the position of one corporate entity in the positioning planes of all five culture performance drivers, a more quantitive awareness of the cultural weaknesses and strengths will be obtained. In addition, it will lead the way towards improved culture performance characteristics.

The resulting understanding through the overall culture map is only part of the benefit. The map itself also ensures continued awareness and action when it is appropriately made visible to management. The map should therefore be displayed in the conference rooms and offices where the managers who contributed to it, regularly meet. The overall culture map enables a broader competitive analysis by including successful competitors. In general, the overall culture map has the potential of upgrading our understanding of the different culture performance trends in almost any subject group consisting of similar corporate entities.

The next chapter will focus on the positioning process and in particular on the strategies that seem to drive repositioning moves.

Reflections
Key messages

Top management forums these days have recognized that there is no unique solution in the corporate world that leads to success under all circumstances. The awareness is dawning that neither centralization nor decentralization is the issue, but that flexible structural adjustments (possibly networks) are needed for particular corporate challenges and visions. In addition, these forums confirm that 'multinational companies must change the way they have managed people over the past 100 years to be competitive in world markets'. What is missing however, is an understanding of how these (in essence: correct) observations should be interconnected in a consistent approach that can be used by management effectively and elegantly to spin out of the traditional management mode.

The 'positioning model' brings together the key culture performance drivers in an almost natural approach that can be used to manage the optimal corporate response to the challenges of tomorrow. It is part of the new way of thinking and acting in tomorrow's organizations, whatever they are. Together with vision engineering it opens the road to creating a vision-culture balance for *every* corporate situation. The two dimensional positioning planes with each two culture forces, of which the relative strengths need to be expressed and visualized, fully exploit people's intrinsic capability of making subtle comparisons. The particular working of the senses and the brain makes humans weak in absolute judgements and strong in judgements by comparison. For example, estimating the temperature in the exact degree Celcius or Fahrenheit is extremely hard and almost always a guess. However, people may sense only a minimal difference in temperature, whenever it occurs. The 'positioning model' is therefore a useful tool in tomorrow's organizations.

Based on the model for the corporate entity, 'the people-model', five culture performance drivers have been indentified, i.e. *structure, involvement, responsibility, identity* and *goal-tuning*. Together, they seem to provide the best counter force for the pressures from the environment. Each culture performance driver incorporates two culture elements or culture forces. *Structure* incorporates entrepreneurship versus control tendencies, *involvement* incorporates alignment and idea development encouragements, *responsibility* incorporates strategic and operational orientations, *identity* incorporates employee versus corporate goal appreciation and *goal-tuning* incorporates external partnership versus internal partnership preferences. Culture dynamics can and should be made visual through the culture positioning map, which needs to be updated and refined continuously by the management team. Competitive culture dynamics should preferably be registered in the same culture positioning map, in essence by showing the positioning of similar companies.

The diagnostics for culture performance drivers have now in principle been dealt with. One is able to determine the current and the desired position of a corporate entity in five positioning planes, How one actually gets from one position to the preferred one will be discussed in the next chapter on 'repositioning strategies'. The real world examples in this chapter have been used to demonstrate the historic dynamics of corporations *and* the logic of the positioning planes. Although these examples may have been appropriate at a certain time for a certain situation, they are not necessarily meant as cases that need to be copied. Quite a few of these examples illustrate situations where management has been re-active rather than pro-active in their decisions to emphasize certain culture forces. Based on the positioning model, the knowledge and insight of management can be used much more effectively, while in addition the timespan of their decisions is being stretched. It will lead to breakthroughs (relative to the current way of operating) when consistently applied in combination with vision-engineering.

In summary, the examples have helped to confirm the positioning model. Now that we have it, further conclusions can be developed on the improvement of the *corporate dynamics quality*. In Chapter 14, a proposed reference for the management of tomorrow's corporate entities has been worked out.

9

Repositioning strategies

The positioning process

'We have to adjust our culture in each market—we are ready to allow the French to run France and the Germans to run Germany ...'. These are the words of Alan Sugar, the highly successful entrepreneur in command of Amstrad. His statement underlines how important culture *adjustment* is to the successful enterprise. It implies that Alan Sugar and his management team consciously assess cultural characteristics and needs. Let us therefore first review the culture positioning process in order to understand how the actual repositioning strategies fit in.

Process steps

The culture positioning process in essence concerns a workshop in which management-judgements on culture performance are quantified. The final results are registered on an overall culture positioning map, as in Figure 29. This map, as we have seen, consists of five dynamic positioning planes, one for each culture performance driver: structure, involvement, responsibility, identity and goal-tuning. Starting with the dynamic positioning plane for structure, one works through the following steps, using Figure 30, as a worksheet:

1 The current position of the corporate entity concerned should be plotted in the respective dynamic positioning plane. The position can be determined by quantifying the presence of its culture elements in terms of basic, medium or high. For example, in the positioning plane for structure, it means one has to estimate the degree of creative 'entrepreneurial activity' and the degree of 'control'.

108   *The Power of Tomorrow's Management*

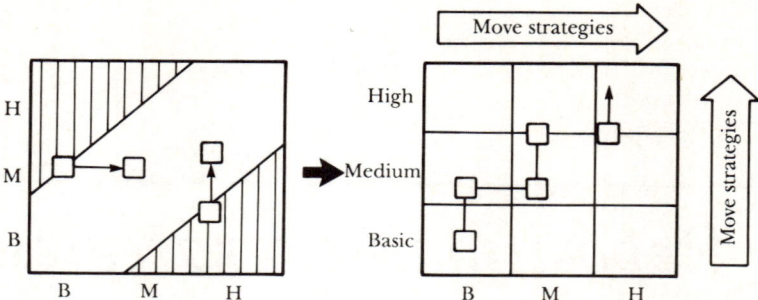

Figure 30   *Culture positioning work-sheet*

2   One should assess the existing position in the dynamic positioning plane and decide on the desired position for the corporate entity to be in. The existing and desired positions one should mark and connect by an arrow in order to show the direction of the *move*. The position of a company is improved when moving closer to the balance diagonal within the dynamic balance area. Over time, a corporate entity will be shown to be meandering upwards around the balance diagonal.

3   Subsequently, one may consider comparing the position of the corporate entity with those of major competitors by plotting their current positions. One should discuss what major conclusions can be drawn in terms of competitive advantages and weaknesses.

4   In order to put a corporate entity into perspective, one should discuss the potential differences with other corporate entities in the subject corporation. It means determining and discussing their positions as well. The success of a corporation is to a certain extent dependent on the degree of internal integration. The culture-match (and vision-match) with internal business partners should therefore seriously be considered.

5   Having identified where to move to (through arrows), one should brainstorm what approaches or strategies would make those moves happen. This task should result in a listing of alternative measures.

6   From the listing obtained during step 5, one should select one to three of the most promising strategies that will most likely drive the corporate entity from the current postioning to the desired position. These key strategies should be worked out in detail at a later stage.

As mentioned before, this six step positioning process should be gone through for all culture peformance drivers. The results can be plotted on the overall culture positioning map. As a result, a management team obtains a clear visualization of the required culture changes. Progress measured at later sessions can be plotted on this map as well.

Move strategies

What makes a corporate entity move to a new position in a dynamic positioning plane? In fact, many of those *move strategies* have been discussed in business literature. But always the question has been: 'what strategy to choose' and 'to whom does it apply'?

One of the major benefits of the overall culture positioning map is the fact that it provides management with the right arguments and rationale for the selection of a strategy. Hence, the culture positioning map can also be used to categorize the different strategies that seem to have been successfully applied in particular companies. The following is such a categorization. Strategies have been sorted by culture performance driver and by culture element. Strategies listed under a particular culture element will strengthen or enforce it. Consequently, this will lead to a move in the positioning plane, either ↑ or sideways →, dependent on the culture element it supports.

Structure-related strategies

Strategies that impact the *structure* of a corporate entity have been sorted by the two structure-related culture elements or culture forces.

Strategies supporting the creative entreprenurial activity; move up ↑.
- Decentralization.
- Diversification.
- Reduction of management levels.
- Creating profit centres.
- Creating quality circles and high performance work groups.
- Moving from functional organizations to product organizations.
- Pushing responsibilities and authority down to lower management levels.
- From individual responsibility to shared responsibility.

Strategies supporting the control activity; move sideways →.
- Centralization.
- Strict internal controls.
- Policies and procedures.
- Permanent audit structure.

- Differentiated authority levels.
- Centralized planning.
- Investment review boards.
- Formalized management system.

Involvement-related strategies

Strategies that seem to have an impact on people involvement, are listed by their particular culture elements.

Strategies supporting the idea development activity; move up ↑.
- Open door policy; everybody is free to talk to any manager.
- Idea exchange media, such as newsletters, electronic mail systems.
- Brainstorming funds.
- Awards and pay for idea-generation.
- Daring goal-setting.

Strategies supporting organizational alignment; move sideways →.
- Fixed and strict planning cycles.
- Regular interactive strategy meetings.
- Applying feedback loops, wherever possible.
- Strategic planning and strategy roll-up network (level by level).
- Only tangible cost/benefits requirements.

Responsibility-related strategies

Strategies that seem to influence the strategic and operational responsibility of managers have been listed below for the respective culture elements.

Strategies supporting strategic responsibility; move up ↑.
- Reduction of management levels.
- Education and training, teaching managers to do planning.
- Allowing some strategic failures and experiments.
- Longer-term profit-related pay.
- Reduction of planning and headquarter staff.
- Job rotation.
- Pay for strategic contributions.

Strategies supporting operational responsibility; move sideways →.
- Standardization.
- Individual accountability.
- Salary based on short term operational performance.

- People selection criteria.
- Detailed operational metrics and measurement.

Identity-related strategies

Strategies that impact on corporate indentity have been categorized as follows,

Strategies supporting appreciation of employee objectives; move up ↑.
- Flexible and part time contracts.
- Allowing multiple employers.
- Job plans to include both corporate and employee objectives.
- Job plans requiring approval of employees.
- People mix the selection criteria.
- Paid leave for social, research, study and entrepreneurial reasons.

Strategies focusing on corporate objectives; move sideways →.
- Strict and standard work contracts.
- People selection and mix; hiring 'soldiers'.
- Limiting the personalities-bandwidth, levelling of characters.
- Adherence to strict formalities (e.g. clothing).

Goal-tuning-related strategies

Finally the strategies, that impact the *goal-tuning* characteristics.

Strategies supporting external goal-tuning; move up ↑.
- Strategic goal exchanges and cooperation with suppliers and customers.
- Strategic goal exchanges and cooperation with competitors and others.
- Being open to outside consultants.

Strategies supporting internal goal-tuning; move sideways →.
- Consolidation and limiting of relations with external organisations.
- Internal and independent definition of core goals.
- Being one's own consultant.
- Strong internal productivity focus.

It's just the beginning ...

Most real world (organizational) strategies can be categorized along the model of the five culture performance drivers. Obviously, management does not have to be limited by the above mentioned strategies. The categories and examples, however, should serve as the feeding ground for additional and more innovative move-strategies.

Due to the continuously changing and evolving business environment, other strategies will certainly be needed and will therefore emerge. It is believed that these strategies can be related to a relatively stable number of culture performance drivers.

Significant opportunities are foreseen by the systematic categorization of successful move strategies through computer systems, as discussed in Part Four of this book.

Reflections

Key messages

Management literature, in particular describing case studies in successful organizational strategies, should now become increasingly meaningful. The positioning model functions as a Christmas tree, in which ornaments (organizational strategies) have their natural place. In other words, the categorization of organizational strategies through the reference structure of the positioning model, provides management with the right arguments and rationale to select or develop appropriate strategies for their organization. This is particularly so once the breakdown of culture performance drivers and culture elements has been memorized by heart. This is the recommendation to every serious reader, i.e. 'to visualize in one's mind the culture map with the five culture performance drivers.' Then 'to project each culture performance driver with its two distinct culture elements or culture forces in a two dimensional positioning plane'. The picture that the reader should have in his mind should look like Figure 29.

The entire culture positioning activity and the selection of repositioning strategies only takes four simple steps per culture performance driver. Two additional steps have been identified in order to provide an appreciation of the positioning of competitors and other corporate entities. The direction of repositioning strategies can simply be marked by an horizontal or vertical arrow in the positioning plane. Each repositioning strategy supports the increase of one culture element or culture force. The breakdown of strategies, based on culture performance drivers and culture forces, will help in developing more effective strategies. People will simply know what to look for. The repositioning strategies make the interactive culture positioning approach complete. Now the understanding of the culture positioning and repositioning needs can then be straightforwardly translated into actions that will improve the corporate entity's capacity to change (culture performance).

10

Managing transformations

One step back

Many companies feel the 'hot breath of change' in their necks. This means that they are becoming impatient with the speed of reorganizations, particularly because these reorganizations are critical plans to increase profits, to substantiate aggressive growth or just plainly to survive. New product development, fast switching of manufacturing operations and the revamping of the sales spirit may not and even cannot take long. Targets are more and more set with a two to three year time span. The long range time span of actions and results is shrinking. The corporate world will look entirely different after three years anyway.

That is why companies like, for example, Philips openly (and rightly so) express their haste. They need successfully to change their organizations into more productive and innovative ones within a time span of about three years. Consequently, tens of thousands of corporate employees have to work differently together using new and more productive processes. At the same time their individual performance in terms of creative contributions, entrepreneurship and the like have to be improved. Is their management crazy? Changes like these used to take eight to twelve years! I think not. These goals are the results of competitive pressures, cool clear-cut analyses and last but not least management vision. So, something needs to be there in order to make these organizational transformations happen in that timeframe.

114 The Power of Tomorrow's Management

From positioning model towards transformation steps

Rather than use the previously defined positioning model for culture performance improvement, one could decide to apply its culture performance drivers in a more *pro-active approach*. But first, let us take one step backwards and recap on the connection between change and the positioning model. This brief journey will underline the logic of such a decision. In Figure 31, an overview of the major evolutionary steps towards culture positioning has been sketched.

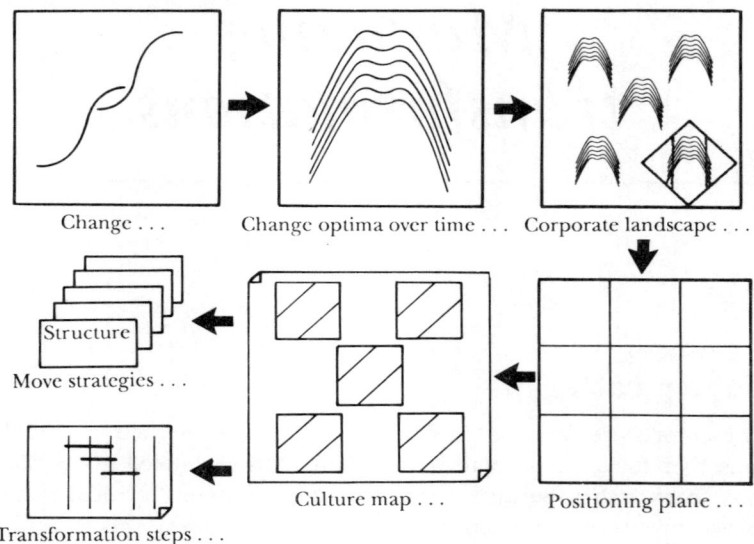

Figure 31 *From 'change' towards transformation management*

Starting from the top left, one finds the foundation of it all: the S-curve phenomenon. It characterizes the essence of change in terms of its continuity, when going through an S-curve, and its discontinuity when jumping from one S-curve to the next. It shows change will go on and on, but along certain phases, each with its particularities and needs. Change in organizations, corporations or nations obviously consists of a whole bunch of these S-curves together.

Overall, change in organizations should show a reasonable balance between 'jumping S-curve' situations and 'sticking to the S-curve' situations. Too much jumping may lead to anarchy, too much sticking may lead to stagnation. This *change-optimum* has been captured in the curve that forms a mountain ridge over time. The dip on the top is where the change optimum is located. It indicates the dynamic balance area between jumping and sticking preferences. The challenge for management is to keep the ball rolling in the dip between its edges on both sides. In fact, if one could 'plot' an organization on a map, one would see a number of these mountain ridges. Each mountain ridge would drive the performance of the overall culture through two culture elements or culture forces, one driving jumping S-curve situations and one encouraging sticking to the S-curve situations. In order to get a clear 'helicopter view', it would be best to fly over this corporate landscape and to take pictures of each mountain ridge. A photograph would then show a mountain ridge dip from a high altitude. What comes out is something that looks like the positioning plane, that is assuming all pictures are taken the same way. The dynamic balance area (the mountain ridge dip) would run diagonally like a band from the bottom left corner to the top right corner. The model of the corporate entity points us in the direction of a few characteristic culture performance drivers based on environmental influences. These culture performance drivers and their positioning planes together finally lead to the culture map. It shows the current and the desired positions of an organization in the positioning planes of the culture performance drivers. Move strategies are then developed to ensure repositioning takes place.

The culture map with the culture performance drivers is entirely based on the change phenomenon. As such, it is best suited to help make change happen quickly. This is particularly so since it is geared towards finding the change optima. Therefore, when companies need to change their organizations in response to new corporate challenges, management should go through transformation steps, that are in line with the culture (and change) performance drivers. Figure 32, shows these transformation steps supported by implementation tasks.

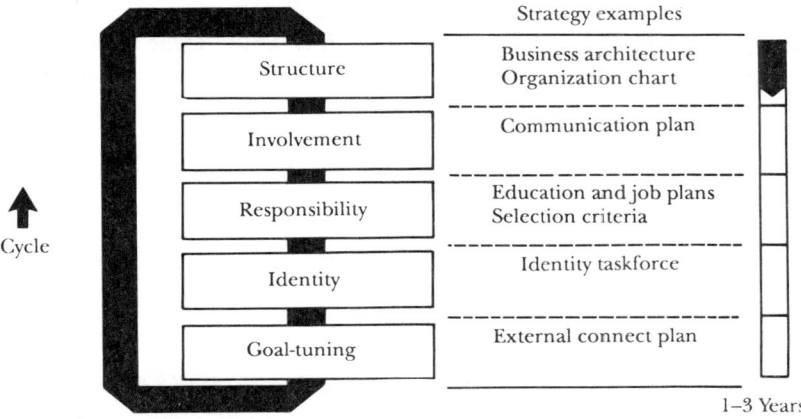

Figure 32 *The transformation cycle*

The right sequence and the right time

When these steps are followed, management should ensure that no critical change performance items are left out. In addition, the sequence with which change performance items are dealt with is optimal. This will result in a more rapidly reacting organization, simply because the basic change performance conditions have been aligned. Management, knowing what steps to follow, can be more creative and better involved when facilitating change throughout the organization, in terms of generating change or move strategies and initiating timing adjustments. Also, the allocation of resources in support of the transformation process can be planned in advance. Unnecessary manoeuvring of people can then be minimized.

Setting the right expectations

Reorganizations may be completed successfully within a time frame of about 1–3 years, dependent on the size of the organization. People will be able to visualize what the transformation steps are. Knowing what is coming will make the 'affected' much more relaxed. The response of people will be in line with expectations that are raised by the transformation plan.

Managing future organizations

After going through all the transformation steps, the next cycle of change will most likely begin. By that time, management should have developed new visions and new transformation- or move-strategies along the patterns of change as projected through the five organizational culture performance drivers. The transformation cycle will trigger leaders to develop follow-on visions for their organizations at the right time. Slipping back into the old situation should not happen, because the momentum of change is maintained by the right timing of management direction. In particular, the issues around the vision-culture balance, as mentioned in Chapter 4, can be prevented.

The management of future organizations will more consciously and proactively focus on maintaining a dynamic balance between culture elements. (Proposition 20)

The leaders and managers of tomorrow will most likely be supported in these efforts by a new breed of consultants. These consultants will make it their job to help improve the organizational and even national culture performance. Their aim is actually to engineer change and culture adjustments. As such, the terms culture engineering or culture engineers seem to capture appropriately the essence of these *new* responsibilities and skills. Organizational dynamics, cybernetics, logic and information technology will be part of their knowledge arsenal, next to sociology and psychology. Their attitude will be pragmatic and action orientated, they engineer, plan and help to implement. Information technology, in particular, will be needed to initiate and maintain knowledge and experience-based data bases or systems, that lead to better predictability of strategy success (see Part Four, Chapter 19).

In conclusion, the engine for transformation management and culture improvements clearly is and will remain: management vision. Culture engineers may help and do some of the work. Organizational momentum is obtained through *move strategies*. The criteria for developing move strategies are provided by culture performance drivers. The performance drivers are quantified in positioning planes through their culture elements or culture forces. And culture elements are derived from change itself. Hence, culture positioning or culture engineering, as an integral part of the 'Power of Tomorrow's Management', offers a breakthrough framework for coping with any future environment.

Reflections

Key messages

Are we manipulating people or organizations when 'culture engineering' concepts are applied? Managers in the past hundred years have done nothing else, probably without realizing it, less consciously and more intuitively. The answer to this question, therefore, entirely depends on the *purpose* of culture engineering. In other words, what is the underlying vision that one may want to achieve? Hence, culture engineering should never be de-coupled from vision-engineering.

The acceptance and achievement of vision is at stake as well as cultural identity. The 'Power of Tomorrow's Management' purposely focuses on the improvement of culture performance, which in fact means the capacity to absorb and realize a particular vision. A vision should preferably be achieved by *using* rather than supressing culture specific characteristics. Culture engineering helps to turn culture specific characteristics into strengths. Furthermore, the ethical quality of a vision (although to a certain extent the product of culture itself) is what makes culture engineering manipulation or not. Managers should prevent the mere rejection of a vision by ensuring 'quality of vision' and a relative closeness to the culture of the environment concerned. Culture engineering should focus on the achievement of vision through an improved organizational response, which can only be *culture specific*. Culture specifics should therefore be turned into success factors or strengths. Corporate transformations are most successfully achieved by the development and implementation of an action plan that covers all culture performance drivers (structure, involvement, responsibility, identity and goal-tuning). Leaders and their visions will determine the success of tomorrow's organizations, not culture engineers. Culture engineers may help leaders to be more effective. From the above, the connection between culture and vision engineering is apparent. It seems like the right moment to focus our attention on the essence of vision and on ways to develop it. After vision engineering, the relative closeness of a vision to the environment concerned, as mentioned above, will be discussed. The relative closeness of a vision is related to the vision-culture-balance spectrum of a corporate entity, which has been developed in Chapter 14, as part of the culture and vision engineering rules.

PART THREE

Vision Engineering

11

Vision, added value and change

Vision in the clouds?

When people think of vision, they regularly associate it with clouds. In other words, one cannot put one's arms around it or squeeze it! Consequently, vision is related to something vague and that in itself is not right! Vision emphasizes the opportunity of dissociating oneself from the limits of today's world to construct an ideal picture. In addition, vision opens the mind and the eye to the overall view, as if observing the world from the top of a mountain. In fact, the better or more detailed a vision in one's mind is, the better that mind knows how to realize it. In a sense, it is how an artist pictures his creation and how a tennis star visualizes his service. The same law applies in corporations and nations. The probability of achieving a corporate vision is to a certain extent dependent on its detail and its contrast. The objective of vision engineering is to determine a process for the definition of a business vision and a model for communicating it to the organization. This is to make sure the organization picks it up, makes it its own and adds value to it by generating supporting visions. The underlying aim obviously is fully to utilize the brainpower of the people in the organization concerned. A business vision eventually should lead to processes that result in sales, profit and whatever has been quantified in measureable goals. As we have discussed extensively in the previous parts of this book, culture plays a key role in the acceptance of a vision.

Vision, i.e. a successful vision, therefore embodies plurality. In other words, it is not a matter of one mind but of many. It incorporates the potential for people and groups of people to redirect and above all to recondition themselves. One of the major challenges for management is to translate vision into controlled action and into supporting activities. At some point in time, resources need to be identified and included in the budget to make things happen. It is important therefore to identify how this translation from mind to matter or from vision to action can take place. The above indicates a delicate balance between the improvement of today's and tomorrow's environment.

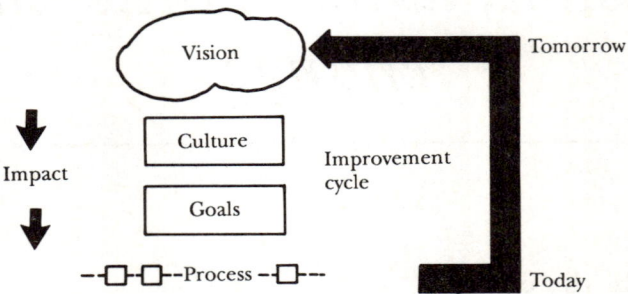

Figure 33 *Balancing the improvement of tomorrow and today*

Vision appearance

In general, visions are simple and easy to understand, otherwise, people would not follow them. Within corporations and nations, top management and political leaders express their visions in terms of straightforward overall achievements, like:

- in five years we will have tripled our sales,
- in three years we will be the number one in our market,
- we will be the lowest cost car producer in Europe,
- we will supply the best quality products,
- we will provide the best product maintenance,
- our future is service, not maintenance,
- we will have reduced our inflation to acceptable standards,
- we will have revitalized the economy and economical growth,
- we will land a man on the moon within the next decade,
- we will have a defence system that makes nuclear weapons obsolete.

In essence, one may conclude that a vision describes what an organization will have achieved once it reaches the future. It is like a self-imposed belief. However, immediately after stating the vision, people will ask the question: 'How'? And obviously, leaders will have that 'how' in mind. In most cases, the 'how' concerns a major shift in organizational resources and substantial additional investment. For example, the corporate leader who claims 'he wants to triple the sales in five years', may plan to invest heavily in sales resources in order to achieve his aim. Peugeot with its vision to become the number one car producer in Europe is substantiating this by major investments in new car development and production facilities. So, vision not only incorporates where or what one wants to be, but also how one thinks one will achieve it. And it is the latter in particular which creates most of the management challenges. Based on the vision-culture imbalance, these challenges revolve around the constructive acceptance of vision. In addition, they drive the culture transformation needs in organizations, as discussed in Part Two of this book.

In one of *Business Week's* cover stories, the above management challenges have been well described by Kenneth H. Olsen, president and founder of Digital, when he says 'my job is to make sure the company has a vision and that everybody follows it'.

Added value: vision's pivot

Success of corporations, societies and people is sometimes based on a very simple quality A young 'ex-employee' in the Netherlands had been unemployed for almost two years. Frustrated by this situation, he developed the simple idea of renting the unused wall space of the numerous sporting centres in the area. He offered this space to all sorts of companies for advertisement purposes and additionally he would take care of the design and the professional production of the advertisement material. Within two years, he was roaming the entire country in search of every new sporting hall, where he offered the same services. After three years, he has bought himself a luxurious house, is driving an expensive car and is planning to build a new office. He is sure of a steady income because every deal consists of a one to five years contract. What really makes him so successful? It is not education, because he only had the very basics. Certainly, he has stamina, but many have and are not successful! In essence, his true *added value* seems to be: the successful *linking of unused wall space* to the need for advertising.

I once organized a vision-development workshop with the well qualified management team of the Dutch city 'Capelle aan den Ijssel', one of the best managed communities in Holland. When we talked about the 'products' of the team, they said: 'well, we built the community hospital and we are creating new industrial activity in the area'! Since my ultimate goal was to make sure that this team would invest in their true strengths, I asked them to confirm whether they were in the real estate or building business.

Obviously, they weren't in either! So, I suggested they reconsider their initial assessment. Their major *added value* turned out to be the successful *linking* of companies and institutions to attractive local arrangements and governmental subsidies, in other words specialized public relations. The Netherlands, for example, consider themselves the gateway to Europe and experts in distribution and logistics. That is apparently what this nation believes to be one of its prime added values. It is therefore not surprising that a significant share of European transport business is in the hands of the Dutch.

The understanding of the true added value of a person, corporation or nation is critical to the successful investment decision or the 'how' of a vision. (Proposition 21)

The identity map

The *identity* of an organization is not always straightforwardly related to its products alone. However, products play a very important part in it, because they are the ultimate output of the corporate entity.

The true added value that an organization provides to its products determines the organizational identity as well. So, when one talks about vision, which says something about what an organization wants to be, one inevitably touches both, that is the core added value *and* the products of an organization. The relation between *core added value* and *products* can be captured in a so-called 'identity map'. The identity map shows the product variety or the number of unique products of an organization versus the amount of its core added values (Figure 34). This map can be used to plot the different companies and their identity changes.

Amstrad, the successful British consumer electronics company that sells anything from hi-fi equipment to microcomputers, has a relatively broad product variety when compared with the amount of internally added value. Its major value added seems to focus on marketing and design specification. Most of the other value added to its products comes from sub-contractors. Distribution and sales are dealt with through, for example, Schneider on the European continent and Sears in the United States, the latter apparently not so successfully. Development and production is mainly done in the Far East. On the identity map, Amstrad is located somewhere on the left. It can be characterized as a modern style company, because the overall trend in corporations seems to be towards more selective core added values. This in itself is an

Vision, added value and change 125

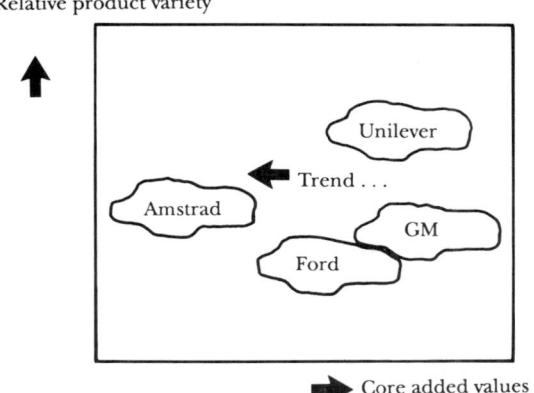

Figure 34 *Plotting companies on the 'identity map'*

interesting development, which seems to be congruent with the trend forecast for the information economy, as discussed in Part Two of this book.

Similar identity changes can be observed in, for example, Unilever, ITT, Chrysler and Ford. Under Harold Geneen ITT grew to a heavyweight multinational with a tremendous product variety and a substantial amount of core added values. Now under its new management, it is reshaping towards a reduced product range and selected added values. Its biggest move has been the sale of its European telecommunications business, which is now grouped under Alcatel. Unilever, the world's largest maker of consumer and personal products, has been handing over the management of some of its factories to third parties. Unilever's true and competitive added values are considered to be in other areas. Chrysler and Ford, in comparison with General Motors, focus more and more on marketing and development as their core added values. The production of their cars mainly consists of final assembly activities. Most of the sub-assemblies and parts are obtained from outside suppliers. General Motors, however, still manufacturers many parts and sub-assemblies itself.

The general trend of companies seems to be going from right to left on the identity map. In other words, to a more selective approach in the identification of core added values. The rationale for companies to reconsider their core added values is based on the general need for companies to respond more competitively to world market changes and requirements. The trend in the identity map is also linked to cultural trends, as discussed in Part Two of this book, because of the required responsiveness to change. The dynamic relation between products and added values as in the identity map highlights the impact of product on added value and vice versa. Product itself is driven by the needs of the customer but also by its definition and performance. Marketing in particular worries about the link with the customer. Management, however, should also be aware of the change in product definition that may result in the need for reinterpretation of the added values in their organizations.

One could summarize the value added as an integral part of vision that seems to be shaped by the following elements:

- product,
- need for corporate flexibility,
- competitive organizational strengths and
- management belief.

Product

Products during the history of our world have evolved significantly. What one did not consider a product in the past is or may become a product in the future. The first products presumably related to the basic needs of life, such as food and clothing. However, today the term product has been stretched and incorporates anything from consultancy to advertisement. One frequently quoted, yet not always understood 'new product', is *information*.

The definition of the information product seems to be maturing rapidly. The information business started off to provide basic information products, for example stock prices on Wall Street through electronic networks. These information products have now evolved and include not only stock prices at any point in time, but also extensive analyses, projections and advice. Many new information products are becoming available on *knowledge* subjects, such as law, medicine, science, technology, bibliographies, finance and product development, just to mention a few! The evolution of products and product definitions should encourage one to consider the following matters during the development of a corporate vision:

- New products are becoming increasingly abstract. They are moving from *physical impact products* to *mental impact products*.

- Every new 'product', as any other product, has a 'price', a 'customer' and somebody who adds value to it.

Vision, added value and change 127

- Not only should 'end products' be considered, but also 'intermediate products' that are handed from one group or one person to another.

- Every organization or group of people is bound together by product, whatever its definition and by their core added values. Both are subject to sometimes rapid change.

It is critical to understand the products and the true added values of an organization. This understanding will lead to the discovery of new products and to the necessary redefinition of core added values.

In conclusion, the evolving product drives the need for the regular assessment and possible redefinition of the core values added and the core skills in a corporate entity. (Proposition 22)

Dutch banks at war

Banks until not so long ago were institutions that provided loans and invested money. These typical money services created specific added values that distinguished banks from any other business. However, banks are increasingly used for very basic money transactions, such as salary payments and the payment of bills. Particularly with the introduction of computers, a growing part of banking services consists of transferring money or rather *money data* from one account to another. These new types of services for an increasing population of clients are eroding the original added values of the banks. In other words, banks are becoming money-data-shufflers. They move data from one account or one place to another.

Then, who else moves data from one place to another? Traditionally, postal organizations have moved data almost literally by carrying mail and later through telegraph and telephone networks as well. It is not therefore surprising that the Dutch PTT with their capability of moving data efficiently decided to invest in the start-up of banking services very much to the anger and fear of the Dutch banks. The banks in turn decided to fight back in three ways. They tried legally to prevent the 'PTT' from moving into extensive banking services. In this they have delayed matters, but not for long. Secondly, they have invested in the development of typically new banking products. And thirdly, they could do nothing else but also invest in data and computer networks. Huge amounts of money are now being pumped into banking systems. This 'parable', which in fact is very much a real world example, shows that an evolving product sometimes cripples the core added values of a corporate entity, like it did in the banking business. In addition, a particular core added value may lead to the definition of imaginative new products, like it did in the Dutch PTT.

In summary, one can safely conclude that the thorough review of both organizational products and core added values opens real perspectives for new business opportunities.

The promise of change

Change, in essence, provides *opportunities* rather than problems! It is needed to make new visions come to fruition. However, the promise for improvement through change very much depends upon the following parameters:

1. the vision detail,
2. a responsive culture,
3. the timely awareness of change.

Vision detail

Not all visions are successful after being 'accepted' by the environment even when the next layers of management responded through the development of supporting goals and strategies. Goals and strategies often do not sufficiently affect the 'roots' of the organization. In many cases, the way people work in the organization and more importantly the way they are measured hardly changes! So, what will those poor people do? They are still being measured in the same old way, they will therefore continue to work in the same old way through the same old processes! And if they don't, they will most likely be penalized for it during their performance review, since that too is still based on old measurements.

Vision should therefore amplify what basic measurements and standards for success are required. It should open the way to a complete overhaul or redesign of operational processes by the redefinition of the basic measurements needed.

Vision should impact on every working person in the organization in terms of how he is measured. (Proposition 23)

'Quell the unrest at the bottom'

Under the leadership of Jack Welch, the dynamic chief executive of the American General Electric Co., GE has significantly improved its global competitiveness over the last couple of years. Welch has been reshaping the corporate culture, making it more growth conscious and less bureaucratic. Many of the lower echelons, however, feel pressed and overworked. But Welch stresses that he wants his employees *to work smarter, not harder*. One of his major challenges therefore is internal communication, because that is what will give him the most leverage. He has to make believers of all of his managers, not just the ones at the top. In order to attract the enthusiasm of the 'lower downs', Welch has invested in an improved training package, has introduced a new reward scheme and has been revamping the employee evaluation system to make it more 'honest'.

From maintenance to service

In a round table discussion between the executives of several major computer manufacturers, it was noted that the technological revolution has led to a reduced need for technical maintenance. As a result, the service industry that used to be concerned with maintenance only, is being redirected from maintenance to supplying overall customer service. This change in vision creates the need for untraditional functions in the service industry, such as marketing. In addition, the skills and measurements of the employees that are required, are no longer as technical in nature. They now seem to focus in addition on finance and administration, on human resource management and on business development. Executives are talking about a change in culture, about collaboration and about intra-preneurship. All seem to be needed to make this new vision in the service industry come to fruition.

In conclusion, successful visions impact on the basic measurements in the organization. These basic measurements function as the fabric of organizational processes. The medium to ensure that these measurements are appropriately adjusted is, of course, the culture of the corporate entity concerned.

A responsive culture

'How to work towards a more responsive culture' has already been discussed in Part Two of this book, where one finds the core concepts of culture performance. Vision and culture engineering, however, are interdependent. This means that they are only effective as long as they are consciously linked. Through the vision-culture (im-)balance (Chapter 4), one knows that certain visions may not be realized when they do not have a reasonable chance of being absorbed by the cultural environment. This refers to the relative closeness of vision to the organizational culture, as first discussed in Chapter 10. On the other hand, a culture can only be adjusted when management vision meets certain quality standards, because vision drives culture change.

Timely awareness of change

A few years ago, a Dutch agency introduced a lucrative new project for the small to medium sized retail business under the name of the 'Best-shop-in-town'. Through an evaluaton of the overall sales performance in a certain area, this project aims to select the best shops in town, which are then offered the opportunity to join the 'Best-shop-in-town' club. At a yearly fee its members get several marketing and advertisement services with the objective of maintaining the 'Best-shop-in-town' status and of course to substantiate further growth. A characteristic part of these services is a yearly market assessment, which allows shops to tune in to the latest local market needs. This is quite in contrast to the usual market study, which in general turns out to be a one-off affair to test the waters for a new business or product. The repetitive market assessment in particular, is the key to the success of this project, especially because shops hardly do any market research. The relatively frequent check on where the market is going and what its needs are almost always provides these 'Best-shops-in-town' with a just-in-time response, that is neither too late nor too soon.

A constant *planning attitude*

The rapid change in the business environment and consequently the environmental challenges and needs can be represented in a 'change and response' trend; see the dotted line in Figure 35. Let us look at the old way of planning, where management determines periodically, or occasionally, what the corporate directions should be, say every two to five years. As devoted managers, they will start to assess the environment. They may find the environmental trend to be going upwards. In response, directions will be developed which are in support of this upward trend, as for example indicated by the solid line for the 'occasional response' in Figure 35. Then after two to five years, management reconvenes in order to develop new directions. Their assessment may now show a downward trend of the environment. New directions are established to accommodate this downward trend. As a result, the management directions are in support of the environmental challenges only once every two to five years, that is at the moment they are established. In fact, between the two to five yearly planning sessions the environment inevitably changes in many ways. The organizational

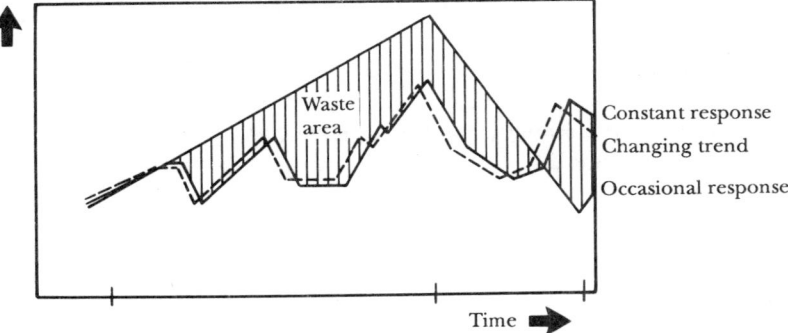

Figure 35 *Change and response trend graph*

efforts that are based on these two to five year directions will most likely be out of phase with the needs of the changing environment and may therefore lose their effectiveness. The so-called effort waste areas in Figure 35 vividly show the distance between the changing environment and the occasional planning direction.

Long term directions (rather than long term visions) tend to be limited in their design. They are based on an appreciation of the environmental changes by people with an attitude, mind-set and belief that are geared to realities at one particular time. The benefits of new understandings and changed views, as matters develop, are simply missed out. In addition, longer term directions may sometimes have the undesirable side effect of conditioning people. As a result, people may be blocked off from alternative solution routes. A flexible planning attitude should therefore be developed by making certain that management continuously evaluates the environment versus the direction set, so turning planning directions into just-in-time answers to any (*business*) challenges that arise. The changing environment can then be responded to accurately. The exact frequency with which this has to take place is dependent on the sort of environment one is dealing with. It may vary from once every minute, to once every week or month. In order to be truly successful one will also have to develop planning directions of a different kind, that in essence are designed for change. Vision, as such, matches this requirement much better than direction. In addition, the way the environment is responded to should differ as well. Most likely, a more decentralized approach will have to be assumed, which at the same time implies that the total measurement and reward fabric of the subject organization will have to be adjusted as discussed under 'vision detail'. This reminds one of the situation in the USSR, where five year plans are common. The efforts of Gorbachev seem to be directed towards the creation of a more responsive economy, which indeed impacts on the basic measurement and reward structure of the socialist system.

A constant planning attitude is essential to successful change and the prevention of wasted effort in corporate entities. The ultimate trick simply is in a continuously evolving awareness of management and in the design for change. (Proposition 24)

Reflections

Key messages

The degree of focus of a direction is much greater than that of vision. The overall impact of directions on organizations, therefore, is much less, more concentrated and in a sense inhibiting. A vision can very well be characterized as an 'in-direction'. Because vision is such an open-ended thinking concept, it tends to impact on the organization in all its facets, assuming its relative closeness to the subject culture. It is therefore not surprising that vision touches important corporate entity characteristics such as core added values and skills, products and culture. Vision in its cloudy disguise turns out to be an unlimited and, until today, under-utilized power-tool.

- Visions manifest themselves as easy to understand conceptions of what the future might be.
- Vision in all circumstances impacts on the core added values and products of a corporate entity.
- Vision should and eventually will impact on every working person in an organization in terms of how he or she is measured.
- Vision requires constant planning, in other words a continuously evolving awareness of management and the design for change.

Constant planning will be the basis for organic change that continuously spreads and grows in an organization. It will be a natural assumption for the biological system analogy, as identified in Chapter 14. A model for the construction of vision will be discussed in the next chapter, based on the findings in this chapter relative to added values and products.

12

The vision model

The body of vision

'The vision model: it may change my way of solving problems'. This is the written comment of one of the branch managers in the group who I talked to on vision and culture engineering.

The 'Titanic' analogy

An organization, a group of people or a person in a sense resembles a ship that sails through the oceans of a particular world. It is relatively vulnerable, because the environmental forces have an unmistakable impact on its wellbeing and on its course. The icebergs that a ship meets on its way have a definite impact on its direction as well. The direction is not based on what its crew sees, once the ship comes close to an iceberg, but on what the crew knows about icebergs. Less than 10 per cent of an iceberg is visible above the surface of the ocean, the remainder is below. The chance of hitting an iceberg is mainly determined by the invisible part under the waterline. It means that the ship has to maintain a respectable distance. Only one ship, the *Titanic*, was considered to be indestructible. The ship seemed to have been so well constructed. The many compartments within its hull would make it practically unsinkable. At least, that is what they thought until the *Titanic* hit an iceberg. Then one of the most tragic shipping catastrophes became fact.

Vision is like an iceberg. It has a definite influence on the course of the corporate entity that it applies to. When corporate entities seem to be undestructable, they may be confronted dramatically with its unexpected impact. The biggest part of vision cannot straightforwardly be seen, it is hidden below the waters on which the corporate entity floats. The way vision appears, in other words, the statement that represents it, is only a small part of its true 'body'. So what is below the surface? What is the true body of vision that one doesn't immediately see?

The 'purpose-driven' vision

The true body of vision contains the so-called strategic progress elements of the corporate entity. They appear in whatever subsection of the corporate entity one chooses to study. Strategic progress elements can be grouped along three dimensions or axes, such as:

- the corporate entity's *purpose*,
- the corporate entity's *process* and
- the corporate entity's means.

The *purpose* of the corporate entity seems to be driven mainly by the awareness of its caretakers. The corporate entity's process and means tend to depend more on change, as we will see later. Figure 36 shows the

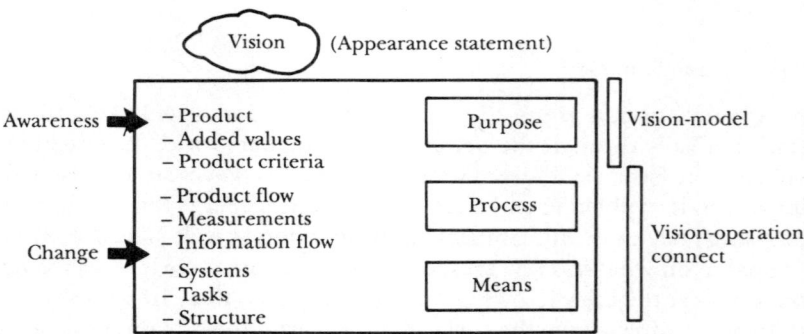

Figure 36 *The total vision in a corporate entity*

relationship between these dimensions and their strategic progress elements.

The names and the descriptions of strategic progress elements relate to items that one normally finds in companies. In case the corporate entity is not a company, but an arbitrary organization or a person, then they should be considered symbolically or figuratively. For example, a product is *anything*, that the corporate entity provides to its 'customers'. A customer is anybody who gets something from the corporate entity

The PURPOSE dimension:

1. The PRODUCT of a corporate entity.
   What is the corporate entity supplying to its customers and what does it *want* to supply?

2. The CORE ADDED VALUES of a corporate entity.
   What values does the corporate entity truly add and what values is it going to add through outside suppliers?

3. The PRODUCT CRITERIA of a corporate entity.
   What does the (quantified) sales volume, range, quality, price, delivery, customer service, etc. of the product look like?

The PROCESS dimension:

4. The PRODUCT-FLOWS that the corporate entity manages.
   What are the basic 'product'* flows between the corporate entity and its corporate partners, such as suppliers and customers?

5. The BASIC MEASUREMENTS needed in the corporate entity.
   The minimal measurements needed to manage the 'product' flows in support of or in line with the product criteria.

6. The basic INFORMATION FLOWS in the corporate entity.
   The necessary senders and receivers of basic measurements within and outside the corporate entity.

The MEANS dimension:

7. The BASIC SYSTEMS in a corporate entity.
   The basic information systems to handle the information flows within and outside the corporate entity.

8. The BASIC TASKS in a corporate entity.
   Whatever cannot be done by a basic information system needs to be done by the human being.

Note: See explanation of 'product' on page 134.

136   The Power of Tomorrow's Management

9   The STRUCTURE within the corporate entity.
    The structure that one needs within the corporate entity to accomplish correctly the basic tasks in the corporate entity.

The culture-purpose connect

The last strategic progress element: 'structure' is not only part of vision, but also part of the corporate entity's culture performance model. It focuses on the maximization of people's response in support of vision. It is the starting point for measures that are there to ensure that people have the right spirit, attitude and behaviour to materialize 'their' (purpose-driven) vision. The strategic progress elements under purpose, process and means each depend on the earlier defined culture performance drivers. For example, structure and involvement seem to be most needed for the achievement of the organizational means. Responsibility is intertwined with the success of process and process design. (Business) partnership and identity are critical when developing the purpose of the corporate entity. It means that an inverse relationship exists between the purpose driven strategic progress elements and the people driven culture performance drivers. This relationship has been worked out in Figure 37.

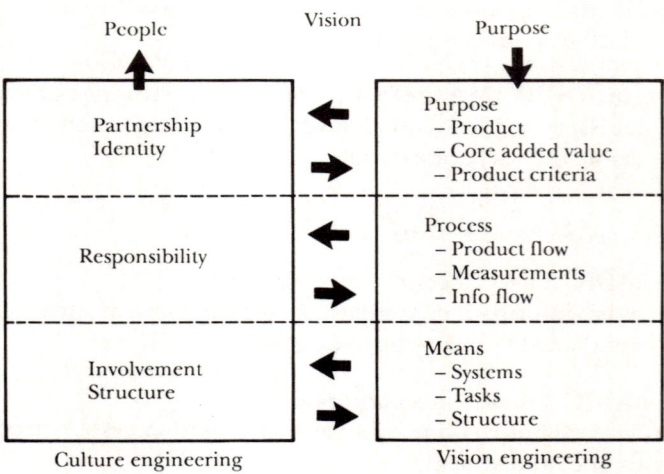

Figure 37   *The culture-purpose connect*

The vision facilitation model

The first three strategic progress elements in the 'total vision' (product, added values and product criteria) together determine the corporate entity's purpose. Through the definition of these elements one ensures that the particular strengths of the corporate entity are identified and connected to its ultimate output and output quality. The vision model provides a logical guideline for the development of the corporate entity's PURPOSE and the three strategic progress elements it contains. The future achievement of the vision model depends on an appropriate level of awareness and the break-throughs that have been incorporated.

The background of the vision model

The vision model is a rational tool that can be used to facilitate and develop the critically needed awareness of the corporate entity's purpose. This awareness is essential to initiate and undertake the right actions. Hence, the logic of the vision model had to be based on the following ground rules,

1   The vision model should be driven by an ultimate goal, for example, as has been formulated in the vision (appearance) statement.

2   It should start to define the 'customers', since they are the ones that drive and in essence *justify* the corporate entity.

3   The build-up of the model should be led by *what one wants* rather than by 'common sense'. There is no better motivator than wanting something. It is also the best way to identify and create break-through potential.

4   Sufficient check and balance situations should be included in order to put the 'wants' into an achievable perspective.

5   The 'wants' should be consolidated in order to keep focus on the essentials. Too many details at the start will smother progress.

These rules have been based on a mix of business reasons and psychological findings on people's behaviour, as discussed earlier in this book. They ensure that people experience the building of the vision model as an eye opener. In other words, people should return to their environment, realizing that there is life beyond the horizon for their own initiatives and ideas.

The construction benefits

The vision model needs to be actually constructed. The vision model 'builders' should be the people who eventually trigger and organize actions in support of the corporate entity's purpose. Hence, when the corporate entity concerns an organization of any kind, the team of corporate entity leaders should participate in the construction of the vision model.

The following items summarize the objectives and at the same time the *benefits* of the vision model construction process. Starting with the most important ones, they are:

- getting meaningful awareness of the corporate entity's purpose,
- facilitating innovation and break-through by 'wanting',
- mobilizing the brains of people,
- getting a picture of interconnects with needed partners,
- getting 'strategic thinking' into teams,
- getting towards 'team aims' and synergy in people's energies,
- simply getting an understanding of each other's aims,
- linking strategy to 'do-goals',
- moving away from paper-pushing-planning.

If the corporate entity concerns one person only, one should add:

- synergizing the different aims one has,
- more effectively converging energy and capacities of one person,
- simply understanding one's own aims.

The 'construction' approach

During the construction of the vision model, some of the steps request the person or the team to list the customers, products, etc., that one would want. In this way, good ideas, although not immediately viable, may surface, to be stored for later use. However, many people are not really used to saying what they want. Sometimes it is because they are too shy to make their choice, but in general it is because they have just never been asked! Managers, in particular, tend to fear these 'free to choose' situations; it gives them the feeling of being out of control. For that reason, the vision model has been designed with sufficient checks and balances to ensure that free choice is channelled into a constructive and realistic sense.

The background of this channelling is 'productive creativity'. It is obtained by an alternating focus that moves from a 'free choice of wants' to structuring and from structuring to a 'free choice' of (bigger) wants continuously, see Figure 38. 'Structuring' concerns the search for matching relations between chosen wants, the quantification of assumptions and eventually the assimilation of wants within existing environmental patterns. In the same way, the fine-tuning of the resulting vision model should take place at a later stage in order to improve its realism and the chance of success.

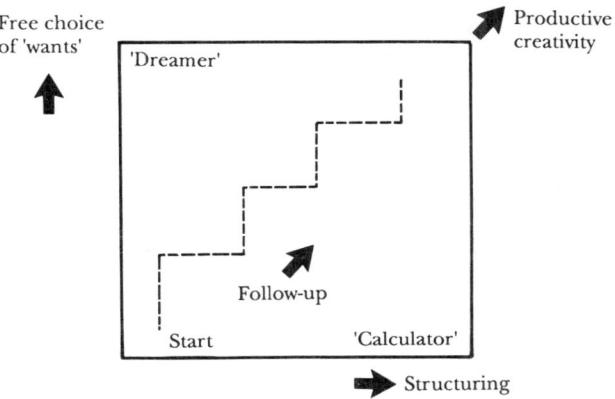

Figure 38 *Productive creativity*

Constructing the vision model

The best way to imagine the construction of the vision model is to place oneself in the shoes of an entrepreneur who wants to start his own business. This advice may not be too difficult to follow because most people between the ages of 20 and 50 have at least once seriously considered doing the same.

The vision of the potential entrepreneur revolves around what he *wants* to achieve in a number of years in terms of,

- business-size;
- customers;
- products;
- added value;
- suppliers and
- orientation within his business; for example: by customer, by product, by function, by supplier, by market, by geography, by major system.

140 *The Power of Tomorrow's Management*

In addition, he will think of the business success factors, such as market positioning, quality, service levels, price, volume, etc.

With the above considerations in mind, nine steps have been defined that lead to the definition of the vision model. These nine steps are,

1   confirmation of the vision (appearance) statement,
2   understanding the environmental impact,
3   defining the customers,
4   selecting products and product groups of the corporate entity,
5   estimating the business potential,
6   identifying the added values,
7   selection of core and non-core added values,
8   establishing potential sources and suppliers and finally
9   the quantification of the product success criteria.

Normally, the initial exercise to establish these steps in a team would take about two to three days to complete. The resulting vision-model-picture has to be clear and simple enough to be used as a base reference and communication tool during any follow-up or rather fine-tuning exercises. It is, after all, a growing awareness, that one should be after. In the following pages, the above steps have been worked out in detail. They tell how the vision model should be built.

Step 1: 'identifying the vision statement'

The team or the person that is about to start the vision process has to decide first what the triggering vision (appearance) statement is. Typical vision statements could be:

- 'a 10 per cent annual increase in earning per share'
  (as from Harold Geneen for the ITT corporation) or

- 'we want to be the lowest cost car producer in Europe'
  (as from Jaques Calvet for the Peugeot-Citroen corporation) or

- 'towards a prosperous economy through perestroika'
  (as from Mikhail Gorbachev for the USSR).

But 'alas', when no vision appearance statement can be identified, the team obviously has a problem:
                    NLWACM or 'no-leader-with-a-clear-message'!
The challenge will be to search for the true leader who can convince this

group of people. Or when the corporate entity concerns one person, then he or she should establish his or her own vision statement in the above format. The great leaders of this world, however, will never be caught in a situation where their people are wondering what the ultimate vision is!

Step 2: 'sorting out the priorities in the environment'

The purpose of this step is to select the important influences in the environment, of which this particular corporate entity is part. This is simply because one's course of action may be determined by it. One has basically two options, either to be led by the environment *passively* in the sense the French writer Emile Zola (1840–1902) may have meant it in his books about 'des Rougon-Macquart', or by taking the initiative *actively* to play a role in shaping the environment.

By reviewing and judging the major events in the environment, one develops an understanding about 'what to react to in the corporate entity', but also about 'what the opportunities are to influence it'. The environmental analysis may therefore turn out to be a 'personality examination', because it reveals the basic attitudes of the contributors in terms of passiveness and willingness to shape! During this step, the outcome of market studies should typically appear, also technological and social developments, the evolving world and country economies, specific directives from top management and projected customer needs. In summary, this step should qualify and to a certain extent quantify the major external drivers that will or *should* impact on the corporate entity. During any follow-up sessions that are geared to fine-tune the vision-model, this step should list the findings on the assumptions that have been used when constructing the model.

The process to be followed consists of two tasks. The first is to make a list of all items or scenarios that might influence the corporate entity. The ideas of the team members (if there is a team) should be made visible. It is important for each team member to know and understand these. Cross-fertilization of the environmental appreciation is indeed one of the anticipated team-building gains during this task. Subsequently, one should select three to five major items that impact on the corporate entity most. Each one should then be worked out or expanded in order to grasp the basics and nature of their potential influence. The best way to do this is to describe and picture the *past, present* and *future* of each item. Thus the dimension of time will be made part of this exercise. Sufficient time should be reserved to do this step properly. Its quality will determine the final quality of the vision model. The outcome of this step will be an environmental summary of the major influences and possible and impossible scenarios. This summary (Figure 39) should be updated regularly. It should preferably not take more space than one sheet of paper.

Environmental influence summary

Major impact items:	Past	Present	Future
1...			
2...			
3...			
4...			

Figure 39   *Amplification of environmental impact items*

Step 3:   'defining the customers'

The purpose of this step is to brainstorm and logically group the customers that people want the corporate entity to have. Again, this step comprises two parts. The first consists of listing the customers that one would want to have, and the second consists of gathering the customers into logical groups. In most cases, people will ask the question: 'which

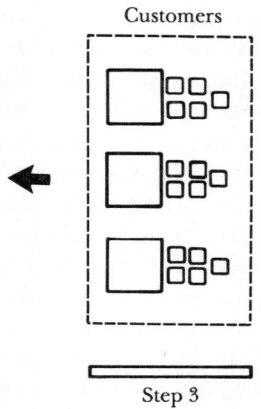

Figure 40   *Customers in the vision model*

groups'? And the answer should be: 'what do *you* think?' In other words, the people, who are responsible for the corporate entity's success, should seriously make a value judgement on how they group their customers, for example, by market segment, by product, by customer type, etc. The grouping exercise in essence functions as a first consolidation and sanity check. The outcome of the entire step consists of, say three to five, key customer groups that have their own identification and name. The customers, who belong to a certain group should be visibly linked to each other. The first part of the vision-model has thus been completed (see Figure 40).

Step 4: 'identifying products and Product Focus Units'

This is perhaps one of the most important steps in the definition of the vision model. The products that the corporate entity passes on to its customers, as well as the product groups, will have to be identified. In fact, one considers here the 'ultimate output' of the corporate entity. Products concern anything that is provided to the customers of the corporate entity. One may have intermediate products in *any* form and end products, such as physical goods, services, consultancy and soforth.

Again, what counts is 'what one *wants* to generate and deliver as products'. When listing the products that people would want to provide, the following alternatives should be considered,

- customer driven products,
- competition driven products,
- supplier driven products,
- substituting products, that replace existing ones in the market,
- technology driven products and
- products based on certain strengths within the corporate entity.

Subsequently, the identified products need to be grouped into product groups or Product Focus Units (PFUs). Each Product Focus Unit should get an imaginative and meaningful identification with the objective to evoke some of its spirit in the minds of the people who may have to materialize them. Again, it is up to the people who participate in this process, to decide which groups make most sense. Product Focus Units will help ensure more specific product-oriented strategic decisions during the next construction steps. The vision-process, therefore, will henceforth relate to each of the selected PFUs. The outcome of Step 4 is an overview of about three to five Product Focus Units. Linked to those are the product ideas, as identified during this exercise.

Step 5: 'sizing the Product Focus Units (PFUs)'

The purpose of this step is to confirm the significance of each Product Focus Unit, with the objective of facilitating any future strategic investment decisions. The significance of Product Focus Units can best be determined by estimating their relative business size coupled with their future potential growth rate. But what is business size? When the corporate entity comprises a company, business size is determined by its total sales potential. In the case of a department, however, business size may be related to costs, simply because its products may not (yet) have a price tag and because of the direct relation between (justified) departmental expenses and their products. In other words, one will first have to agree on what exactly business size is going to refer to. The business size for each Product Focus Unit is expressed as a percentage of the total corporate entity size, that is of all PFUs together. It may boil down to estimating the current sales or cost volume of each Product Focus Unit. The outcome in the vision model will be a percentage for each PFU, as part of the total (100 per cent), i.e. of all PFUs together; (see Figure 41).

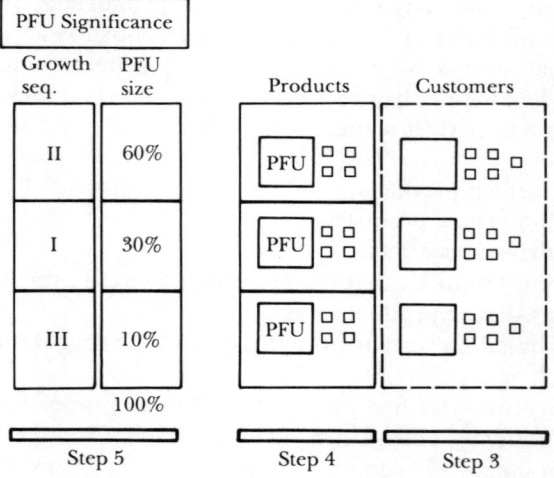

Figure 41 *Products, product focus units and PFU significance*

The next task is to define the potential growth rate of the PFUs by selecting the fastest grower, the second fastest grower and so on. This is a critical step, because the growth rate expectation in fact shows the future potential of the PFU. The growth rate expectation may change significantly in a relatively short period of time, as opposed to the PFU-size. For example, the breakthrough of a certain technology may dramatically improve the growth potential of a PFU and of course its significance almost overnight. Hence, the growth sequence is one of the elements in the vision model that has to be closely watched in the follow-up sessions. The growth rate of the PFUs will be registered in the vision model by their growth sequence. The first PFU will be the one with the highest growth rate, the second PFU will have the second highest growth rate and so on.

Step 6: 'identifying added values'

The purpose of this step is to define the currently available and actually needed added values for each Product Focus Unit in the corporate entity. This exercise will eventually contribute to the decision as to where to get the necessary added values *from*.

Added value relates to a particular (sometimes unique) set of skills, capacity, positioning, expertise or resource that is in essence required successfully to generate and deliver products to customers. Added values may vary from specific public relations skills, contacts, production capacity and market channels to the expertise in a certain field. Core added values are provided by the corporate entity itself. Non-core added values are obtained through added value suppliers. Core added values should therefore preferably be unique, competitive and hard to find elsewhere. In this step, the major added values per Product Focus Unit should be listed. One should start with about three added values that are

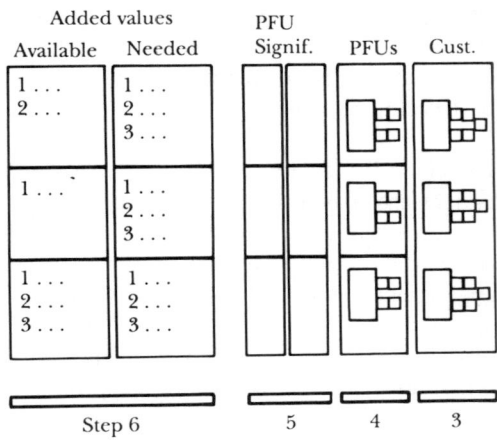

Figure 42 *Added values in the vision model*

146   *The Power of Tomorrow's Management*

actually needed for each Product Focus Unit and subsequently those that are currently available per PFU within the corporate entity itself. The results are incorporated in the vision model 'to be', as in Figure 42.

Step 7: 'selecting core and non-core added values'

When a corporate entity does not have the added values it needs to deliver the products of its choice, there are several ways of obtaining them. They have been summarized below, starting with the least committing and ending with the most committing alternative.

- *Subcontracting* particular added values to vendors and suppliers. The Amstrad company is a well recognized example of this approach, 'buying' much of what it requires.

- Setting up *joint ventures* through which certain added values may be obtained. For example, the Japanese steel industry in particular, Kawasaki Steel, has expanded into an entirely different product range through joint ventures (e.g. silicon wafers).

- Through *acquisitions* a company can get the added values it needs to ship their future products. Both General Motors and Daimler Benz, for example, have acquired several high-tech companies to give them the technologies needed for their future products.

- By *investing* in the development of the required added value within the corporate entity. This will cause *organic growth* of the organization. Many companies, such as for example the Digital Equipment Corporation, have (in the past) demonstrated this preference, in Digital's case by developing the technology they needed themselves.

There are several reasons for selecting one of the above alternatives. Some corporate leaders are driven by a preference for *organic* growth, which is growth from within the organization. Organic growth has a considerable impact on the corporate entity, because it relies heavily on organizational change processes in order to cope with the development challenges. Success will depend on specific cultural characteristics of the organization. Other corporate leaders are led by a preference for size and volume. As a result, they will opt for the development of *acquisition strategies*. ITT under Harold Geneen grew this way to a respectable size. Again, success here depends on specific cultural characteristics as well. Each of the above alternatives has its background and requirements for particular cultural characteristics. It is obvious that the connections with culture positioning emerge from these discussions; they will, however, be discussed later.

In general, the following two criteria can be applied for the selection of the above alternatives for *each* of the added values, as listed per Product Focus Unit,

- Product Focus Unit *significance* and
- *the uniqueness of the* particular *value added*.

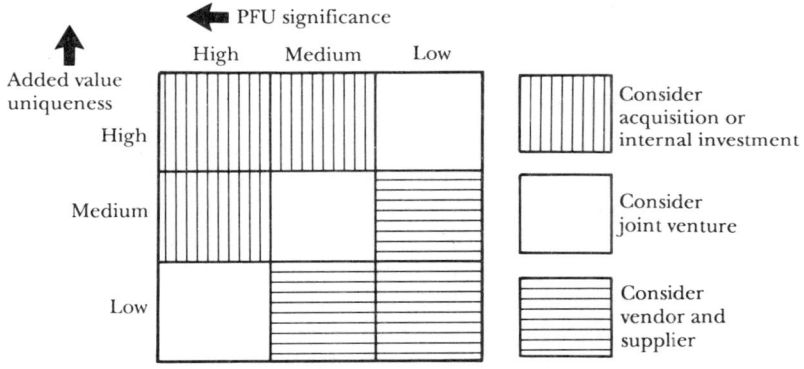

Figure 43 *Added-value-supplier 'positioning plane'*

In Figure 43, these criteria have been plotted in an added-value-supplier 'positioning plane'. The uniqueness of the added value concerned can be either high, medium or low. 'High' relates to situations where the added value cannot be provided anywhere else in the business world. An added value with a 'low' uniqueness means it is generally available and not very special. Also PFU significance can be quantified in terms of low, medium and high, that is based on the previously established PFU growth sequence coupled with the PFU sizing. Product Focus Units that do not have a tremendous sales potential nor a promising growth rate, will not encourage management to invest in corporate acquisitions or in internal development. This is particularly so when the added values required for the PFU can be obtained anywhere in the business world. In this case, it is wise to consider to 'buying' the added values from vendors and suppliers.

The various combinations of PFU significance and added value uniqueness lead to three recommendations in total for the sourcing of the required added values. According to the added-value-supplier

148 *The Power of Tomorrow's Management*

'positioning plane' in Figure 43, the recommendations are:
- to consider vendors and suppliers,
- to consider joint ventures,
- to consider acquisitions or internal development investments.

Only in the last case, may the required added values actually be turned into *core added values*. The rationale for acquisitions rather than for internal investments seems mainly dependent on cultural strengths and weaknesses and on the cultural range, as will be discussed in Part Four of this book. With the recommendations at hand for the sourcing of the required added values, one is now ready to identify *alternative* 'suppliers' in the vision model.

Step 8: 'identifying suppliers'

Knowing what type of suppliers to go after (internal investment, acquisition, joint venture, vendor), one can start to brainstorm the alternative 'suppliers' for the particular added values required. It should result in several possible business partners for each Product Focus Unit, that have been grouped in the columns for internal investment, acquisitions, joint ventures and vendors, wherever appropriate. Needless to say, both *internal* as well as *external* business partners may be identified! The outcome of this step has been sketched in Figure 44. The major part of the vision model and the corporate entity's purpose has now been completed. It is important to realize that this picture not only incorporates the ideas but also the preferences of its 'designers'.

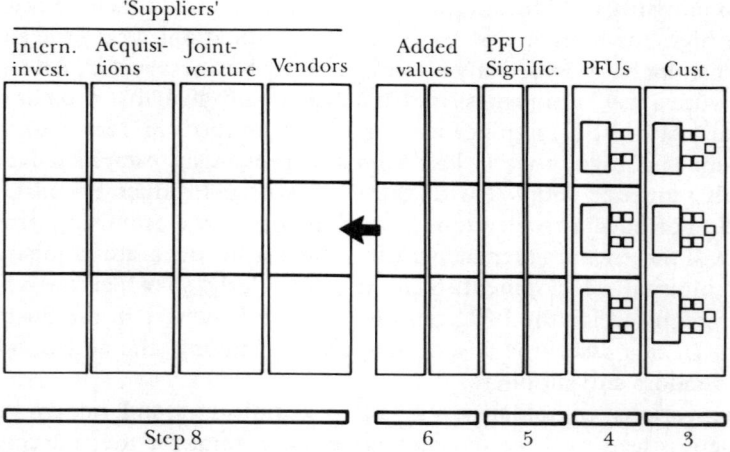

Figure 44 *The complete vision model*

Step 9: 'Product criteria or measurable goals to work to'

The next challenge is to create the right *incentives* or *measurable goals* to mobilize the kinetic energy of the corporate entity, in other words to get it moving. These measurable goals will be the criteria for success, the criteria for organizational performance, the criteria for rewards and the criteria for process design and tool selections. Hence, it is logical that these criteria are related to the ultimate output of the organization: the products and Product Focus Units. One should try to put oneself in the place of the customers, as they have been selected, and question why they would want one's product? This step therefore focuses on the definition of the product criteria in terms of,

- product functionalities,
- product appearance,
- product price,
- product margin,
- product quality,
- product delivery,
- product availability,
- total product sales volume,
  etc.

These elements should be identified as well as possible, even when realizing that not all expertise and information may be available to define them appropriately. However, people do know more than they are consciously aware of.

Success only through follow-up

The purpose of the vision model is to create a structured awareness of the key elements that seem to drive the successful corporate entity. When awareness is heightened people tend to undertake much more meaningful actions, because they then realize what it is all about and what their own shortcomings were when creating the vision model. It will lead to an effective allocation of the right resources, for example in the area of strategic marketing and finance to resolve these shortcomings and to improve the quality of the model. The vision model is a *dynamic model*, not only because of the corrections and adjustments required, but also because change and events in the environment (such as wars, technological breakthroughs, new products, economic disasters, oil crises, etc) result in the need to update it continuously. In addition, the continued involvement of people in the fine-tuning of the vision-model will elevate their alertness for new business opportunities and breakthroughs.

In conclusion, the development of the vision model for a company underlines the fact that products and customers are not just a marketing or engineering concern but a total corporate entity concern. Specialist functions, like, for example, marketing and engineering, are strong in generating new ideas, quantifying of ideas and professionally implementing ideas. Their activities, however, should be driven by the corporate entity's purpose and not vice versa.

Focus networks

The best way to create a follow-up structure is to agree and define focus networks, consisting of key contributors within the organization. One of the advantages of focus networks is that they are independent of the existing organizational structure. Anyone who can significantly contribute, should be part of it. Hence, the follow-up of the vision model itself could well be structured through,

- a focus network aiming at the customer base developments,
- a focus network aiming at product development and
- a focus network aiming at the supplier base development.

These focus networks should be responsible for the connection with the operational world in terms of concept development, environmental analysis, performance measurement and strategic progress. As such, the focus networks should also be rewarded for the performance and progress in their area. The chairpersons of these teams should be members of an overall focus network, that is responsible for the update and development of the vision model itself. Based on these suggestions, the vision model may help to break through unnecessary hierarchies in historically developed organizations.

Reflections

Key messages

I have often had the opportunity of addressing groups of 'corporate citizens' on vision engineering. I prefer a short interactive brainstorming session at the start, which seems to switch the minds of those attending to whatever they have in their memories on the subject. The following catchwords capture what these people believe vision is:

- Idea;
- Think;

The vision model   151

- New concept;
- Adaptability;
- Imagination;
- Planning;
- Forward thinking;
- Perspectives;
- Anticipation;
- Picturing success;
- Open mindedness;
- A dream;
- Provocative/controversial;
- Creativity.

The results of several groups were very consistent. Remarkably, vision did not seem something for leaders only. It is everyone's tool. It is flexible, it translates the picture of future achievement into today's environment and it breaks through current senses by being provocative. But in every case the question came up: 'how to turn vision into *action*'.

The nine step process of building a vision-model, as discussed in this chapter, shows how to lead the way. Starting with 'what we do it all for' and ending 'by developing the basic resources needed', straightforwardly transforms vision from a transcendental phenomenon into a world of clear-cut and ordered tasks. This will be increasingly important when moving from a 'shaping' to a 'creating' world (Chapter 14).

- The complete vision picture covers the awareness driven purpose of an organization, as well as the change driven processes and means.
- Each 'corporate entity' has certain strategic progress elements that are grouped along three dimensions: the purpose-dimension, the process-dimension and the means-dimension.
- The construction of the vision model comprises a logical and understandable definition of the strategic progress elements along the purpose-dimension, such as products, core added values and product criteria.
- There is an inverse relation between strategic progress elements and the five basic culture performance drivers, as defined in Part Two of this book.
- There is no better motivator than *wanting* something. It is also the best way to create breakthroughs. We should exploit the wanting-power of people better.

The vision-model is the foundation of the vision-operation connection (Chapter 13), that talks about creating change in a corporate entity.

13

The vision-operation connection

The most common issue in planning

During one of the vision development sessions that I organised, the question came up: 'how does a woman find the man of her dreams?' And somebody immediately answered: 'by *adjusting* her dreams!' And this intuitive reaction indeed grasps the essence of success. Nine out of ten people find their spouse this way and not by intensifying their search, not by trying harder. The idea is to start off with a dream and then to proceed by adjusting it based on findings, experiences, needs and the environment. By the way, dreams cover both the visions of the ideal partner as well as the way the partner is found. How many girls have not dreamt of finding their prince, as in the movies? And how many girls have actually met their spouse that way? The same, of course, applies to men as well. The key in the above is the continuous updating and adjusting that is required. Success is very much related to flexibility and continuous restructuring. For example, *perestroika* or restructuring in the USSR will only be successful therefore if it means a continuous *perestroika*.

The most common issue in planning is as trivial as the above. To come up with a vision or a strategy is not really the issue. The issue is in translating strategy into effective and controlled action, or in other words: translating strategy into success. We know that success is related to flexibility and the management of continuous change, but what are the core contributors to success? And also, what *is* success?

The success-cube theory

From what we have previously discussed in this book, one may conclude that both vision and culture should be considered the key contributors to success. But that as a conclusion is not sufficient. In order to materialize success, one obviously needs also to allocate specific resources. In other words, resources through culture will translate vision into action. Hence, success is based on vision, culture and specific resources.

Vision and culture can be considered as the platform for success. Based on this platform, resources will help to erect the so-called success-cube for the corporate entity, as in Figure 45. The success-cube represents the maximum interaction between the three key success contributors. Their combined outcome is the *success vector* that functions as the quantified measure or standard of success. In fact, it *represents* success!

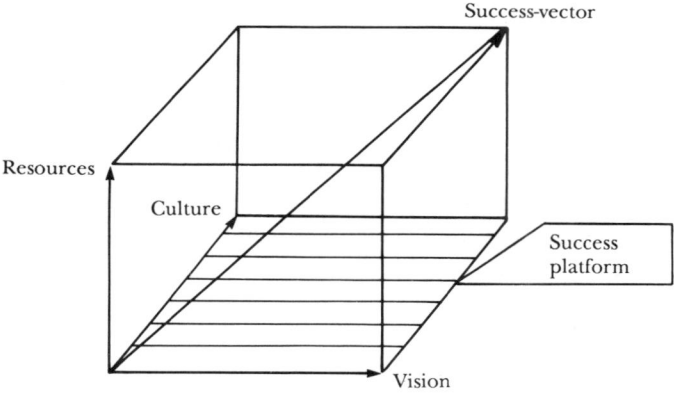

Figure 45 *Success-cube for the corporate entity*

The success vector

If the success vector is the standard of success, then it must incorporate the goals that have been defined as *product criteria* in the previous chapter. This is simply because they are a quantification of the vision model's standards of success. At the same time, the success vector will include the culture repositioning goals, as discussed in Part Two of this book, and finally the *resource goals*, such as skills and capacity.

The length of the success vector in the success cube is maximized when goals related to vision, culture and resources have been met. The success vector will shorten in the event that the goals of one of the success contributors have only partly been realized. Theoretically, one may compensate this (to a certain extent) by overachieving through the other success contributors. For example, in the event that the culture repositioning goals have not been fully met, one may compensate by overachieving the goals related to vision and or resources. In order to ensure maximum success, it makes sense to identify the contents of the success vector first and then to work towards it. The success vector will then turn from a resultant into a success driver and goal-set.

Translating strategy into action

Through the success-cube, we have in broad terms defined the 'translation of strategy to success'. The main purpose of the success-cube is to show the relationship between vision, culture, resources and the success vector. The question now is 'how to translate strategy into controlled and effective action'. The latter seems particularly to relate to the appropriate allocation and control of resources, such as, for example, people, systems, tools, capital, technology and knowledge. In effect, resources function as the action agents for the success-cube. Resources are by definition scarce, which results in their economical distribution. But there are more allocation criteria that impact on the effective use of resources. Especially when dealing with people, the allocation of resources depends on cutural needs. It should therefore be resolved through culture positioning. The following examples seem to illustrate current rules of thumb used when allocating innovative resources or change agents.

Development resources

The development of software systems is a fairly complicated matter. It not only deals with computer design constraints but also with end-user requirements that seem to be driven by historical business processes. And as we have discussed before, historical processes tend not to be optimally structured! Software development firms that have made it their business to do the above, are obviously very dependent on success. They must find ways to increase the success rate of their developments in order to make profit. So, how do they do it? Companies like, for example, Hoskyns in the United Kingdom, tend to limit the size of their development groups to not more than three to five people. These groups are responsible for the total project and consist of several different specialists. For the professionals in those companies, it is fairly easy to get an approval to do such a project, as long as they don't break the sizing rule. Any proposals for bigger sized projects need to go through a tough approval cycle that involves most of the management.

The grocery-concept

I have several times helped the management of a distribution organization in developing and implementing their vision. At one point we were discussing unconventional solutions specifically in relation to the development of a simplified operational process that could well be systemized. Past experience showed this to be very difficult, the outcome had never been satisfactory. The results of the brainstorming session seemed to turn the team on. Some of the items were,

- 'power to the people',
- sub-contract major parts of the distribution responsibiity,
- implementing 'profit centres',
- pay for 'group-performance',
- pay for ideas,
- systemize everything.

These ideas eventually led to the introduction of the very simple and at the same time very interesting 'grocery-concept'. The grocery-concept aims to simulate the grocery, where one or perhaps a few people run the entire business. The grocer is responsible for procurement, goods receipts, administration, sales, advertisement, etc. No way can a grocer be tempted to make his business and administrative process too complicated. And no way can he allow fatal administrative errors to occur, it would simply kill his business.

The idea was to set up a pilot that would implement the grocery concept in the distribution environment. A very few people were to be made responsible for all physical and administrative activities for a well defined set of part numbers. The challenge in terms of workload would have to be made considerable, thus providing the incentive to simplify and systemize the operational process where possible. On the other hand, the group would be measured and rewarded for their cost and quality performance, as if being a profit centre. Based on the above, the following guidelines were compiled in order to manage strategic developments in a manageable and controlled environment,

- break 'success' down into clearly defined *success-lumps*,
- minimize the number of people allocated to realizing each success-lump,
- create challenges in terms of workload and complexity, but give a carte blanche to develop, modify and improve,
- reward the entire group for overall group performance,
- define performance in terms of cost, service, profit, etc.,
- if possible, create internal or external competition.

'Change success cubes'

Managers in organizations should not only be concerned about short term profits but should also position their organizations for continued success. This positioning requires investments to be made now that may not immediately pay off. The incentive for management to make these investments is in the way they are measured. For example, Harold Geneen (ITT) changed the standard of success for his managers into: 'a 10 per cent annual increase in earnings per share.' In order to achieve this 10 per cent increase every year his managers indeed had to invest in the development of new products and new processes. Since these investments or change projects are not always part of the daily routine and challenges, they tend to be neglected. I therefore asked a group of fairly senior operational managers to list the major success factors for strategic change projects. The outcome was surprisingly simple:

1   the *right* resources should be made *available*,
2   the project and project outcome have to be well *defined*,
3   sufficient *awareness*, *support* and *review* has to be ensured.

It is remarkable how these success factors match the key contributors in the success-cube. 'Having the right resources' obviously relates to *resources*. 'The definition of the project and project outcome relates to *vision*. 'Sufficient awareness, support and review' is all intertwined with *culture*. The difference between these items is a matter of scale. In other words, strategic change projects or investments can be represented by their own success-cube or change success-cube (Figure 46). This success cube has its own change success vector, which depends on the

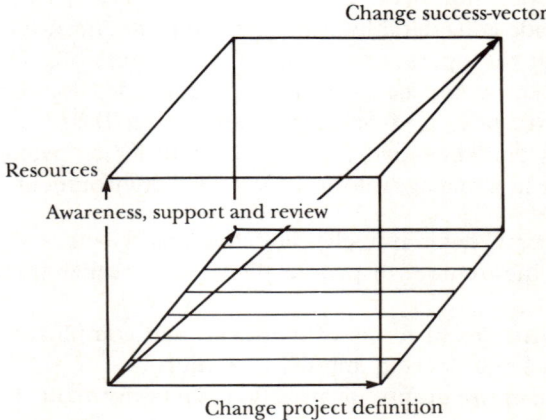

Figure 46   *The change success-cube*

success factors just mentioned. Many change success-cubes may be required to materialize the success cube of the total corporate entity. The leaders of the corporate entity will have to ensure that each success factor is satisfied. Firstly, the change definition and completion criteria need to be identified. Secondly, the progress review process and support structure during the change project-life-time needs to be agreed and followed up. And finally, the resources have to be made available. In the majority of cases, this is most effectively done by including the required resources (people, training and development, etc.) in the yearly budget. Obviously, this will have timing implications. In addition, the corporate entity leaders will have to coordinate the initiation and linking of the different change projects in support of the success-cube for the total business entity. Change projects are therefore essential to the realization of vision.

The completion of the total picture

Once the purpose of the corporate entity has been defined through the vision model and the product criteria, a start should be made with the development of,

> the corporate entity's *process* and subsequently,
> the corporate entity *means*.

This activity can only be triggered by the leaders of the corporate entity. The organization will have to do the actual work on these. People's major tools will be the 'limited resource commitments', such as change projects, that are initiated to develop product-related strategic progress elements, such as product flow, measurements, information flow, systems, etc.

In summary, key responsibilities of leaders in a corporate entity are,

- to build and expand the awareness of the vision model,
- to facilitate and improve cultural awareness,
- to initiate and support change,
- to instill the *right sequence* of strategic progress elements,
- to ensure that *change success* factors are met.

Simplifying processes

Several times, managers have assured me that in order to cope with the increased complexity of today's and tomorrow's world, they need to simplify the processes that govern their operations. And they are right!

In many cases, the efficiencies projected in computer system proposals, for example, do not materialize because of historically evolved processes that are too difficult to simplify. People seem to be hung up on them. The mere suggestion of change gives them the feeling of losing ground and control.

So how does one simplify corporate entity processes in a responsible manner? There is only one way to do it successfully and that is to start from scratch by 'growing' the corporate entity from its roots upwards. This can be achieved by drawing the *total picture*, in other words, by redefining all of the strategic progress elements. A completed 'vision-model' is conditional for the successful development of the strategic progress elements that are related to the process and means of the corporate entity. For example, the required added values and the 'product' are essential in establishing a 'customer' and 'supplier' base. And through customers and suppliers, the most straightforward product flow can be developed, which is then used for the definition of the necessary measurements.

Obviously, when defining measurements, one should only focus on those that are essential to the successful movement of products from suppliers to (end-)customers. The more (unnecessary) measurements one defines, the more complicated the final corporate entity process will turn out to be. Measurements in turn, will lead to the senders and receivers of information and thus to the information flow. Based on the corporate entity process, the next three strategic progress elements (systems, tasks and structure) can be determined, representing the *means* of the corporate entity. At this point, 'standard' systems, that normally would not fit the old operational processes, will have a reasonable chance of being applied successfully. In any case, the newly established corporate entity process, through its straightforward definition, will greatly simplify system development. Then whatever cannot be handled effectively by a system will have to be done by man. The outcome in terms of tasks indeed determines the basic performance measurements of the people in the corporate entity. Finally, the corporate entity's structure is developed as a compromise between tasks and culture.

In conclusion, by following these broad outlines for the definition of the total picture, the resulting corporate entity process and means will be based on reason and break-through rather than on history and prejudice. The last two seem to be the most quoted causes for operational processes that are too complex. De Bono, as referred to in Part One of this book, would characterize old processes as thinking pattern traps. The sequence of determining the strategic progress elements functions as the trick to escape these. It ensures that people get an opportunity to dissociate themselves from the currently soaked-in process–constraints without overlooking the essentials.

Reflections

Key messages

Many organizations experience the strangling impact of over-optimization in its segments. The performance aims of such organizational segments do not often sufficiently relate to the overall objectives of the organization, nor do they support the needs of the end-customer. Segments, in that case, tend to live their own life and measure their success relative to their internal business partners only. Over time, this results in a wealth of often unnecessary measurements and business practices, that seem to justify and prove the segment's performance, but miss showing the true impact on the end-customer.

At that moment, the overall management should redefine the organizational purpose through the vision model in order to realign these segments and directly relate them to the needs of the customer, as expressed in the product (success) criteria. Every segment may then develop its own organizational purpose, but based on these overall product (success) criteria. The vision model is customer and product driven. It provides a well balanced approach to cutting out many of the inefficiencies that may have historically crept into the organization. Its impact will eventually be reflected in a reduced amount of organizational measurements, in fewer policies and procedures and in a simpler task-set. The regained simplicity will make quality and creativity possible again.

This redefinition of the organizational purpose will have to be supported by appropriate strategies that lead to a suitable improvement in the associated culture performance.

- According to the success-cube theory, success of corporate entities can be represented by a cube, of which the dimensions are: vision, culture and resources. Vision and culture together form the success platform of this cube.
- Corporate transformations can be achieved by 'bite-sized' change activities that may be identified as 'change-success cubes'. The three dimensions of change-success cubes represent the changes in definition, management awareness and resources.
- Management should be concerned with the facilitation and coordination of these change-success cubes. Overall success will depend on a continuous wave of change-success cube initiations. This wave will never end, because it is driven by a constantly moving environment.
- Simplification of corporate processes can only be achieved by re-growing the corporate entity from its roots upwards. The roots of an organization are in the organizational purpose. The vision-model and the complete vision picture are essential guides in this rebuilding process.

PART FOUR

Improving the Vision-Culture Balance

14

Vision and culture engineering laws

Towards a biological system

The 'Progress Spiral'

In the previous chapter, we identified vision together with culture as the platform for success of corporate entities. And on that platform, vision comes first. According to the success cube theory, one then progresses towards success through the allocation of resources. One may explain this movement towards success by comparing it to the turning of a screw. The torque rule, in Figure 47, shows this dynamic and progressive relation between vision, culture and resources. It concerns a continuously revolving emphasis on vision, culture, vision, culture, etc., that is made possible by the efforts of the right type of people resources. As a result, one observes a spiralling movement upwards in the direction of increasingly greater success. This movement can be identified as the *progress spiral* of a corporate entity.

But what is really happening here? Is the evolution towards corporate entity success a smooth flow of events? When we go back to the vision-culture balance, as in Chapter 4, we understand that vision causes an imbalance with the existing culture every time. In the event of relative proximity' to the environment the culture transforms by absorbing the vision during its achievement process. The art of management is to maximize the vision-jump or in other words, to create the greatest possible imbalance without the rejection of the vision by the cultural environment. It is to create the greatest possible progress in one go. Culture engineering helps in making the existing cultural environment

164 *The Power of Tomorrow's Management*

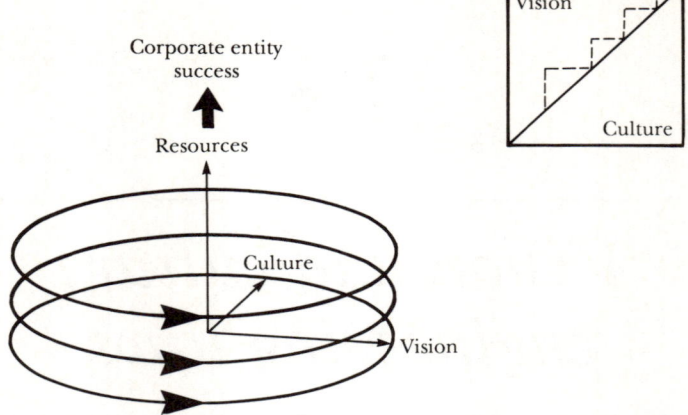

Figure 47 *The 'progress spiral'*

more receptive and indeed has a smoothing effect on the evolutionary process towards greater corporate entity success. However, each imbalance situation, created by vision, may be like a small revolution. This leads to an important proposition on the management process, as identified in this book.

Vision and Culture Engineering (VCE), as the 'Power of Tomorrow's Management', will speed-up the evolution of the corporate entity by making revolutionary achievements manageable. (Proposition 25)

The above conclusion opens the way to an improved understanding of the dynamics and evolutionary stages of the corporate entity. As we will see, its evolution very much resembles that of biological systems.

The 'Vision-Culture balance Spectrum'

Each corporate entity goes through several characteristic vision-culture balance stages, as in Figure 48. Together, these stages form its path of evolution.

One of the first stages is that of survival. In the survival stage, the vision and the culture of a corporate entity are of a specific kind. They are entirely geared to maintaining and if possible increasing the probability of continued life. The norms within that culture and the type of visions are down-to-earth and tend to be reactive. Such a corporate entity acts like a herd of wild horses that is continuously in search for

Vision and culture engineering laws 165

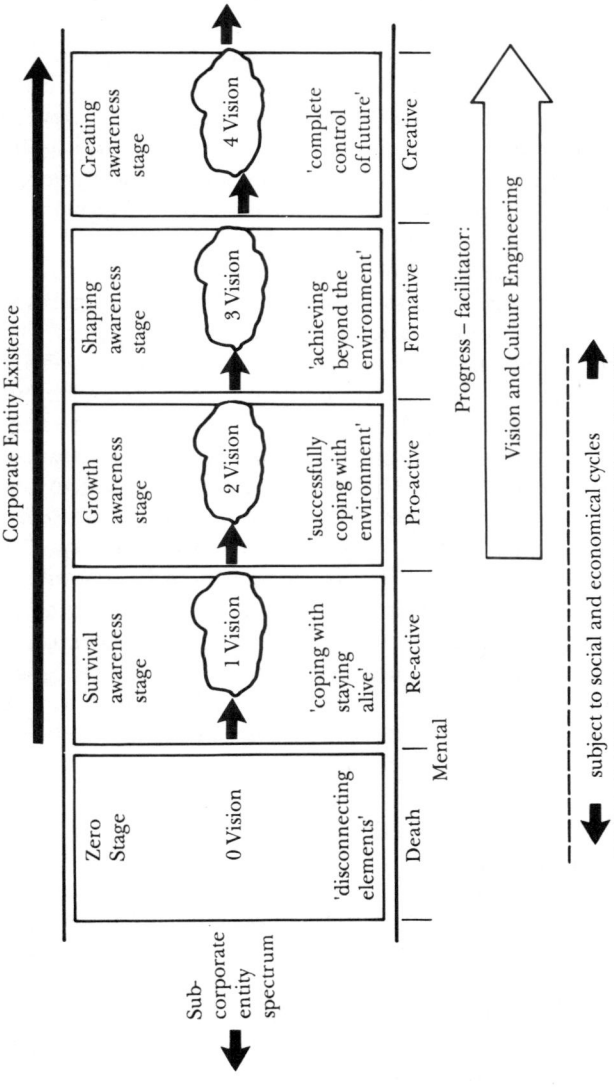

Figure 48 *The vision–culture balance spectrum*

food and that is challenged by climatic conditions beyond its control. The survival stage is reflected in a basic awareness that seems related to survival and staying alive. Once a corporate entity masters its survival, it will enter the next stage, which can be characterized as the stage of growth. At that time, a corporate entity successfully copes with environmental challenges. Having built up a surplus in resources, it will be able pro-actively to invest in growth. This is reflected in a certain growth awareness. Particularly at this stage, corporate entities develop the need for vision and operating culture. As a result, an urge will emerge to manage and engineer its culture more consciously in support of a growth oriented vision. Then, as always, some achieve this growth and some do not. The ones that do move on to a next stage.

The growth stage is followed by a stage that can be characterized by 'shaping'. Corporate entities in this stage have developed the power to break through the environmental influences and cycles. They, in fact, are able to 'shape' the environment. An awareness of creation develops in the corporate entity, in particular around achievements that lie beyond the environment. This stage can only be passed successfully by significantly refining and improving skills related to vision development and culture optimization. Vision engineering and culture engineering capabilities mature during this stage and become part of the *core* added values. The most advanced stage, with all its possible (and impossible) gradations for corporate entities to come into, is the 'creation' stage. It is a stage where corporate entities show an almost complete control of their future. Creations of any kind may eventually be achieved. Vision and culture engineering have advanced into a spring-like progress spiral, where revolutionary visions are seamlessly processed in a highly performing and responsive culture. It is the ideal stage to be in for every type of corporate entity, whether it concerns a person, an organization or a nation.

The Net-Force of Change

But what lies beyond the 'creation' stage and the 'survival' stage? Both are at the far ends of the vision-culture balance spectrum. They are not, however, the last stages for corporate entities to be in. When corporate entities slip backwards from survival, they come into a 'zero stage'. This will first manifest itself as mental death, which is characterized by the loss of coherent awareness of the totality of the corporate entity. The 'zero stage' will cause disconnections between the elements within the corporate entity. It almost resembles physical death. Each of the elements in the corporate entity will at one time have evolved through their own (sub-)corporate entity spectrum. When the corporate entity

Vision and culture engineering laws 167

evolves beyond the creation stage, it may become part of a new total with its own spectrum as well.

But what now causes the move from stage to stage in this spectrum? I like to call it the 'net force of change' (Figure 49). This net force of change is the result of two antagonistic forces: the 'pull of death' and the 'push of life and spirit'. Death relates to *no* change as much as spirit

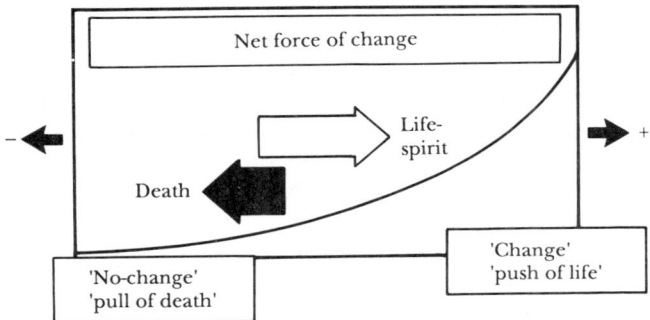

Figure 49 *The net force of change*

relates to progress and change. The closer one is to the zero stage, the stronger the pull of no-change or death will become. On the other hand, the further a corporate entity moves to the right, the stronger the push of spirit will manifest itself. Thus, the net force of change will become stronger when the corporate entity moves to the next evolutionary stage. As such, evolution will gain momentum and speed when the corporate entity progresses to the right of the spectrum. As we have discussed before, vision and culture engineering will be required (and even become conditional) from the growth stage onwards to the right. They will literally increase the push of spirit and life. As such, vision and culture engineering (VCE) will speed-up the evolution of corporate entitites. The analogy of the above to evolution in nature very much shows that corporate entitites are part of it and as such follow the same characteristic patterns.

Measuring perspectives for management

The four evolutionary stages can be used by management to determine in what stage a particular corporate entity is. As a result, culture performance and vision can be tuned to the evolutionary window of needs. When comparing, grouping or competing with other corporate entities, one should ensure one looks for similarly positioned ones. A difference in stage may be exploited, but only if (as we will later see) it is to the benefit of all partners. If one had to make a distribution of all corporate entities in the world, one would presumably still find the majority in the 'growth stage' or lower. However, as we have concluded before, the further corporate entities come, the faster they evolve.

The big difference

How does the Vision and Culture Engineering (VCE) approach support and expand traditional and proven management concepts, such as Management By Objectives (MBO)? We know that the key attribute of the MBO concept is the development of a clear set of objectives by management. The rewards of people (or employees) are related to the achievement of those objectives. Consequently, a certain degree of self-control may emerge in order better to manage progress versus these objectives. Management creates incentives by setting goals and by connecting these to a reward system. One could distill the above classical view on managment to an approach, that is essence is based on:

- brains;
- a finite world;
- an objective world;
- discontinuity and
- targets.

It relates to brains, because of the calculted method of connecting objectives to rewards. It is a finite world, because of a horizon that is determined and limited by these 'objectives'. It is an objective world, because of the minimized encouragement and involvement of subjective people powers by a fixation on a predetermined goal-set. The peaking pattern of goal-setting itself tends to drive a notion of discontinuity. And finally, targets, not their backgrounds, seem to be the dominating factors.

Vision and Culture Engineering (VCE) aims to expand these characteristics principally, to ensure the continued performance of corporate entities in the brave new world of the information age society and the information age economy, but also with the objective of creating a greater evolutionary momentum for the corporate entity. Through the development of a certain 'vision-model', rather than objectives, and by the improvement of culture performance, management will create an early awareness and involvement process. It will lead to the immediate build-up of an atmosphere that increases the chance of creating breakthroughs. Achievement will be seen as part of an evolution and

Vision and culture engineering laws 169

continuous progress will be base for rewards. VCE will stretch the classical management view towards a world of:

brains and guts;
infinite horizons;
objective and subjective people powers;
continuity in the very long term and
targets that have been related to the *why* ...

The management role will be expanded from vision developer to vision and culture facilitator. And managers will turn into status-free managers, being part of several people-networks.

Changing a traditional trend

The above 'characteristics' of Vision and Culture Engineering (VCE) invite an assessment of possible trend changes relative to breakthroughs. Let us assume that management sets its objectives at a certain moment in time. In Figure 50, this moment has been identified along the X-axis. The objectives may relate to a specific organization.

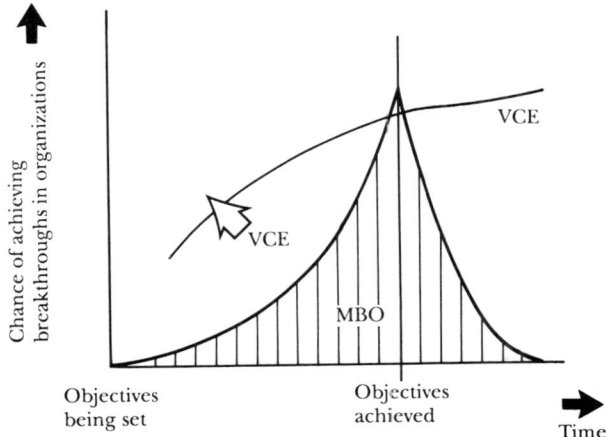

Figure 50   *The big difference*

In the traditional management approach, the involvement of the organization will gradually increase between the time the objectives are set, and the time the objectives are achieved. As a result, people may eventually build up their incentive level to contribute to the achievement of the objectives. Also, because their reward system is related to this achievement. The incentive level may peak just before or at the moment that the objectives are met. Thereafter, the incentive level will most likely collapse. It will only build up again when closing in on a next set of objectives. The assumption here is that the incentive level depends on the degree of involvement and the reward system. More important is the following proposition.

The chance of achieving any breakthroughs is related to the level of incentive and as such to the timing and method of people's involvement. (Proposition 26)

Hence, the chance of achieving any breakthroughs in the traditional management approach will also peak around the time the objectives are met. The following, however, may demonstrate the potential of the above proposition.

In the past, product engineers developed new products alone. Having completed the design, they 'threw it over the fence' to the manufacturing engineers, who had to make sure that the product could be manufactured and assembled to a good standard of quality and at a reasonable cost. In most cases, the design needed significant rethinking by the product engineer in order to improve its manufactureability. Once this costly and time consuming redesign process was completed, the manufacturing engineer arranged for the necessary tooling and the product could be launched. The next person to stumble over the product design would be the service engineer. He had to fix a product that was hard to fix because it did not meet *his* requirements at all. Companies decided to do the obvious. The product had to be designed by the product engineer together with the manufacturing engineer, the service engineer and even the customer. By early involvement, new breakthroughs could be achieved in the area of design, manufacturing, service and use.

In summary, the difference of VCE, as driven by its typical characteristics, lies in the chance of achieving breakthroughs at an early stage and in a continually rising probability of encouraging breakthroughs.

Competitive culture engineering rules

To be honest, this section is the outcome of a presentation about culture engineering to a well qualified English management team. After the presentation, the general manager asked me how actually to establish the scoring when positioning the organization in the positioning plane of a certain culture performance driver. What I assumed to be commonsense, wasn't really seen as such.

Culture engineering, as opposed to vision engineering is indeed more

Vision and culture engineering laws   171

qualitative in character. To a certain extent, this is compensated by the fact that awareness is sufficient as a result. This awareness will be based on a notion of where one thinks the corporate entity is and should be positioned in the positioning plane. Over time, as contributors get a better appreciation of cultural strengths and weaknesses, their judgement will mature and become more refined. Based on this reasoning, one should start with fairly broad scales, for example, high medium and low, before using scores between 0 and 10, to position oneself along the axes of the positioning planes for structure, involvement, responsibility, identity and goal-tuning.

Positioning grid

Another approach is to establish a positioning grid for a certain industry, a group of nations, a group of individuals and so on. The positioning grid is nothing more than a large positioning plane, in which the particular positioning planes of companies, nations, individuals, etc. fit (see Figure 51). As a result, one is able to create the entire known culture

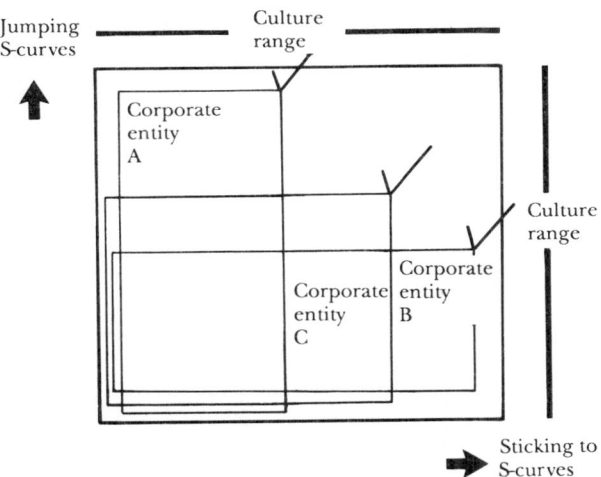

Figure 51   *Positioning grid and culture range*

range for a certain culture performance driver in a certain industry, group of nations, etc. One may capture a good deal of the existing evolutionary stages, as they have been discussed in Chapter 14. The culture range is determined by the extremes along the axes in the positioning grid. It will actually help in defining a rating scale for the corporate entity concerned. In the last chapter of this book (Chapter 19,

172 The Power of Tomorrow's Management

'framework for the future'), I will suggest an approach to develop a position grid more thoroughly by gathering real life examples through a predetermined information pattern. The process of developing a positioning grid and its rating scale consists of the following steps.

One should start with the identification of the corporate entities that one will have to operate next to. For example, when looking at national culture performance, one may consider the European nations or the third world nations. When considering industry, one may look at the car industry, the publishing world and so forth. And when it concerns individuals, one may look at the individuals who have to work together in a team. In the second step, the selected corporate entities are plotted in the positioning grids for each of the culture performance drivers, such as structure, involvement, responsibility, identity and goal-tuning. The best way to do this is to start plotting the extreme cases along the axes of the positioning grids. Those in particular will function as a reference for the other members in the group. Then, based on the number of corporate entities and their assumed spread in the positioning grid, one is able to decide a rating scale. A rule of thumb would be to choose a scale maximum that is about twice the total number of corporate entities plotted. For example, if the group consists of four 'car-companies', then each of the axes would show a scale of zero to eight. The remaining (non-extreme) corporate entities can subsequently be included in the positioning grids.

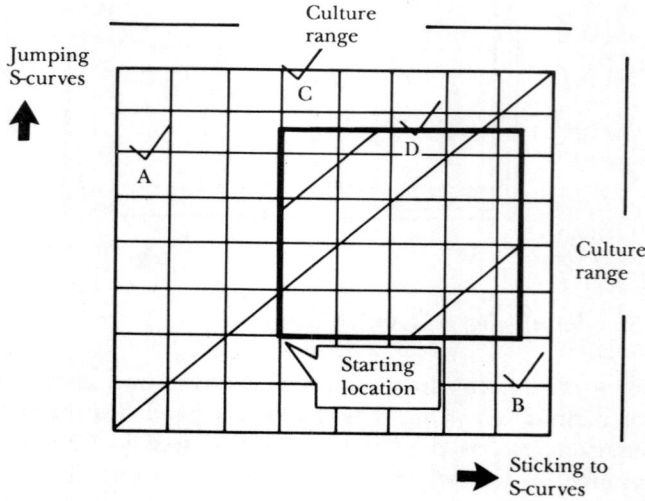

Figure 52 *Positioning plane in positioning grid*

Knowledge of the particular corporate entities obviously determines the quality of this positioning task. It is therefore recommended (and interesting) to invite 'authorities' on the selected corporate entitites, who can actually help and advise during this positioning task.

The last positioning task is to plot one's own corporate entity in the positioning grid(s). Its location, or rather its 'starting location' in each positioning grid, will have to be identified in order to develop the positioning plane that is going to be used for the management of the culture performance improvement tasks in the subject corporate entity itself. The target, obviously, is to come close to and to meander around the dynamic balance diagonal of the grid. The resulting positioning plane, as developed from the starting location in the positioning grid, should allow that to happen (Figure 52). The size of the positioning plane should therefore be dependent on the distance between the starting location and the dynamic balance diagonal. Then, having drawn the positioning plane in the positioning grid, the grid itself may function as the measurement scale, in particular the part that is enclosed by the positioning plane.

All in all, the positioning grid helps in determining a competitive culture performance scale that is based on the positioning of other similar corporate entities. Side benefits of this exercise are,

- the increased confidence of the contributors;
- improved knowledge of the total culture range possibilities;
- the appreciation of competitive cultural strengths and weaknesses.

Hence, the positioning grid not only supports the definition of a realistic culture performance scale, it also provides the possibility of competitive culture engineering.

Reflections

Key messages

In 1988, the Industrial Bank of Japan expressed unprecedented and straightforward criticism of US industry, blaming the corporate culture of certain American companies for the loss of America's international competitiveness. They based their conclusions on the performance of 23 industries over a six year period. In particular, the tendency to ignore long-term goals for the sake of short-term successes was highlighted.

In Far Eastern companies, very long-term visions and plans are common. Industries and money suppliers are willing to take a decade of loss or modest profits to capture market share and associated successes.

174   The Power of Tomorrow's Management

It is not unusual for Japanese companies to deal with very long range plans or visions, in some cases spanning up to 150 years! The belief in continuity in those companies generates the confidence to make and plan for long term deals.

- Successful companies in the future will ride on the 'progress spiral' of corporate entities that consists of a continuous and alternating focus on vision and culture. During this ride, the resources are the action agents.

- Over time corporate entities may 'spiral' through a four stage evolutionary spectrum of vision-culture balance situations, i.e. from survival to growth, from growth to 'shaping' and from 'shaping' to 'creation'.

- The VCE or Vision and Culture Engineering process helps corporate entities to evolve from one evolutionary stage to another.

- The Vision and Culture Engineering process aims to stretch the scope of traditional management views and may as a result improve the chance of creating new breakthroughs.

- Vision should be built through a sliced approach, in which culture engineering functions as a transformation planning pause.

- Culture engineering may help in the competitive positioning of corporate entities.

15

In nations

Culture performance: more visible

The business success of Japan has not only focused attention on the Japanese corporations responsible and their business approach, but also on the relative homogeneity of Japanese culture. Typical characteristics are its tendency to strive for consensus, the continuous adjustment to the needs of the social and business environment, their tolerance (within limits) of new ideas and the synergetic support of national goals. Together they distinguish Japan from other cultures.

Based on the messages in this book, one may conclude that there are particular elements that ignite and materialize the potential of national cultures. And those are not just sound economic measures. It requires a certain country spirit and drive that is mobilized by (national) culture performance drivers. At the same time, the performance of national cultures is subject to change through interaction, as result of the evolving situation in the world both economically and culturally. For example, countries like Taiwan and Korea are developing an increasing impact on the world's economy. Their successful passion for economic expansion is having inevitable repercussions on the effectiveness and performance of other national cultures.

Managing national culture performance

The much referred to internationalization of trade is amplifying the above interactions. In fact, it emphasizes the overall distribution and development of resources, capacities and cultural strengths in the world of today and tomorrow. Countries, as corporate entities, will, and should, eventually react to it. First by nurturing an increased awareness of their relative economic and culture performance position in the world and secondly by developing conscious and more outspoken measures to change and or exploit their country's economic and cultural strengths.

Margaret Thatcher has not only tried and succeeded to change the economic performance of the United Kingdom. She has also addressed the improvement of specific elements in its national culture that appeared to be vital for economic growth. These elements included anything from the de-unionization of society to the basic ethical values of the people, such as honesty and integrity. Mikhail Gorbachev is very much following a similar path by trying to restructure the system in the USSR and by trying to change basic workforce attitudes. The challenge of adjusting the national culture in order to make it more competitive again has led to more openness or *glasnost*.

Diversity

This envisaged trend of improving the performance of national cultures by no means implies that all national cultures will eventually evolve into one successful model. The opposite, I believe, is true. Cultural diversity may well become greater as countries manage to develop and exploit particular culture performance niches.

Europe

The significance of the economic power of Europe seems to be possible in spite of a fair amount of duplication of effort as a result of national interests. The European Community (EC) is successful in its current configuration perhaps due to the continued diversity of the contributing national cultures. In other words, the economic co-existence in the European Community has not eroded the capability of its members to initiate national measures needed to protect (to a certain extent) their own interests. The flexibility and resilience of the European Community, as a whole, is possible as a result of the relative independence of its member nations and of the alternative views and solutions that these nations generate. The further unification of the European market in 1992 will merely simplify and improve the effectiveness of its total operational process. Its cultural diversity will remain; in fact, the resulting overall and internal competitiveness will then be accentuated even more.

USSR

It is not surprising that the Soviet Union under Gorbachev is evidently loosening the rein on its partners in Eastern Europe, in order to achieve a similar resilience as in the European Community. Unlike his predecessors, Gorbachev says he will tolerate more diversity, letting each regime try out its own solutions in relation to *perestroika*.

In summary, the above two examples relate to Part One of this book (Chapter 3), where the corporate entity has been introduced. The conclusion, to strive for one accepted vision that is shared by different corporate entities and which is coupled to management's acceptance of culture specific solutions, seems to run in parallel with this discussion.

Facilitation

In summary, the above noted trend of intensified interactions between world nations, will generate an increasing demand for the means successfully to adjust the culture performance of countries relative to other countries. Through Vision and Culture Engineering (VCE), country leaders and their teams will indeed have an opportunity to manage these culture changes in a structured and more predictable way, By focusing on vision and culture performance, these leaders may be able to plot and facilitate competitive and even better balanced transformation strategies.

Positioning a nation for success

The vision and culture engineering process in nations, in principle follows the same steps as in any other corporate entity. The difference is in the contributors, in the scale of the application and perhaps in the particular emphasis on culture engineering. For example, the differences in opinion on ethics, political preferences and human relations will strongly influence the choice of move strategies that are needed to reposition a nation in a culture positioning plane.

Drivers and contributors

Political leaders and their teams are the drivers of new political scenarios. Those scenarios may well be established by using Vision and Culture Engineering (VCE-)concepts, particularly because they will help to structure and facilitate the development of an accepted scenario. Country leaders may use Vision and Culture Engineering effectively to involve the ministries, institutions, industry and last but not least the people in the country. In addition, governments may be encouraged to initiate a culture performance advisory board, or 'think-tank', that assists and advises the government on culture performance improvement matters. Typical tasks of such an advisory body would be,

- the definition of new culture performance drivers;
- positioning grid comparisons with competitive country cultures;
- development of repositioning strategies;
- proposal and implementation of move-strategies;
- analysis of successful repositioning experiences;
- grooming national leaders for 'positioning tasks'.

Outline of the final approach

The following generic steps summarize the process of applying Vision and Culture Engineering concepts in political and country arenas,

- obtaining a 'quantified' understanding of the country's culture performance strengths;
- development of an overall vision-statement;
- development of the national culture map and repositioning needs;
- increasing the dimensions of vision (along strategic progress elements)
- installing a culture performance advisory board;
- managing vision and culture transformation processes.

Success factors

Vision and Culture Engineering on a national level, as any other approach, has its own success factors. They are fairly critical, because national awareness may not be fooled for long. Some of the most obvious and sometimes hard to achieve success factors are in order of priority,

- no *hidden* objectives for 'power';
- opening the way to productive creativity;
- amplifying and choosing constructive leaders;
- follow-up.

Reflections

Key messages

Political and economic events in the world of today and tomorrow will be increasingly interdependent. With Europe struggling towards unity, with the USSR in search of a new economic spirit, with the USA trying to recapture its business leadership and with the Far East positioning itself for long term success, the focus must be on the establishment of new and winning visions and on the making of supporting cultural environments. The use of Vision and Culture Engineering concepts, therefore, cannot and will not be limited to corporations only. Nations, like companies, should be considered as corporate entities. They only differ in scale. Vision and Culture Engineering efforts will therefore flow over to nations and their national leaders in order to help them manage their environments in a more predictable and competitive way.

16

In corporations

Formidable change agents within

Corporations need change in order to survive, which is why successful corporations belong to the most inspiring change agents. For corporations, there are not many (legal) ways to hide failure. Their success is measurable, for example in earnings per share or profit. So in order to continue to achieve success, they need to innovate, invest, change processes, change technologies, change business partners, change strategies, change attitudes, change behaviour, change culture performance and change people. One additional delicate problem tends to arise: change has to become more and more acceptable and smooth. Ruthless change may backfire through resistance, low morale, procrastination, less change, loss of time, lack of innovation, rebellion and so forth. It does not mean however that change has to be minimal, but it means people have to be made part of it, even when they are affected.

In response to very competitive overhead percentages of, for example, Toyota, Ford Europe has successfully reduced its administrative and financial overhead costs by putting the problem to the people themselves. As a result, they were allowed to co-engineer the plan and the approach to achieve this goal, while in some cases they knew it would impact on themselves to the extent of causing redundancies.

The massive AT&T corporation under Jim Olsen and his successor is being reshaped in order to make it more competitive, again by lowering its costs and by reversing the downward trend of its revenues. Olson worked out a version of the vision model in his team and assured total support by asking each member personally to confirm his commitment in front of the team. Within a year and a half, the company had made big gains. One of the decisions (unusual for AT&T) was to buy part of Sun

Microsystems Inc. in order to obtain its well developed microprocessor, instead of developing one themselves. This decision, which had been based on an assessment of AT&Ts true core added values, allowed the R&D savings to be poured into other efforts. But Olson still had major problems left to be tackled. The spirit and loyalty of the employees has to be brought back again after lay-offs and redeployment in a company that used to cherish its employees from the cradle to the grave.

The above are classical examples of change in corporations, where the framework of Vision and Culture Engineering could have been successfully applied. In fact, the increased competition between companies, the faster change in technology and the coming information age, where people's motivation will almost directly be linked to success, all make a framework for managing accepted change inevitable. From now on, we had better make change attractive, especially because it is the basic ingredient for the success of any corporate entity in the long term. The management of vision and culture performance, therefore, is not an art that should be mastered by the top management of a corporation alone, but by all levels in the corporation including the individual employee (in search of his or her own destiny). It should be part of,

- strategy planning cycles and budget preparations;
- re-organizations, organizational networks and change programmes;
- quality and productivity programmes;
- competitive culture performance positioning.

The future mob

A dragon may be waiting around the corner of time, pointing toward another opportunity for the application of Vision and Culture Engineering. It is the future mob of *employed* professionals, who will be looking for another job, say, in about ten years time. Already, the supply of professionals who have just left university, is more than the demand in the business world, mainly as a result of the birth wave right after the second world war. It means that corporations can afford to hire graduates. Graduates not having a significant corporate imprint can easily be moulded into a shape that fits the existing corporate culture. The problem of assimilation is still manageable and the corporate culture has a reasonable chance of staying untouched. However, demographic projections show that around the year 2000 the demand for professionals may be bigger than the supply of graduates. Many new employees will then come from other corporations bringing with them a different culture. Corporations (and employees) will then be faced with three major challenges,

1   how to assimilate employees coming from different cultures,
2   how to exploit the potential of the cultures they bring and
3   how to maintain the good elements of an existing culture.

These challenges can only be overcome by confrontation, that is, by trying to get an understanding and awareness of the home culture *and* the alien culture. That awareness should be created objectively without too much prejudice. Culture engineering, coupled to vision engineering, is designed to channel those situations and backgrounds into constructive actions.

In search of a suitable partner

Organizations are continuously evaluating and linking up with business partners inside and outside their corporation. Acquisitions, partnerships, joint ventures are in, but are they really successful? Studies show that many mergers, acquisitions and joint ventures simply do not work. Part of the problem is the lack of an appropriately formulated business strategy, the other part is people. In particular, how to get people from different companies to work together effectively in the right structure, sharing tasks and exchanging knowledge and skills. Sometimes, acquisitions do not even get a chance to materialize just because of cultural differences. Elsevier, a rich Dutch publishing concern, developed a perfect vision on what they needed to realize their corporate goal for growth: 'acquisitions'. They set their eyes on a somewhat smaller but successful Dutch publishing group Kluwer. So, Vinken, the chairman of Elsevier, gave the order to buy. What in his mind seemed like a simple business deal turned out to be a time-consuming nightmare: Kluwer said 'No'! Not over their dead body!' Weeks of (much publicised) fighting finally drove Kluwer into the arms of the Wolters Samson publishing group. In the meantime, every judicial trick had been tried to keep Elsevier off their backs. Elsevier bought whatever shares they could get, but in the end did not succeed in getting the majority. The deal was off ... What happened? The background to Kluwer's rejection was its distrust of the culture and vision in Elsevier. Kluwer had built up a strong identity of its own that after all seemed a better match with the culture of Wolters Samson. Hence, for companies who plan any acquisitions, it certainly makes business sense to work and check the culture and vision match first.

The application of Vision and Culture Engineering can help in mapping the culture performance differences that may hinder acquisitions, joint ventures and the like. We have seen in the 'Competitive culture engineering rules' (Chapter 14) that corporate cultures have their particular range. Corporations that take over other corporations have to ensure that the range of their culture is congruent with the range of the 'culture to be hosted'. In fact, any cooperation with external as well as internal business partners should be preceded by a check on the culture match. It means that a culture match should be ensured for each of the identified culture performance drivers, such as structure, involvement, responsibility, identity and goal-tuning. In figure 53, three

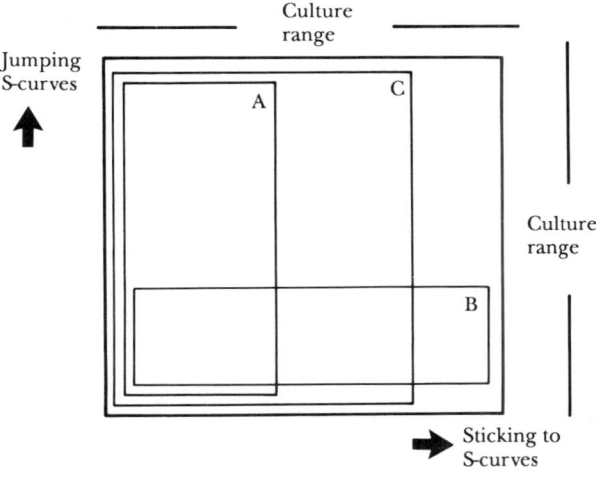

Figure 53 *Culture performance match in the positioning grid*

possible companies with typical culture ranges have been sketched in a positioning grid. The culture range of company A, for example, has a totally different orientation from the culture range of company B. This seems to resemble the Elsevier-Kluwer case. It would therefore be highly risky to try to marry these two cultures. However, company C, although it has a different culture range, has a fairly reasonable chance of absorbing or matching the culture of company A. Figure 53, in fact, shows that culture positioning has the potential for being applied effectively when assessing and preparing for acquisitions and joint ventures. Not surprisingly, culture engineering will resolve the people problem. On the other hand, vision engineering with its vision model seems like an appropriate tool that can be used to facilitate the right awareness of the required added values and how they should be obtained.

Reflections

Key messages

Organizations of tomorrow will be designed to cope successfully not only with tasks, but also with change. The management of new-age organizations, in order to deal with both tasks and change, may well split into two management disciplines. One that focuses on knowledge and skills management and one that deals with task management. Knowledge and skills managers care about the growth and allocation of individual people resources in an environment of change. In other words, they worry about the 'how', when people are considered.

Task managers will be responsible for the day-to-day management of people networks or in other words, cross-functional, cross-knowledge and cross-level teams. One could say, task management worries about the 'what'. Vision engineering is important to both disciplines. For the knowledge and skills manager, it is a way to manage the growth of the individual people resources (see Chapter 17, In careers). The task manager may use vision engineering to facilitate the direction of the people networks that he task-manages. The knowledge and skills manager together with the task manager may use culture engineering to establish the most effective operating culture for a particular task-network or task-team. In tomorrow's companies, vision and culture engineering will be used in a whole host of situations, related not only to management, but also to match-making in all kinds of business partnerships. Hence, business partnerships within or between companies will be subject to a conscious form of both vision and culture engineering.

17

In careers

What do you want to become?

When one asks youngsters what they would like to become or what they would like to study, one usually gets the answer: 'I don't know!' The kids who consistently claim to know what they want, really stick out! The choice they finally make tends to be based more on 'what they stumble over' rather than on 'what they want'. OK, they may like the job they have eventually opted for in the business world, but the underlying drive and wanting seems to be missing at the start. This motivational problem creates unnecessary efficiency losses and absorbs corporate and individual investments to resolve it.

Not only youngsters, but also established employees in corporations are subject to similar situations. Not many corporate employees do really know what they want. They sail in the direction in which the wind is blowing. One thing is sure in the corporation of tomorrow, when it is struggling with change, people will frequently move from one job to the other during their working life. Organizational networks of people and resources that are created to achieve a certain goal, have a predictable time span and lead to the movement of employees from one network to the other. In light of this example, the term 'education permanente' is not to please the people but a *must* to prepare employees for new business challenges and new network memberships. Wouldn't it therefore be nice if one could help people in establishing what they *want* to do! If that could be done, people would be much more productive, efficient and happier right from the start. Then whatever is invested in those people would have a much better pay back, simply because the employee will be behind it with full committment. Let me put it this way, corporations and organizations in their struggle for change will be forced to do this in order to maintain and increase their overall competitiveness. The aim should be to get a *happy* employee. Not by giving him amusement, music or anything of that kind, but by giving him the challenge that he wants and that he can cope with.

The employee career system

The question obviously is 'how to make employees happy' or in other words 'how do they obtain the challenge that they want and can cope with?' The best way is to provide a guidance framework that channels their wants and creates sufficient awareness on the feasibility of what they propose for themselves to do. The vision model, as discussed in Part Three of this book, has the potential to guide individuals through the steps of a 'wanting-evolution'. It starts with the task of finding an overall vision statement, that forms the base of the exercise. Then it suggests an appreciation of the environment which will underline the individual's dependence on the environment and which may trigger unexpected opportunities. The vision model is truly kicked off by the question to determine the 'customers' that the individual would like to deal with or provide something for. Then the individual can pick his or her products, determine his or her business potential, evaluate what added values are needed and at last decide where he/she gets them from.

The nine steps, that lead to the vision model, form the blue print of a stimulating career planning tool. So, if personnel or human resource departments want to increase their contributions to the success of the corporate entity concerned they should transform themselves into 'people potential' facilitators by helping employees to use appropriately the vision engineering process for themselves. The pay-back is in terms of improved productivity, less training investment and more effectively spent training resources. Simply because at that time the training requirements are the result of productive creativity and as such based on true wants and needs. Obviously, the finally developed vision model may function as a base for personnel selection. The much discussed but not always implemented employee profile data bases would gain in their applicability and added value, when there structure would be based on the personal vision model. It means that neither management nor the human resource function should establish this data base, but the employees themselves. Through an interactive computing approach, a vision model system could lead to an honest and useful assessment by the employee of where he or she wants to go. Also it will help to identify what investments are needed in terms of education, skills, experience, etc.

Where do I fit?

In order to be successful, it is good to know and understand what one's personal inclination is. How one reacts to things and what one's basic approach is when being asked to do something. This awareness may lead to actions towards becoming more effective, for example, by searching for environments to work in. For example, environments where one finds particular attitudes that one as an individual seems to be lacking. The ultimate goal again is to increase the chance for success and the success rate, which is in the interest of both the individual and the corporate entity that the individual is part of.

The culture engineering process, like the vision engineering process, can be used for personal development purposes. It allows one to position oneself along the five proposed (or any newly identified) culture performance drives. It rationalizes one's judgements on personal inclination and weaknesses and points one in the direction of more effective change ingredients. In addition, the selection of the preferred and most stimulating working environment can be based on the same findings.

Judgements on personal inclinations and/or on the different environments may not be infallible. But the structure that culture engineering offers ensures that attention is consistently focused on a number of well-defined criteria, that can be found in any corporate entity at any time.

Reflections

Key messages

As I have noticed in several workshops, the dormant desire of people in organizations is to be in command of their own future. This seemed to be prevented particularly by the lack of guidance on how to obtain and exercise independence in personal goal-setting. The most productive form of bringing competitive power to the people is therefore to hand them the right tools and structure to become the architects of their own destiny. The structure for the definition of one's own destiny, as encompassed by Vision and Culture Engineering, can be as strong as the structure that is provided by religion. However, it needs to be coupled to the belief that people can achieve whatever they can embrace and justify in their vision. There is no doubt in my mind that both vision engineering and culture engineering provide a key framework for growing that vision for personal success tomorrow.

People may decide to leave the company or move to another job based on the outcome of the vision and culture engineering approach. Should this worry companies? In my view, no! Those people sooner or later would have decided to leave anyway. Or worse, they may have stayed but then been completely demoralized and frustrated, which would have been much more destructive.

18

Preparing managers for tomorrow

Some basic steps

The first challenge with every new concept or idea is to start using it. A number of straightforward steps will have to be taken, in order to lay the foundation for tomorrow's success. Whatever senior management aims to achieve, they should clearly visualize the final result! It is like playing a tennis match. When you think of what you need to do in order to make the perfect service, you are most likely to fail. It is not the reminder that you have to bend your knees, stretch your body and hit the ball as high as possible, that makes you successful. What really works is to visualize in your mind where you want the ball to come down and with what speed. At the same time you should trust your body to work it all out and go for it. It explains why people with an appalling technique are sometimes able to deliver a good shot.

So, before senior management decides to 'go for it', they should make certain they know what it is that they want to achieve by applying vision and culture engineering. Learning the potential of VCE, however, should precede visualization, simply because more may be possible after understanding it.

Consistent management messages

Very effective in an organization are the personal messages, aims and views of senior management. It takes away the mental barrier for other management to initiate further action. Therefore, the introduction and use of VCE should be openly supported by senior management. But what is more important is that the messages should be consistent over time. These messages will have to be repeated over and over again, because it takes a fair amount of time for an entire organization to absorb and implement a new way of thinking and dealing. Obviously, management cannot afford to change its messages significantly during this process, because doing so will certainly encourage the sceptics and confuse the supporters. Since consistent senior management messages are so important, appropriate attention should be spent on the initial formulation and the timing.

Training and education

We may learn from the experience of New United Motor Manufacturing Inc. (NUMMI), a joint venture between General Motors and Toyota, where rule simplication and flexibility are the key drivers of productivity and quality improvements. It is interesting that the employees of NUMMI go through extensive training and education sessions first. These are not only to prepare the employees for the new job but more specifically, training is designed to help people cope with a different workstyle. People are in a sense reconditioned to the work in an environment with a new dimension: freedom to initiate and improve!

Training or rather education is one of the prime factors in the successful implementation of vision and culture engineering. The organization really has to understand the background and the why first. Then the actual 'how to do it' should be addressed through simple workshops. The target-groups and the timing should be calculated to ensure balanced implementation. This is to prevent unnecessary and unproductive confrontations between those 'who do know' and those 'who do not'. Follow-up training sessions to measure the results, understand the findings and confirm the continued application of VCE should be planned in advance.

Success breeds success

In order to prevent the reinvention of the wheel, success stories from other parts of the organization should be used. This will also stimulate cross-fertilization and create a certain amount of internal competition. Success stories and other typical findings or results are in most cases an under-utilized encouragement for the rest of the organization. Newsletters, presentations, computer-bulletins. video tapes and computer networks (like those between universities) are some of the most popular (and state of the art) success carriers.

Culture laboratory

The first steps towards actually testing longstanding economic theories in a laboratory environment have been taken. It seems that research with animal and human subjects in such areas as consumer behaviour is gaining respectability. Laboratory environments are normally associated with technical applications and testing. Extending its use to traditionally cloudy subjects seems logical considering the new wave of interest in culture and behaviour. This is especially so, since corporations are becoming more and more aware of the potential impact of improved corporate cultures. Hence, corporations may apply the laboratory concept in their own organizations. By testing certain cultural strategies in a controlled organizational environment through so called pilot programmes or try-outs, it is possible to assess their use and applicability in other parts of the organization.

The workshop reference card

Workshops are important tools for managers in their facilitation role. It is for this reason that I have included a super-summary of the vision and culture engineering workshop approach in the form of the VCE reference card in this chapter. It can be used by facilitators, by workshop participants and by those who want to be reminded (on demand) of what the key elements of vision and culture engineering are.

A workshop is an impacting approach of learning to understand, appreciate and apply the vision and culture engineering way of thinking and acting. The following cycle for both vision and culture engineering could well be used to obtain a practical working knowledge of the VCE-concepts. In each case, however, one should tailor the workshop structure to the needs and expectations of the audience concerned.

For both Culture and Vision, one should consider the following steps:

1 Introduction of concepts (lecture)
2 Application workshops (related to the personal environments)
3 Links to the business environment (lecture)
4 Application workshops (related to the business environment)

192   *The Power of Tomorrow's Management*

Vision and Culture Engineering
'The Power of Tomorrow's Management'

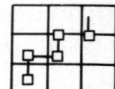

Reference
Card
1

Vision engineering

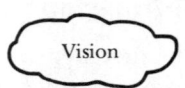

First topic
- Identify the *vision statement* of the top-leader in the particular *corporate entity* . . .

Second topic
- Establish the three to five major environmental impact items; sketch their relevance in the past, today and in the future.

Impact	Past	Now	Future
1 . . .			
2 . . .			
3 . . .			

Third topic
- Determine the 'wanted' *customers*.
- Develop the 'wanted' *products*.
- Estimate the '*product significance*'.
- Identify 'added values' needed.

PFU = Product focus unit (product group)
CG = Customer group

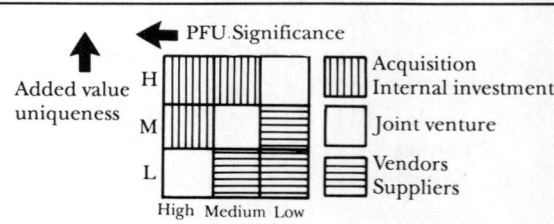

Fourth topic
- Determine how to obtain the required *added values*.
- List the potential added value *suppliers* in the *total picture*.
- Brainstorm the *success factors*.

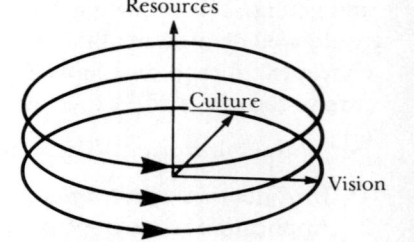

Fifth topic
- Ensure *follow-up* of the assumptions in support of the *progress spiral*.
- Relate vision to culture performance needs
- Develop the subsequent *strategic progress elements*, as part of the organizational *process and means* . . .

Resources

Culture

Vision

Preparing managers for tomorrow 193

Vision and Culture Engineering

'The Power of Tomorrow's Management'

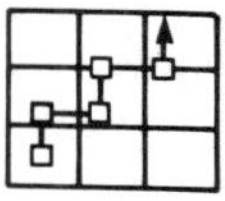

Reference Card 2

Culture Engineering

First topic
- Identify the target *corporate entity*, i.e.
  - a nation;
  - a corporation or an organization;
  - an individual, and
  its *total vision picture* (*Reference Card, side 1*).

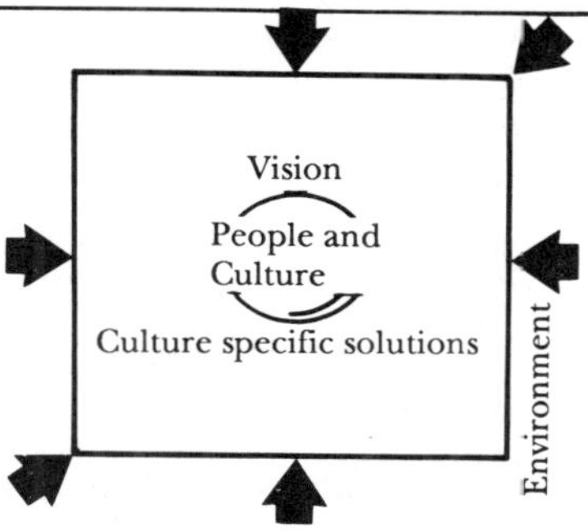

Vision
People and Culture
Culture specific solutions
Environment

Corporate entity model

Second topic
- Determine the current and the desired position in the *positioning plane* for each culture performance driver (the objective is to meander around the balance diagonal).
- Give a *score* for each *culture-force* to define the position in the positioning plane of a culture performance driver.

Culture perf driver

Jumping S-curves: High / Medium / Basic
Positioning plane
Basic Medium High → Sticking to S-curves

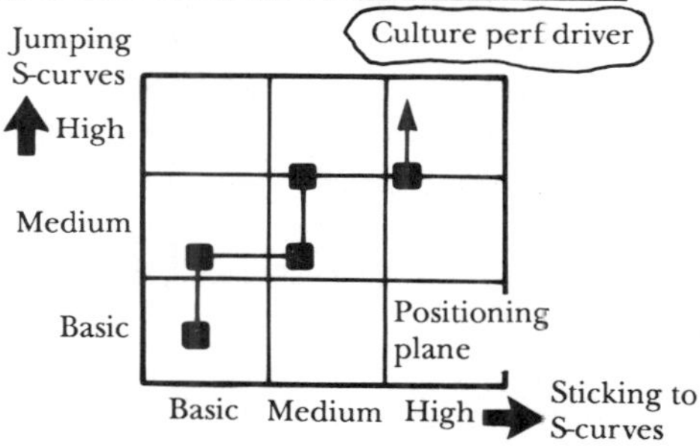

Culture-forces

Culture performance driver:	Jumping S-curves:	Sticking to S-curves:
• Structure	▲ Entrepreneurship	► Control
• Involvement	▲ Idea development	► Alignment
• Responsibility	▲ Strategic	► Operational
• Identity	▲ Employee goals	► Corporate goals
• Goal-tuning	▲ External	► Internal

Move-strategies

Third topic
- Develop and choose '*move-strategies*' to get from the current to the *desired position* in the 'positioning plane'.
- Show total result in a '*culture map*' and use it as a *visible reference* for follow up.

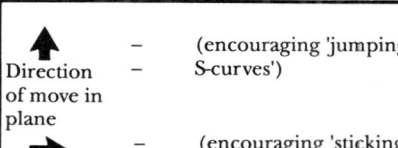

Direction of move in plane
↑ — (encouraging 'jumping S-curves')
→ — (encouraging 'sticking to S-curves')

Change, only through awareness

The essence of vision and culture engineering is in creating a convincing level of awareness, which will stir the need to do the 'right' thing. Often I have seen situations where methods were enforced or where people were nodding to show their agreement to do certain things in certain ways. Initially encouraged I found out that within the next month or so those same people seemed to have forgotten all about it. Why? It turned out that 'when it is not in people's hearts, it will not be in their heads'. So, the challenge for 'tomorrow's management' will be to achieve awareness in the 'guts' of people.

Impact on managers

After having gone through the culture positioning steps, managers will sense a natural drive to confirm the assumptions they made about *their* environment. Thus culture engineering will create a genuine and more meaningful impetus for management to walk round the office or shop floor to find out what happens there and what seems to drive or bother people there. Another result is that managers will be much more interested and open to new strategies and trends in other successful businesses, simply because they know *what* they are looking for. Business success stories, for example, will therefore be studied with a different attitude.

In short, the formulation of culture repositioning goals will lead to a conscious and subconscious search for new cultural highways. (Proposition 27)

Through vision engineering, management will develop a more structured curiosity and business drive to confirm the significance of the Product Focus Units (Chapter 12) in their corporate entity. In addition, they will start to scrutinize the core added values of their corporate entity, which may result in their reselection or rejection based on true economic and strategic rationales. Managers will be eager to carry out the same process with their own people, because they can best tell their own people by having them go through the same process.

In conclusion, the potential for overall and team performance will encourage the application of vision and culture engineering. Not projects or programmes, but 'real awareness' will truly drive the necessary actions. (Proposition 28)

19

Framework for the future

Culture expert framework

Vision and culture engineering, through culture positioning, provides a base for further quantification of corporate, national or in general corporate entity cultures. In fact, the development of artificial intelligence applications on computers has resulted in relatively simple tools that can be applied to interpret real life data by means of induction techniques.

Induction techniques make simple conclusions possible; they help

1   to identify relevant decision criteria or attributes,
2   to *prioritise* decision criteria or attributes based on *true* data.

In other words, the outcome of these types of applications is a set of rules. In the case of culture engineering, these rules may lead to advice on which move strategies (Chapter 9) could be used in particular circumstances. Examples of these circumstances are:

- the particular group, of which the corporate entity is part;
- the particular individual or group of individuals;
- the particular success or performance improvement aimed for;
- the rituals and hymns in the subject corporate entity;
- the particular *position* in the different positioning planes.

Computer systems that use induction techniques to determine general rulings require the registration of sucessful move-strategy-decisions, as well as the associated circumstances or attributes related to those move strategies.

The framework that culture engineering provides through its positioning planes for each of the culture performance drivers, indeed allows for the development of such a system in the foreseeable future. In fact, several possible systems may be identified, i.e. one for nations, one for specific industries and one for individuals. The structure of these systems and their files should be built around the following lines of thinking:

Proven decision:
- successful move strategy

Attributes:
- culture positioning indicators (Chapter 9);
positioning plane
starting and ending positions
- culture indicators before the move-strategy was applied;
rituals and *hymns in the corporate entity*
- success and overall performance target aims;
growth, profit, innovation, etc.
- corporate entity indicators and properties;
corporate sector, group of nations, group of individuals
size of the corporate entity

In order to ensure the consistency of data that is registered in the system, an unequivocal questionnaire should be developed to gather that data above. At any point in time, however, one should be able to add more attributes, when it turns out that the existing ones are insufficient for the identification of one unique successful move-strategy. In practice, it means that firstly the system should be initiated through the analysis and registration of historically proven move-strategies, obviously using a pre-determined questionnaire. Once that has been done, the 'expert-system' is geared to generate its first conclusions and/or recommendations. From then onwards, all further successful move strategies and their attributes should be registered. In this way, the applicability of the culture expert framework or system will be expanded. At the same time, the recommendations generated will mature, specifically after new attributes have been added.

The result will be a medium in which tremendous knowledge is gathered in a structured and logical way. This medium may function as a strategy decision system for corporate entities. But what is more important, it improves the understanding of culture performance trends in this world. This understanding may lead to the development of more realistic scenarios for culture events. Also, the culture (re-)positioning accuracy and scale may be improved over time. A culture expert system will be another way to maintain the right level of awareness through the possiblity it provides to shape the future and to prepare for tomorrow's success.

Tomorrow ... the 'association'

The combination of culture and vision is something very personal. People are proud of it and people's thinking and behaviour are determined by it. The management or rather *engineering* of culture and vision, even with the objective of increasing its performance and overall competitiveness, may touch the very pride of the people concerned. Therefore, help will most likely be needed in objectively driving the process of creating awareness and culture adjustment.

The role of a culture engineer as consultant, will be to teach the process and to guide people in its use. The aim should be to make people and organizations self-sufficient in applying it. Extreme discretion and confidentiality should obviously be guaranteed. The culture engineer and not the manager of the team will likely operate as a team facilitator, primarily to encourage the free contributions of the team members. An additional role of the culture engineer is to consolidate the end-results objectively.

Culture positioning sophistication

The quality of the culture positioning process may be greatly improved if reference cultures and their positions are available. In other words, a data base with culture positioning data of other corporate entities may open the way to an overall improvement in the general culture performance of a corporate entity group through cross-fertilization. In addition, inputs on new culture performance drivers and their culture elements will increase the sophistication of culture (re-)positioning in general. These inputs should preferably come from top managers in industries, corporations and nations.

The 'association'

Relative to the achievement of success for nations, corporations of any kind and individuals it is in the interest of these corporate entities to create a continuous focus of the refinement and improvement of culture performance and positioning models. Obviously much further work has to be done still.

This book, therefore, not only has the purpose of postulating a new approach to improving the chance of success for corporate entities, it is also meant to inspire the initiation of a VCE association, that professionally works on and worries about the improvement of the performance level of corporate-entity-cultures. This association should ensure culture performance progress,

- by organizing *world vision and culture engineering conferences* in order to gather and exchange inputs or reflections on move-strategies and new culture performance drivers;

- by building and improving 'real world' *culture performance models*, that contain data and intelligence on the success of the different groups of corporate entities;

- by developing the *vision and culture engineering* concept with the objective of creating effective help on culture performance adjustments and as a spin-off the development of a *newly emerging engineering discipline;*

- by proliferating *positioning* and *awareness concepts*, through media such as printed matter, video, interactive computing, human facilitators and human integrators, that are accessible to any 'corporate entity';

- by developing and providing *positioning-tools*, that help people in appropriately applying and visualizing vision and culture engineering.

What is more *humane* than 'to help people to prepare for success tomorrow' ...?

PART FIVE

Appendices

Appendix 1
Propositions (page number)

1 Alignment refers to having an organization or a group of people constructively accept and build on a given vison. (6)

2 Corporate awareness refers to a shared understanding of the corporate future, identity and culture by management and other people in the organization. (7)

3 Awareness concerns the mismatch between the 'observation' and the 'reference vision in people's minds'. This mismatch leads to corrective change actions (driven by the creative subconscious), that are geared to align 'what one observes' to the 'vision in one's mind'. (14)

4 The 'corporate entity' comprises (any number of) people, who are tied together in a group by a certain commonality in their vision of the future and by a common operating culture. They face the challenges of a common outside environment. (22)

5 One and the same vision may create different solutions in companies with different corporate cultures. (23)

6 The assumption is that a certain logic or rule exists underlying management trends, with which corporate repositioning efforts can be explained and anticipated. (28)

7 There is a natural tendency towards the (re-)establishment of a balance between vision and culture, once a vision has been introduced. This balance is achieved either through the absorption of the vision in the culture or by the rejection of the vision. (32)

8 The improvement of the vision-culture balance and the application of the associated culture and vision engineering processes, as in Parts Two and Three of this book, will help managers to grow towards a new set of values and success factors, such as:

the importance of heart (or guts) as well as brains;
the appreciation of an infinite rather than a finite world;
the need for a subjective as well as an objective world;
the endorsement of continuity;
the support of targets. (41)

9 As a result of change within corporate entities and the environment, the cultural characteristics of corporate entities will have to be adjusted in order to maintain or improve corporate entity success. (50)

10 By adjusting the vision, strategies and actions in a corporate entity, one will also impact on its culture. (53)

11 Culture performance can be explained on the one hand as the capacity to cope with sophisticated visions. On the other hand, culture performance refers to the time it takes to absorb a new vision. (55)

12 The challenges of tomorrow will fuel the need for new management tools, one of which is a framework for the repositioning of corporate culture and the development of change strategies. (58)

13 The effort-result curve cycle indicates that companies over time will have to cope with continuously succeeding S-curves. As such, they are moving through an alternating cycle of continuities and discontinuities. (64)

14 Culture performance drivers determine the inclination of people within corporate entities to stick to S-curves or to jump S-curves through two culture elements or culture forces. (67)

15 Structure is one of the key culture performance drivers, because it impacts on how people operate together in any organization. (75)

16 People involvement is the second key culture performance driver. (75)

17 Responsibility (strategic versus operational), as a key culture performance driver, is increasingly important for maintaining responsive and 'state-of-the-art' corporate entities. (77)

18 Corporate identity, linked to employee identity, is and will become even more a key culture performance driver. (77)

19 Goal-tuning with external and internal partners is the fifth and (for the moment last identified) major culture performance driver. (78)

20 The management of future organizations will more consciously and pro-actively focus on maintaining a dynamic balance between culture elements or culture forces. (116)

21 The understanding of the true added value of a person, corporation or nation is critical to the successful investment decision or the 'how' of a vision. (124)

22 The evolving product drives the need for the regular assessment and possible redefinition of the core added values and the core skills in a corporate entity. (127)

23 Vision should impact on every working person in the organization in terms of how he is measured. (128)

24 A constant planning attitude is essential to successful change and the prevention of wasted effort in corporate entities. The ultimate trick simply is in a continuously evolving awareness of management and in the design for change. (132)

25 Vision and culture engineering (VCE), as the 'Power of Tomorrow's Management', will speed up the evolution of the corporate entity by making revolutionary achievements manageable. (164)

26 The chance of 'achieving breakthroughs' is related to the level of incentive and to the *timing and method of people's involvement*. (170)

27 The formulation of culture repositioning goals will lead to a conscious and subconscious search for new cultural highways or strategies. (194)

28 In conclusion, the potential for overall and team performance will encourage the application of vision and culture engineering. Not projects or programmes, but 'real awareness' will truly drive the necessary actions. (194)

Appendix 2
Glossary of Terms

Alignment Refers to an organization or a group of people constructively accepting and building on a given vision.

Artist environment Characteristic state for the corporate entity to be in, i.e. when a high appreciation of individual goals is coupled with a low appreciation of overall corporate entity goals. It relates to the culture performance driver 'identity'.

Awareness A mismatch between what people sense (see, hear, feel, etc.) and the 'sub-conscious' reference vision in their minds.

Change cube The relationship between three vectors (the 'definition of change' vector, the 'management awareness, support and review' vector and the 'resources' vector) that leads to successful change. The first two vectors should be considered as the 'platform of success'.

Change optima The dynamic balance over time between a discontinuity preference (jumping S-curves) and a continuity preference (sticking to S-curves) in an organization.

Constant response The constantly developed awareness of environmental change that is reflected in strategy adjustments.

Corporate entity Any number of people who are tied together in a group by a certain commonality in their vision of the future and by a certain operating culture. They face the challenges of a common environment.

Corporate family Characteristic state for the corporate entity to be in, i.e. when a high appreciation of individual goals is coupled with a high appreciation of corporate entity goals. It relates to the culture performance driver 'identity'.

Cross-fertilization phase The second phase on the effort–result curve, where a basic potential for performance improvement is exploited through a natural or planned process of cross fertilization of results and findings.

Culture A dynamic system of dependent items, such as environment, ethics, vision, values, strategies, attitudes, behaviour and actions. By adjusting vision, strategies and actions one also, therefore, impacts culture.

Culture engineer A facilitator who helps managers and management teams to develop new vision-culture balance situations by using the vision and culture engineering approach.

Culture map The visualization of all positioning and re-positioning efforts of a corporate entity, i.e. for each of its culture performance drivers e.g. structure, involvement, responsibility, identity and goal-tuning.

Culture performance The capacity of a corporate entity to cope with sophisticated new visions coupled with the time it takes to absorb these visions into its culture.

Culture performance driver A culture performance driver is a typical set of strategies, e.g. structure, involvement, responsibility, identity and goal-tuning, that determines the inclination of people within a corporate entity towards a preference for discontinuity (jumping S-curves) or a preference for continuity (sticking to S-curves) through two culture forces or culture elements.

Culture range The range between the extremes in a group of corporate entities, as included in a positioning plane for a certain culture performance driver.

Dynamic balance area The fruitful, and at the same time manageable, imbalance between either a preference for discontinuity (jumping S-curves) or continuity (sticking to S-curves) in a corporate entity, in particular in relation to vision-specific needs.

Dynamic enterprise Characteristic state for the corporate entity to be in, i.e. when a high creative entrepreneurial activity is coupled with a high degree of control. It relates to the culture performance driver 'structure'.

Effort-result curve or S-curve The graphed relation between 'effort' (on the X-axis) and 'performance' (on the Y-axis) in the shape of a stretched 'S'. Three distinct phases can be distinguished, i.e. the maturation phase, the cross-fertilization phase and the exhaustion phase.

Exhaustion phase The last phase on the effort-result curve, where a natural potential for significant performance improvement has been exhausted.

Goal-tuning The fifth culture performance driver for a corporate entity (after 'structure', 'involvement', 'responsibility' and 'identity'), which is determined by two culture forces, i.e. the 'tuning of goals with external (business) partners' and the 'tuning of goals with internal (business) partners'.

Hyperactive enterprise Characteristic state for a corporate entity to be in, i.e. when a high creative entrepreneurial activity is coupled with a minimum degree of control. It relates to the culture performance driver 'structure'.

Identity The fourth culture performance driver of a corporate entity (after 'structure', 'involvement', and 'responsibility'), which is determined by two culture forces, i.e. the 'appreciation of individual goals' and the 'appreciation of corporate entity goals'.

Identity map The identity of corporations plotted on a graph in terms of their product variety and number of core added values.

Involvement The second culture performance driver of a corporate entity (after 'structure'), which is determined by two culture forces, i.e. the 'idea development activity' in a corporate entity and 'alignment'.

Maturation phase The first phase on the effort-result curve, where a basic approach for potential performance improvements is being developed and matured.

More impact Increased usefulness at a certain effort, in particular as a result of a culture-performance improvement.

Move strategy A strategy that relates to a specific culture performance driver which improves the balance between two culture forces.

Opportunity sharing company Characteristic state for a corporate entity to be in, i.e. when a high level of goal-tuning with external (business) partners is coupled with a high level of goal-tuning with internal (business) partners. It relates to the culture performance driver 'goal-tuning'.

Optimal participation Typical state for a corporate entity to be in, i.e. when a high level of idea-development activity is coupled with a high level of organizational alignment. It relates to the culture performance driver 'involvement'.

Paradox-equilibrium area The same as the dynamic balance area, where neither of the two culture forces is too dominant but where a certain imbalance has the preference because of the 'change' it causes. The 'paradox' refers to the need for two culture forces that are (to a certain extent) antagonistic. The 'equilibrium' relates to the need for both culture forces, but in a manageable (im-) balance.

People model The corporate entity model, where external and internal influences drive the need for a particular set of culture performance drivers, such as structure, involvement, responsibility, identity and goal-tuning.

PFU PFU stands for Product Focus Units. PFUs are logical groupings of products in a corporate entity, that require specific added values and investment decisions.

PFU significance The importance of a Product Focus Unit in terms of its current money or £ volume (sales, revenue, budget) and its overall growth rate.

Portfolio environment Typical state for a corporate entity to be in, i.e. when a high level of strategic responsibility is coupled with a high level of operational responsibility. It refers to the culture performance driver 'responsibility'.

Positioning grid A positioning grid concerns a positioning plane which incorporates more than one corporate entity. The grid itself is based on the number of corporate entities and the location of these in the positioning plane. It is helpful in establishing a culture range and a sense of improvement that is related to other corporate entities.

Positioning plane A two-dimensional plane (or graph) for a particular culture performance driver, that can be used to plot the relative existence of two culture forces or culture elements in a corporate entity. Based on the position in the plane, one can identify the need to re-position to an improved balance between these culture forces.

Productive creativity Productive creativity is an approach that may lead to breakthrough by allowing people to think unlimitedly based on what they want. However, once the wanting exercise has been completed one goes through a structuring process to bring the 'wants' into a realizable perspective.

Progress spiral The evolutionary process towards corporate entity success via a continuous and alternating focus on vision, culture and resources.

Responsibility The mind culture performance driver for a corporate entity (after 'structure' and 'involvement'), that is determined by two culture forces: the 'strategic orientation of people' and the 'operational orientation of people'.

Sine-curve phenomenon The sine-curve like split in management effort, that moves from vision development towards the facilitation of a positive and supporting organizational response.

Soldiers environment Characteristic state for the corporate entity to be in, i.e. when a low appreciation of individual goals is coupled with a high appreciation of corporate entity goals. It relates to the culture performance driver 'identity'.

Structure The first culture performance driver for a corporate entity determined by two culture forces: the 'degree of creative entrepreneurial activity' and the 'degree of control'.

Success cube The relationship between three vectors (the 'vision' vector, the 'culture' vector and the 'resources' vector) that leads to successful change. The first two vectors should be considered as the 'platform of success'.

Total consensus Characteristic state for the corporate entity to be in, i.e. when a modest idea development activity in the corporate entity is coupled with a high degree of organizational alignment. It relates to the culture performance driver: 'involvement'.

Total fragmentation Characteristic state for the corporate entity to be in, i.e. when a high idea development activity in the corporate entity is coupled with a low degree of organizational alignment. It relates to the culture performance driver 'involvement'.

Trader company Characteristic state for the corporate entity to be in, i.e. when a high degree of goal-tuning with external (business) partners is coupled with a low degree of goal-tuning with internal (business) partners. It relates to the culture performance driver 'goal-tuning'.

Traditional environment Characteristic state for the corporate entity to be in, i.e. when a modest strategic orientation is coupled with a high degree of operational emphasis. It relates to the culture performance driver 'responsibility'.

Vault company Characteristic state for the corporate entity to be in, i.e. when a low degree of goal-tuning with external (business) partners is coupled with a high degree of goal-tuning with internal (business) partners. It relates to the culture performance driver 'goal-tuning'.

Vision-culture balance The not always stable equilibrium between vision and culture in any corporate entity. The phenomenon causes a natural tendency towards the (re-) establishment of a balance between vision and culture once a vision has been introduced. This balance is achieved either by the absorption of the vision in the culture or by the rejection of the vision.

Vision-culture balance evolution spectrum A five-staged evolution pattern for vision-culture balance situations in corporate entities. It covers the 'zero stage', the 'survival awareness stage', the 'growth awareness stage', the 'shaping awareness stage' and the 'creating awareness stage'. Progress along this spectrum can only be achieved by some form of vision and culture engineering.

Vision model   A workshop model, that can be used by management teams of any kind to determine the purpose of their corporate entity. It covers customer groups, product focus units, product significance, added values, investment needs and suppliers.

Appendix 3
Bibliography

'Action 86 saves Matsushita from too large a drop in profits'; Boer de E., *Financieele Dagblad*, 19 February, 1987.
'A linking of like minds'; McEwan F., *Financial Times*, 8 October, 1987.
'And speed will cut expert system costs'; Kehoe L., *Financial Times*, 14 August, 1986.
'And then came the hard part'; Thomas D., *Financial Times*, 27 July, 1987.
'Alvey at the crossroads'; Fishlock D., *Financial Times*, 12 August, 1986.
'America, Europe and Japan: a time to dismantle the world economy'; Thurow L., *The Economist*, 9 November, 1985.
'America's most successful entrepreneur'; Petres P., *Fortune*, 27 October, 1986.
'Anatomy of a shake-up'; Collin R., *International Management*, September, 1986.
'A new generation begins to make its mark'; *Financial Times*, 31 August, 1988.
'Apple decentralizes into four divisions'; *Financial Times*, October, 1988.
'Apple's growth could stay stunted for a while'; Lewis G., *Business Week*, 10 June, 1985.
'A spoon full of terror helps the firm turn round'; Cane A., *Financial Times*, 3 June, 1987.
'AT&T: the making of a comeback'; Keller J., *et al., Business Week*, 18 January, 1988.
'Avoiding a cancer of arrogance in a high-tech start-up'; Gibb R., *International Management*, October, 1987.
'A question of accountability'; Levitt M., *Financial Times*, 4 September, 1987.

'A quiet coup at Daimler-Benz';   *Time*, 27 July, 1987.
'Back to the future';   *Economist*, 27 June, 1987.
'Billions for internal network of Philips';   *NRC*, 13 May, 1987.
'Blue collar workers in the boardroom: putting business first';   Hoerr J., *Business Week*, 14 December, 1987.
'Breaking the multinational mould: how DEC snuggled up to its customers';   *International Management*, November, 1985.
'British Airways jolts staff within a cultural revolution';   *International Management*, March, 1987.
'Can Jack Welch re-invent GE?';   Harris M., *Business Week*, 30 June, 1986.
'Can John Sculley clean up the mess at Apple?';   Wise D., *Business Week*, 29 July, 1985.
'Can Steve Jobs do it again?';   Hafner K. M., *Business Week*, 24 October, 1988.
'Ceramic materials in West Germany';   *Techneiuws/Bonn*, September, 1987.
'Chen works for IBM on parallel computer';   *Computable*, January, 1988.
'Coming to a new awareness of organisational culture';   Schein E., *Sloan Management Review*, 1984.
'Compagnie Bancaire emerges from the shadows';   Delamaid D., *International Management*, March, 1987.
'Companies to be self-accountable';   Colitt L., *Financial Times*, 9 October, 1987.
'Competitive advantage';   Porter M., *Free Press*, 1985.
'Competitive advantage through information';   Porter M., *Harvard Business Review*, 1986.
'Confessions of an advertisement man';   Ogilvy D., Pan Books, 1987.
'Co-operation in Europe: absolutely essential';   *Computable*, 3 April, 1987.
'Corporate anthropology: a new phenomenon in the consulting world', Lier van F., *Financieele Dagblad*, 26 March, 1987.
'Creating a laboratory for financial services';   Simonian H., *Financial Times*, 12 August, 1987.
'Chrysler zooms up-market with Lamborghini';   Bruce L., *International Management*, October, 1987.
'DEC goes charging into the office';   Peterson T., *Business Week*, 26 May, 1986.
'Detroit's new mentors in managing Americans: the Japanese'; Schwartz J., *International Management*, September, 1986.
'Different treatment of females in man-driven corporate cultures'; *Financieele Dagblad*, 22 October, 1987.

'Digital Equipment: a step ahead in linking computers';   *Business Week*, 21 April, 1986.
'Diversity is the secret weapon';   Smart T., *Business Week*, 14 December, 1987.
'Do-it-yourself systems with Artificial Intelligence on a micro computer';   Milman J., *IEEE Compcon*, 1984.
'Do headquarters earn their keep?';   Skapinker M., *Financial Times*, 2 October, 1987.
'Drive, he said';   Betts P., *Financial Times*, 27 July, 1987.
'Elsevier's merger strategy not necessarily heaven';   Boer de E., *Financieele Dagblad*, 1987.
'Enterprise Dynamics';   van der Erve M., Sijthoff, 1986.
'Everything can be done a little better tomorrow';   *Financieele Dagblad*, 20 August, 1987.
'European youths not ambitious enough';   *Computable*, 31 October, 1986.
'Europe's chipmakers pull out of a long losing streak';   Peterson T., et al., *Business Week*, 30 June 1986.
'Ex-employee re-strained from using information;   Davies R., *Financial Times*, 9 October, 1987.
'Expert systems: a key for productivity explosion';   Beynals B., *Telegraaf*, 21 November, 1987.
'Faith behind Japanese spirit';   *Financial Times*, August, 1988.
'Flexible company structures heavily impact labor market and management';   Groot E., *Financieele Dagblad*, 20 November, 1986.
'Ford's idea machine';   Gelman E., *Newsweek*, 15 December, 1986.
Fokker considers manufacturing airplanes in the USA';   *Financieele Dagblad*, 16 July, 1986.
'Ford's Bruce Blythe has a blank check and a mission';   Treece J., et. al., *Business Week*, 24 December, 1987.
'GAK successfully advised companies on reducing illness-absenteeism';   *Financieele Dagblad*, 5 March, 1987.
'Gorbachev tightens reins, vows greater democracy';   *Financial Times*, 3 October, 1988.
'Gorbachev unveils revolutionary economic reform';   Cockburn P., *Financial Times*, 26 June, 1987.
'HAS set for take-off';   Kuperus G., *Holland Herald*, 1987.
'How Carlzon gives the customer what he wants';   Lester T., *International Management*, October, 1987.
'How far can Philips elbow its way into the U.S.?';   *Business Week*, 2 March, 1987.
'How Ford hit the bull's eye with the Taurus';   *Business Week*, 3 June, 1986.

'How Ford used inituitive design to break free of committee cars'; *Financial Times,* 28 September, 1988.
'How IBM is fighting back'; Harris M., *Business Week,* 17 November, 1986.
'How some companies avoid cultural pitfalls'; Dixon M., *Financial Times,* 14 August, 1986.
'How will the Gorbachev show play in Eastern Europe?; Echikson B., *et al., Business Week,* 18 January, 1988.
'How Perstorp persuades the managers to innovate'; Arbose J., *International Management,* June, 1987.
'How Tonka toys with its European range'; *Financial Times,* 1 September, 1988
'Industrial break-throughs threaten market positions'; Boogert H., *Telegraaf,* 10 June, 1987.
'Innovation as a way of life: how leading companies do it'; Parry C., *International Management,* February, 1986.
'Innovation: the attackers advantage'; Foster R., Pan Books, 1987.
'In search of excellence'; Peters J., *et al.,* Harper & Row, 1982.
'Interdependent networks favoured over hierarchies'; *Herald Tribune,* 16 June, 1988.
'Is profit-sharing the best way to get Europe back to work'; Skapinker M., *International Management,* September, 1986.
'Is traditional management dead?'; Piper A., *International Management,* January, 1986.
'Jack Calvet: another Lee Iacocca?' Melcher R., *Business Week,* 9 March, 1987.
'Jack Welch: how good a manager?'; Mitchell R., *Business Week,* 14 December 1987.
'Japan's energetic search for creativity'; Berger M., *International Management,* October, 1987.
'Japanese bank launches attack on American Corporate Culture'; *Financial Times,* 18 July, 1988.
'Keeping up with the company was not the most challenging task'; Kuin D., *Financieele Dagblad,* 19 August, 1987.
'Kicking the single-product habit at Kodak'; Helen L., *et al., Business Week,* 1 December, 1986.
'Kodak is trying to break out of its shell'; Buell B., *Business Week,* 10 June, 1985.
'KP cracks a hard nut'; Leadbeater C., *Financial Times,* 3 June, 1987.
'Lack of innovation threatens small business'; *Financieele Dagblad,* 1987.
'Lateral thinking'; de Bono E., Pelican Books, 1977.
'Level of investment in Holland too low'; *Financiele Telegraaf,* 12 December, 1986.

'Levy's new designs for Renault'; Bernier L., *International Management*, October, 1987.
'LULU is home now'; *Time*, 17 June, 1985.
'Maxwell meets with Elsevier tomorrow'; Snoddy R., *Financial Times*, 12 August, 1987.
'Make room in the labs for economists'; Smith E., *Business Week*, 1 December, 1986.
'Management: it's top-down and bottom-up'; Keuning D., *Financieele Dagblad*, 26 March, 1987.
'Managing entrepreneurs requires special skills from top management'; London van H., *Financieele Dagblad*, 23 April, 1987.
'Marriage of true minds behind Anglo-Dutch success'; *Financial Times*, July, 1988.
'Merger trend intensifies'; Cane, A., *Financial Times*, 15 October, 1987.
'Move over Boone, Carl and Irv – here comes labor'; Berstein A., *Business Week*, 14 December, 1987.
'Mrs Thatcher and Europe'; *Financial Times*, 18 November, 1987.
'New study find high level of cynicism among US & Euro workforces; *International Management*, October, 1985.
'New top-structure with Daimler-Benz'; *Financieele Dagblad*, 4 July, 1986.
'New thrust towards the ceramic engine; *Financial Times*, 6 September, 1988.
'Old practices that distort decisions'; Dullforce W., *Financial Times*. 1 July, 1987.
'Organisation structure Hoogovens IJmuiden changed considerably'; *Financieele Dagblad*, 22 September, 1987.
'Part of the scenery, but not yet part of the culture'; Garnett N., *et al.*, *Financial Times*, 2 August, 1986.
'Patrick Gunkel lives in a world of lists, dazzling intellectuals'; Stipp D., *The Wall Street Journal*, 4 June, 1987.
'Perrot to Smith: GM must change'; Pederson D., *Newsweek*, 15 December, 1986.
'Philips gets a truly different structure'; Boer de E., *et al.*, *Financieele Dagblad*, 14 September, 1987.
'Philips wants to change organisation considerably'; *Computable*, Feburary, 1987.
'Picking the cherries in Asia'; *Financial Times*, 1 August, 1988.
'Pratt & Whitney's stall is turning into a tail-spin'; Mitchell R., *Business Week*, 17 December, 1987.
'Preaching in the market place'; *Financial Times*, 18 July, 1988.
'Profit related pay, not such an easy option'; *Financial Times*, 11 September 1987.

'Productivity program saves millions'; Honpis N., *Excellence*, February, 1986.
'Psycho-Cybernetics'; Maltz M., Pocket Books, 1969.
'Re-inventing the corporation'; Naisbitt J., *et al.*, Warner Books, 1985.
'Scenarios: shooting the rapids'; Wack P., *Harvard Business Review*, December, 1985.
'Service Industry Round Table'; Mum R., *Computer/Electronics Service News*, November, 1987.
'Simple logic that can bring reward'; Butler S., *Financial Times*, 12 October, 1987.
'Sensing your way up the S-curve'; Lawson T., *International Management*, October, 1986.
'Small businesses are stressed'; *Telegraaf*, 1987.
'Search for a miracle cure'; Alexander C., Time, 20 May, 1985.
'Soviet athletes: if you can't beat 'em, imitate 'em'; *Herald Tribune*, 30 September, 1988.
'Strategies for UK electronics'; *Financial Times*, 1988.
'Successful decentralization requires special leadership qualities'; *Financieele Dagblad*, 30 April, 1987.
'Taking on the toughest market'; Palmer J., *Time*, 30 March, 1987.
'Technology transfer'; Marsh P., *Financial Times*, 30 October, 1986.
'The big three get in gear'; Koepp S., *Time*, 24 November, 1986.
'The family approach to revamping systems'; *Financial Times*, 29 July, 1988.
'The high flight of KLM'; Berg van den A., *Intermediair*, 25 September, 1987.
'The Honda way'; Garrison L., *Time*, 8 September, 1986.
'The information business'; Field A., *Business Week*, 25 August, 1986.
'The Japanese forge ahead to tackle the world problems'; Berger M., *International Management*, March, 1987.
'The legal profession: Paddling with the tide': Hughes R., *Financial Times*, 15 October, 1987.
'The London street trader who would like to be as big as Sony'; *International Management*, September, 1986.
'The mind of a marketing maverick'; *International Management*, October, 1987.
'The new Alcatel power house: so far so good'; Bruce L., *International Management*, October, 1987.
'The ten commandments for management'; Twijnstra A., *Financieele Dagblad*, 21 May, 1987.
'The trouble with take-overs'; Lorentz C., *Financial Times*, 1987.
'Today, decision in Kluwer take-over battle'; *Financiele Telegraaf*, 14 August, 1987.

'Unilever aims to bolster lines in U.S.'; Nelson M., *The Wall Street Journal*, 19 June, 1987.
'USSR—New thinking for foreign trade'; Special Advertisement section, 1987.
'Volvo's drive for shorter cycles'; Lorentz C., *Financial Times*, 26 June, 1987.
'Wall Street votes with its feet'; Kaletsky A., *Financial Times*, 5 December, 1986.
'What is a guy like this doing at McKinsey's helm?'; *Business Week*, 13 June, 1988.
'White collar productivity management'; *Management Decision*, 1986.
'White collar robots go to work'; Kehoe L., *Financial Times*, 5 August, 1986.
'White collar: the employees' side'; Fitz-Enz J., *International Management*, May, 1986.
'With or without Gorbachev reforms are coming'; Shevenko A., *Herald Tribune*, July, 1987.
'Who said take-overs were dead?' Rudolph B., et al., *Time*, 23 March, 1987.
'Why budgies fell foul of Boots' bottom-line'; Parkes C., *Financial Times*, 4 September, 1987.
'Why Hewlett-Packard looked East for its computer innovation'; Yanchinstei S., *Financial Times*, 1 July, 1987.
'Why Kodak is starting to click again'; Helen L., *Business Week*, 23 February, 1987.
'Why managers today have a tougher task of managing complexity'; Hill R., *International Management*, August, 1986.
'Why small can still be beautiful;' *Financial Times*, 3 October, 1988.
'Why the spark has gone'; *Financial Times*, 1 July, 1988.

Index

Added value, 123, 145
Added value supplier 145, 147
Ahmet Aykac, 40
Airbus Industries, 25
Alcatel, 125
Alignment, 101, 107, 124
Apple, 28, 44, 84
Appreciation of corporate goals, 94
Appreciation of employee goals, 94
Artistic environment, 96
Associative interacting, 16
Atari, 84
AT&T, 99, 180
Awareness, 13, 14

Boots, 88
British Airways, 27
British Midland bank, 40

Calvet, Pierre, 12, 33, 140
Chernobyl, 93
Chrysler, 77
Club Méditerranée, 88
Competitive culture engineering, 170
Consciousness, 12
Constant planning attitude, 130
Continuity-discontinuity paradox, 64
Control structure, 69
Core added values, 145
Corporate awareness, 7
Corporate culture, 52
Corporate entity, 21
Corporate family, 96
Cosa nostra, 98
Creative entrepreneurial environment, 69
Creative sub-conscious, 13
Cross-fertilization, 61
Culture engineer, 117

Culture expert system, 196
Culture forces, 73
Culture performance, 54, 67
Culture performance drivers, 67
Culture performance lines, 54
Culture positioning map, 103, 167
Culture positioning process, 107
Culture range, 171
Customers, 134, 142

Daimler-Benz, 101
De Benedetti, Carlo, 5
DeBono, Edward, 15, 158
Deming, 49
Digital (DEC), 82, 100
Disestablishment, 40
Drucker, 49
Dutch Ministry of Economical Affairs, 11
Dynamic balance area, 65, 68
Dynamic positioning plane, 68

EDS, 101
Effort-result curve, 59
Elsevier, 182
Employee career system, 186
Environment, 141
European Technews, 11
Exhaustion phase, 62
Expert framework for culture, 195

Focus networks, 150
Fokker, 25
Ford, 40, 125
Fuji Xerox, 82

Geneen, Harold, 102, 125, 140, 156
General Electric, 128
General Motors, 92, 101, 125

Goal-tuning, 78, 98
  with external partners, 98
  with internal partners, 98
Goal-tuning related strategies, 111
Gorbachev, 5, 26, 32, 140, 176
Great Depression, 36
Gunkel, Patrick, 16

Heineken, 99
Hewlett Packard, 23
Hoogovens, 83
Horizontal goal-tuning, 99
Hoskyns, 154
Hyperactive enterprise, 81

Idea development, 85
Identity, 77, 94
Identity map, 124
Ideonomy, 16
Industrial age, 55
Information age, 56
Information product, 4, 56, 126
Internal communication, 10
Involvement, 75, 85
Involvement related strategies, 111
ITT, 102, 125

Japanese corporate culture, 27
Jobs, Steven, 44
Jumping S-curves, 63, 65
Juran, 49

Kanter, 22
Kennedy, John F., 12
Keynes, 36
Khrushchev, Nikita, 32
KLM (Royal Dutch Airlines), 97
Kluwer, 182
Kodak, 28, 82
Korea, 175

Laffer, 51
Lamborghini, 77
Lateral thinking, 14
Levy, Raymond, 93
Lotus, 23

McDonnel Douglas, 25
McKinsey, 85
Maltz, 12
Management by objectives, 168

Management trends, 27
Mao, 74
Matsushita, 89
Maturation phase, 60
Means driven dimension, 135
Mirvis, 22
More-impact, 50
Move strategies, 71, 109

Naisbitt, John, 22
NASA, 93
New Deal in management, 36
NeXT, 44
Nippon T&T, 82
Nissan Diesel, 82
Nordberg, 88
NUMMI, 190

Olsen, Kenneth H., 30, 123
Operational orientation, 89
Opportunity sharing company, 100
Optimal dynamic enterprise, 81
Optimal participation, 87

People model, 75
People's Express, 84
Perestroika, 152
Performance drivers, 60
Perot, H. Ross, 101
Perstorp, 88
Peters, 50
Peugeot-Citroën, 12
PFU significance, 144
Philips, 37, 83, 88, 99
Planning process, 38
Po-device, 15
Portfolio environment, 92
Positioning effort, 70
Positioning grid, 172
Post industrial age, 56
Prestowitz, 25
Process-driven dimension, 135
Product, 126, 134, 143
Product criteria, 135, 149
Product Focus Unit (PFU), 143
Progress spiral, 163
Purpose-driven dimension, 135

Reference vision or picture, 13
Renault, 83, 93
Responsibility, 76, 89

Responsibility-related strategies, 110
Rigid enterprise, 82
Roosevelt, 36

SAS, 28
Sculley, John, 84, 89
S-curve, 59
S-curve jump, 63
Self-management, 39
Shell oil company, 18
Siemens, 99
Sine pattern, 4
Smith, Roger, 92
Soldier environment, 97
Strategic orientation, 89
Strategist environment, 91
Structure, 74
Structure-related strategies, 109
Sub-conscious, 13
Success-cube, 153, 156
Success vector, 153
Sugar, Alan, 40, 107
Sun Microsystems, 180
Supplier, 135
Synergy, 24

Taiwan, 175
Tateishi Electronics, 82
Thatcher, 5, 40, 176
Thinking and guidance framework, 7
Thurow, Lester, 102

Tice, Louis, 12
Titanic, 133
Total consensus, 87
Total fragmentation, 87
Trader company, 100
Traditional environment, 92
Transformation steps, 115

Unilever, 102, 125
Uniqueness of added-values, 147

Value flexibility, 57
Vander Klugt, C., 88
Vault company, 101
VCE Association, 197, 198
Vertical goal-tuning, 99
Vision appearance statement, 122
Vision-culture balance, 31
Vision-culture balance spectrum, 164
Vision engine, 12
Vision-jump, 31
Vision model, 137
Vision statement, 134
Volvo, 83

Wack, Pierre A., 18
Waterman, 50
Welch, Jack, 128
Why-issue, 38

Zola, Emile, 141